DESIGNING CRITICAL LITERACY EDUCATION THROUGH CRITICAL DISCOURSE ANALYSIS

"*This is a wonderful and exciting project that focuses a new and helpful lens on teacher education. The idea of having teachers use critical discourse analysis to explore various aspects of their experience is novel and potentially ground-breaking. I have total confidence that educators will find this book incredibly useful.*"

Catherine Compton-Lilly, University of Wisconsin-Madison, USA

"*The authors have taken critical literacy into teacher education. Writing as teacher research-ers and critical discourse analysts they outline their approach to designing literacy education that explicitly works for social justice. The book is based on a year of their lives as teacher educators engaging with the complexity of shaping ethical teacher identities and the politics of educating critically reflective practitioners. As well as telling credible and critical stories of their own work they demonstrate an approach to critical discourse analysis and make a strong case for why this is central to critical literacy.*"

Barbara Comber, Queensland University of Technology, Australia

Uniquely bringing together discourse analysis, critical literacy, and teacher re-search, this book invites teacher educators, literacy researchers, and discourse analysts to consider how discourse analysis can be used to foster critical literacy education. It is both a guide for conducting critical discourse analysis and a look at how the authors, alongside their teacher education students, used the tools of discourse analysis to inquire into, critique, and design critical literacy prac-tices. Through an intimate look at the workings of a university teacher education course and the discourse analysis tools that teacher researchers use to understand their classrooms, the book provides examples of both pre-service teachers *and* teacher educators becoming critically literate. The context-rich examples high-light the ways in which discourse analysis aids teachers' decision making in the moment and reflections on their practice over time. Readers learn to conduct discourse analysis as they read about critical literacy practices at the university level.

Designed to be interactive, each chapter features step-by-step procedures for conducting each kind of discourse analysis (narrative, critically oriented, multimodal), sample analyses, and additional readings and resources. By attending to the micro-interactions as well as processes that unfold across time, the book illustrates the power and potential of discourse analysis as a pedagogical and research tool.

Rebecca Rogers is Professor of Literacy Education and Discourse Studies at the University of Missouri–St. Louis, USA.

Melissa Mosley Wetzel is Associate Professor in the Department of Curriculum and Instruction at the University of Texas at Austin, USA.

DESIGNING CRITICAL LITERACY EDUCATION THROUGH CRITICAL DISCOURSE ANALYSIS

Pedagogical and Research Tools for Teacher Researchers

Rebecca Rogers, Professor
Melissa Mosley Wetzel,
Associate Professor

 Routledge
Taylor & Francis Group

NEW YORK AND LONDON

First published 2014
by Routledge
711 Third Avenue, New York, NY 10017

Simultaneously published in the UK
by Routledge
2 Park Square, Milton Park, Abingdon, Oxon OX14 4RN

Routledge is an imprint of the Taylor & Francis Group, an informa business

Library of Congress Cataloging-in-Publication Data

Rogers, Rebecca (Rebecca L.), 1959– Designing critical
literacy education through critical discourse analysis : pedagogical and research
   tools for teacher researchers / by Rebecca Rogers, Melissa Mosley Wetzel.
      pages cm
   Includes bibliographical references and index.
1. African American children—Education (Elementary)—United States.   2. Language arts
(Elementary)—United States.   3. Literacy—United States.   4. Critical pedagogy—United
States.   I. Mosley Wetzel, Melissa.   II. Title.
   LC2778.L34.R76 2013
   371.829'96073—dc23   2012047534

ISBN: 978-0-415-81059-3 (hbk)
ISBN: 978-0-415-81061-6 (pbk)
ISBN: 978-0-203-07086-4 (ebk)

Typeset in Bembo
by Apex CoVantage, LLC

Printed and bound in the United States of America by Publishers Graphics,
LLC on sustainably sourced paper.

For Sofia, who is teaching me about language and literacy acquisition. You inspire and enrich my life in so many ways.
—Rebecca Rogers

For my brother Joshua, who thought I would write.
—Melissa Mosley Wetzel

CONTENTS

PREFACE

If you are reading this book, you probably have interests in critical literacy, teacher education, discourse analysis, and/or teacher research. You may read this book as a teacher researcher in order to learn applications of tools of discourse analysis or perhaps you were drawn to our focus on teacher education in literacy. Or you may be a seasoned discourse analyst looking to expand the kinds of critical discourse analyses you conduct. We have kept these different audiences in mind as we wrote this book.

We wrote it in order to explore the complexity of critical literacy in teacher education and to share what we have learned by drawing on discourse analysis as a tool for both pedagogy and research. *Critical literacy* refers to approaches to literacy education that seek to both disrupt unjust texts and social practices and use literacy to reimagine and redesign new possibilities (Lewison, Leland, & Harste, 2007; Luke, 2012). Most scholars who study critical literacy focus on K-12 classroom settings or K-12 students' literacy practices in their communities. However, we know very little about how pre-service teachers themselves gain the pedagogical knowledge for critical literacy (for exceptions, see Dozier, Johnston, & Rogers, 2006; Mosley, 2010). If teacher educators in the field of literacy will influence current pedagogy, we need more and better research drawing on these frameworks to define what teachers should learn and should know how to do (Darling-Hammond & Bransford, 2005). Further, discourse analysis in literacy research has become an increasingly popular set of theories and methods but there are few examples of discourse analysis contextualized within teacher education settings, especially as a research and pedagogical tool.

To demonstrate how we use critical discourse analysis in service of our teaching, we chose four approaches to highlight in this book: narrative analysis, building tasks analysis, critical discourse analysis, and multimodal discourse analysis. We might have chosen others. Indeed, there are many varieties of critically oriented discourse analysis that may be equally as productive. However, in practical terms, these are the approaches we work with in our teaching and research (Rogers, 2011). For teachers of Critical Discourse Studies working in university-based contexts, among students who may be seeking a more stable body of "how-to" expertise, we wanted to offer a model of how such open-ended approaches to inquiry may be taught. The appendices at the end of the book do just that. We hope *Designing Critical Literacy Education through Critical Discourse Analysis* will spark debate and discussion in the field about the teaching and learning of critical discourse studies.

In Chapter 1, we introduce our purposes of the study as well as the theories of critical literacy we draw on throughout the book. Chapter 2, *Inside the Design of our Teaching and Research*, explores the context and methods of the study as well as the traditions of discourse analysis and teacher research. Chapter 3, *Narrating Literacy, Identity and Culture: Narrative Analysis*, describes narrative approaches to discourse analysis and illustrates how we used cultural narratives—both spoken (autobiographical) and written (literature)—in our classroom to create a community of practice responsive to culture, race, power, and language diversity. Chapter 4, *Inquiry into Linguistic Diversity: Discourse Analysis*, draws on a building tasks analysis to analyze a student-centered inquiry into language variety and assessing oral reading that emerged generatively during our instruction. Chapter 5, *Practicing Racial Literacy: Critical Discourse Analysis*, illustrates through a critical discourse analysis the process that teacher education students used to explore their own racial histories. Finally, performative literacy practices are the focus of chapter 6, *Performing Literacy: Multimodal Discourse Analysis*, here, we analyze teaching practices of the pre-service teachers in a tutoring practicum. In Chapter 7, *Conclusions*, we bring the book to a close by reflecting on the role of discourse analysis in critical literacy education.

Chapters 3 through 6 include detailed appendices that are an accessible guide to doing critically oriented discourse analysis in educational studies.

In essence, we prepared a multi-layered text. If you are primarily interested in teacher research, or critical literacy in teacher education, you might read the book without much interest in the detailed appendices. Indeed, there are few book-length accounts of designing critical literacy within university settings, particularly in teacher education, so this may be compelling enough. However, if you are interested in the theories and methods of critical discourse analysis, you will want to spend time with our appendices. Each chapter focuses on a different approach to critical discourse analysis and, embedded in each chapter, are references to a set of appendices that feature the tools associated with that approach. The appendices are cumulative so that you will be able to deepen your skills as a discourse analyst as you progress throughout the book. For example, Chapter 3 focuses on critical narrative analysis. The appendices in this chapter include: Choosing a Type of Narrative Analysis, How to Identify Themes in a Narrative Analysis, Locating Narrative Structure, Creating Transcripts, Identifying the Clause as the Unit of Analysis, Analyzing Positioning, and A Guide to Conducting Narrative Analysis. In the appendices associated with later chapters, we cycle back to some of the ideas presented in Chapter 3 but build on them. For instance, we illustrate additional ways of segmenting texts and creating multimodal transcripts. Each chapter includes a "guide" that walks you through the steps for conducting a different approach to discourse analysis and additional readings and resources to support and extend the approach highlighted in the chapter (see Table 1.2 in Chapter 1). This structure makes the book an interactive guide to conducting critical discourse analysis as you can "try out" the steps in conducting discourse analysis as you are reading the book. If you are short on time and want to learn more about conducting critical discourse analysis, you could just read the appendices. However, we think the beauty of our approach is the nesting of critical discourse analysis within a year-long teacher research project. We are hopeful that this structure will be appealing to those new to discourse analysis. And, more seasoned practitioners will find the discourse analysis situated within the longitudinal context of a year-long course to be a refreshing change from most discourse analysis studies.

For us, the intersection of the foci of this book created a space that stretched our thinking about what the theories and methods of critical discourse analysis that we use in our research have to say about our work as teachers and teacher educators. As we weave in and out of the praxis in our teacher education classroom, we demonstrate through our context-rich examples the ways in which discourse analysis aided our decision making as teachers in the moment as well as looking back at our practice over time. We show how we used discourse analytic frameworks to guide our thinking about classroom practice and, in a parallel fashion, encouraged our students to do the same. What results is an intimate look at the workings of a critical literacy classroom as well as the discourse analysis tools that teacher researchers use to understand their classrooms. Throughout, we invite you to consider, along with us, how discourse analysis may foster critical literacy education.

We could not have written this book if not for the generosity of our students, who shared their learning and development with us each day. For the most part, they did not mind the continual running of the tape- or video-recorders, our open-ended questions or our requests for the records of their learning. They shared their materials and reflections with us, knowing that the more we understood about how learning evolved, the better we may teach them and reach our future students. We also thank Naomi Silverman for her encouragement and support in pursuing and completing this book project.

—*Rebecca Rogers*
—*Melissa Mosley Wetzel*

References

Darling-Hammond, L., & Bransford, J. (2005). *Preparing teachers for a changing world: What teachers should learn and be able to do* (1st ed.). San Francisco, CA: Jossey-Bass.

Dozier, C., Johnston, P., & Rogers, R. (2006). *Critical literacy/critical teaching: Tools for preparing responsive teachers*. New York, NY: Teachers College Press.

Lewison, M., Leland, C., & Harste, J. (2007). *Creating critical classrooms: K-8 reading and writing with an edge*. New York, NY: Taylor & Francis Group.

Luke, A. (2012). Critical literacy: Foundational notes. *Theory into Practice, 51(1)*, 4–11.

Mosley, M. (2010). Becoming a literacy teacher: Approximations in critical literacy teaching. *Teaching Education, 21(4)*, 403–426.

Rogers, R. (2011). Becoming Discourse Analysis: Constructing Meanings and Identities. *Critical Inquiry in Language Studies, 8(1)*, 72–104.

1
DESIGNING CRITICAL LITERACY EDUCATION THROUGH CRITICAL DISCOURSE ANALYSIS

Introduction

Critical literacy education is not possible without inquiry into discourse practices: an examination of the relationships between language, power, and identities. In this book we report on a year-long experiment in our teacher education classroom, which began with our exploration about how teaching and learning within a literacy practicum may support the learning and practices of our students, elementary education majors at a Midwestern university. We situated our class in an urban elementary school near the university that would challenge our pre-service teachers to think about their own language, identity, culture, and beliefs as well as provide them with experiences designing literacy practices for African-American students using a variety of pedagogical frameworks. We found, both in the moments of instructional decision making and during the long hours of poring over transcripts together, that discourse analysis was critical in the teacher research model we followed. In fact, we make the case that critical literacy is not possible without discourse analysis. Throughout the book we illustrate how we brought discourse analysis to life within our teaching, learning, and research.

We begin with a vignette from an interaction of three pre-service teachers who are drawing on tools of discourse analysis to think about the text *Iggie's House*[1] (Blume, 1970). The context is a book club group activity that we, the teacher educators, designed around books that featured White protagonists who in one way or another, were working towards racial justice. The book club group included three participants from our class: Leslie who is White, Tonya who is African-American, and Chelsey who is also White. They are early in their first discussion of the book, and are focused on Winnie, the protagonist, who resists her family and community who are not-so-welcoming to a new neighbor, an

African-American family. Leslie raised her eyebrows and peered down at the book. She began:

> Leslie: I think, I feel like, especially when the other day, and while I was reading it, I almost feel like I am this little girl.
> Tonya: Really?
> Leslie: Like, well, because I feel like, um, when she when she talks about like, like um, ok, when she talks about things like people aren't supporting her, when she has these ideas and they're not the same as her parents. I feel like that situation is really similar to me sometimes, if I try to talk to my parents or like friends, like that aren't in the education program about different like social justice type things, they don't really understand it.
> Tonya: I think that's interesting.

In this interaction, Leslie engaged in a textual analysis of the book by relating her own experiences of growing up in a family who had different ideas about "social justice type things." To either bring Leslie's attention to another read of the book *or* to gain a deeper understanding of her position, Tonya drew on a set of tools that she developed throughout the class, tools that we will refer to as "critical literacy"—the questioning of language, identity, and social practices in events in which print and literacy are involved. Here, she questioned Leslie's identification with a character who is White within a book that re-centers whiteness in an exploration of race and racism (see Rogers & Christian, 2007 for a closer analysis of this book).

In the moments that followed, Leslie continued to look intently at her book and at Tonya, as Tonya offered her narrative of how she had read the story.

> Tonya: Um, I think I can see how maybe you could feel that, but I didn't feel that at all.
> Leslie: You didn't? What did you feel from the book?
> Tonya: I definitely didn't feel like I was in the book.
> Leslie: What did you feel like?
> Tonya: This little, this book made me upset. I don't like to read books where nothing happens.
> Leslie: Right, but she's still, she's still in my mind. She's like a growing activist, but she can't do anything right now so it's a waste of time!

From Tonya's view, this was a book in which "nothing happens." Her textual analysis identified the kinds of anti-racist work that Blume (1970) portrayed in the character of Winnie. Tonya emphasized that Winnie was a small child who was beginning to construct tools to work for racial justice but who, at this point in the book, had not yet taken action. Leslie continued to lean towards Tonya, and gave her her full attention, carefully thinking about Tonya's idea. In the next set of interactions, we heard Leslie's use of agreement, for example, the phrase "mmmhmmm," to indicate she was listening to Tonya's read of the text:

> Tonya: To explore, well not a waste of time, like I had reflected on that too, but it was interesting to have the author explore her emotions [Leslie: mmmhmmm] about the subject, but what about the African-American family? [Leslie: mmmm] I don't think that's fair at all. Because they were the ones that were suffering, the signs got placed in their yard [Leslie: right]. There are no Black people around. How do they feel? And it was all about, "Winnie this, and Winnie this, and she has to go through this, and she did this," and very descriptive about her bushy hair [hands go up to hair], and the way she dressed, and the way she played, and she chews two wads of gum at a time [Leslie: laughs] and it was like, you can identify with that character [Leslie: right] but if you have to identify with one of the Black characters, you really couldn't [Leslie: mmmm].

Leslie indicated through her close attention to Tonya's read of the story that she was using inquiry into language to build multiple perspectives when reading, a tool of the community of practice that we will further describe in this book, a community built around common engagement with narratives, cultural knowledge, beliefs about literacy teaching and equity, and positions around social action. This is but one example of how our teacher education students engaged in the critical reading of narratives (their own, those in literature and class narratives) and how we, in turn, critically analyzed their learning using discourse analysis, an iterative process we will demonstrate throughout the book.[2]

Leslie and Tonya were two of fourteen participants in our teacher education class. These students spent a year with us in an urban elementary school where we located two of their literacy courses. The participants were mostly White, middle-class to upper-middle-class women, with the exception of two male students and one African-American female student. The participants were either in an undergraduate degree program, double majoring in elementary education and one other major, or post-baccalaureate students in a Master's program in elementary education. The context of the study was an elementary school in an urban neighborhood in a large, Midwestern city where we held our literacy classes and practicum during the year when the study took place. The elementary school served a mostly African-American population and was not far from the university, a private university with high research activity and high academic standards. We were fortunate to have students from different geographical locations and backgrounds in our program, as well as students who had a range of educational experiences (e.g., urban, rural, private, and public).

Critical Literacy: Roots and Recent Work

Critical literacy refers to approaches to literacy instruction that place an emphasis on helping people develop agency so that they can accomplish goals they deem important and resist the coercive effects of literacy (Dozier, Johnston, & Rogers, 2006; Freire, 1973; Janks, 2002; Luke, 2012; Rogers, Mosley, & Kramer, 2009). Critical literacy educators use analysis, cultural critique, and social action to dismantle unjust practices and to construct agentic narratives alongside their students (Rogers, Mosley, & Folkes, 2010). Critical literacy has deep roots in community and adult education around the world. Indeed, the instructional practices of many literacy campaigns in postcolonial countries were rooted in critical literacy (e.g., Abendroth, 2009; Freire, 1973; Kozol, 1978; Weber, 2001). In the United States, the citizenship schools organized by Septima Clark and Myles Horton from the Highlander Center used methods of popular education, an early precursor to critical literacy, to teach African-American adults to read and write in order to pass the voter registration test (Horton, 1998). An important reminder from these literacy campaigns is that literacy education is always a response to particular social and political conditions.

Critical literacy in contemporary contexts sprang from critical pedagogy, the educational manifestation of critical social theory (e.g., Adorno & Horkheimer, 2002; Bowles & Gintis, 1976; Callinicos, 1995). In the 1980s, scholars such as Henry Giroux, Peter McLaren, Ira Shor, and Paulo Freire created a bridge between critical pedagogy and critical literacy education (e.g., Giroux, 1988; McLaren, 1988; Shor & Freire, 1987). And in adult education there continues to be steady calls for critical literacy (e.g., Brookfield, 2005; Degener, 2001; Demetrion, 2005; Heaney, 1992). However, there are only a limited number of portraits of teachers practicing critical literacy (e.g., Auerbach, 2001; Purcell-Gates & Waterman, 2000; Rogers & Kramer, 2007; Shor & Freire, 1987; St. Clair & Sandlin, 2004). In pre-kindergarten through twelfth grade education (PK-12), critical literacy education is still a relatively new phenomenon, only being documented since the 1980s. But scholarship in this area is slowly mounting, at all educational levels. See Table 1.1 for recent critical literacy scholarship by educational level.

Critical Literacy in Teacher Education

Critical literacy has taken longer to find its way into teacher education perhaps because many researchers of critical literacy practices were first studying other teachers' practices before their own. Yet, we see critical literacy in teacher education as a necessary corollary to the project of critical literacy education in PK-12 and adult and community education. This is an educational project that has been taken up for some time in Australia. Indeed, the federally funded Christie Report (Christie et al., 1991) advocated the inclusion of critical literacy as a core component of teacher education programs. While the proposal was

TABLE 1.1. Recent Work in Critical Literacy Education

Early Childhood/Elementary

Aukerman, M. (2012). "Why do you say yes to Pedro but no to me?" Towards a critical literacy of dialogic engagement. *Theory into Practice, 51(1),* 42–48.

Bourke, R. (2008). First graders and fairy tales: One teacher's action research of critical literacy. *The Reading Teacher, 62(4),* 304–312.

Flint, A., & Laman, T. (2012). Where poems hide: Finding reflective, critical spaces within writer's workshop. *Theory into Practice, 51(1),* 12–19.

Labadie, M., Mosley, M., & Rogers, R. (2012). Opening spaces for critical literacy: Introducing books to young readers. *The Reading Teacher, 66,* 1–11.

Silvers, P., Shorey, M., & Crafton, L. (2010). Critical literacy in a multiliteracies primary grade classroom: The Hurricane Group. *Journal of Early Childhood Literacy, 10(4),* 379–409.

Vasquez, V., & Branigan-Felderman, C. (2012). *Technology and critical literacy in early childhood.* New York, NY: Routledge.

Middle Grades

Beach, R., Thein, A. H., & Webb, A. (2012). *Teaching to exceed the English Language Arts Common Core State Standards: A literacy practices approach for 6–12 classrooms.* New York, NY: Routledge.

Comber, B., Nixon, H., Ashmore, L., Loo, S., & Cook, J. (2006) Urban renewal from the inside out: Spatial and critical literacies in a low socioeconomic school community. *Mind, Culture, and Activity: An International Journal, 13(3),* 228–246.

Enciso, P. (2011). Storytelling in critical literacy pedagogy: Removing the walls between immigrant and non-immigrant youth. *English Teaching: Practice and Critique, 10(1),* 21–40.

Huang, S. (2011). Reading "further and beyond the text": Student perspectives of critical literacy in EFL reading and writing. *Journal of Adolescent & Adult Literacy, 55(2),* 145–154.

Johnson, E., & Vasudevan, L. (2012). Seeing and hearing students' lived and embodied critical literacy practices. *Theory into Practice, 51(1),* 34-41.

Kinloch, V. (2012). *Crossing boundaries: Teaching and learning with urban youth.* New York, NY: Teachers College Press.

Locke, T., & Cleary, A. (2011). Critical literacy as an approach to literary study in the multicultural, high school classroom. *English Teaching: Practice and Critique, 10(1),* 119–139.

Park, J.Y. (2012). A different kind of reading instruction: Using visualizing to bridge reading comprehension and critical literacy. *Journal of Adolescent & Adult Literacy, 55(7),* 629–640.

Pirbhai-Illich, F. (2011). Aboriginal students engaging and struggling with critical multiliteracies. *Journal of Adolescent and Adult Literacy, 54(4),* 257–265.

Adult, Family, and Informal Learning Studies

Johnson, L., & Rosario-Ramos, E. (2012). The role of educational institutions in the development of critical literacy and transformative action. *Theory into Practice, 51(1),* 49–56.

(*Continued*)

TABLE 1.1. (*Continued*)

Morrell, E. (2008). *Critical literacy and urban youth: Pedagogies of access, dissent, and liberation.* New York, NY: Routledge.

Pahl, K., & Rowsell, J. (2011). Artifactual critical literacy: A new perspective for literacy education. *Berkeley Review of Education, 2(2)*, 129–151. http://escholarship.org/uc/ucbgse_bre

Rogers, R., Mosley, M., & Folkes, A. (2009). Standing up to neoliberalism with critical literacy. *Language Arts, 87(2)*, 127–138.

Social Media

Burnett, C., & Merchant, G. (2011). Is there space for critical literacy in the context of social media? *English Teaching: Practice and Critique, 10(1)*, 41–57.

Gainer, J. (2010). Critical media literacy in middle school: Exploring the politics of representation. *Journal of Adolescent & Adult Literacy, 53(5)*, 364–373.

Reid, J. (2011). "We don't twitter, we Facebook": An alternative pedagogical space that enables critical practices in relation to writing. *English Teaching: Practice and Critique, 10(1)*, 58–80.

Teacher Education

Johnston, P. (2012). *Opening minds: Using language to change lives.* Portland, ME: Stenhouse.

Jones, S., & Enriquez, G. (2009). Engaging the intellectual and the moral in critical literacy education: The four-year journeys of two teachers from teacher education to classroom practice. *Reading Research Quarterly, 44(2)*, 145–168.

Mosley, M. (2010). Becoming a literacy teacher: Approximations in critical literacy teaching. *Teaching Education, 21(4)*, 403–426.

Rogers, R. (in press). Coaching teachers as they design critical literacy practices. *Reading and Writing Quarterly.*

Rogers, R., Mosley, M., Kramer, M. A. & LSJTRG (2009). *Designing socially just learning communities: Critical literacy education across the lifespan.* New York: Routledge.

Souto-Manning, M. (2010). Playing with power and privilege: Theatre games in teacher education. *Teaching and Teacher Education, 27*, 997–1007.

Tate, S. (2011). Equity and access through literacy development and instruction: The use of critical text to transform student writing and identity within a research seminar. *English Teaching: Practice and Critique, 10(1)*, 199–208.

not formally adopted, many teacher education programs feature components of critical literacy (Luke, 2000). There are reports of critical literacy in teacher education (e.g., Clarence-Fishman, 2001; Comber, Thomson, & Wells, 2001; Dozier et al., 2006; Johnston, 2012; Leland, Harste, Jackson, & Youssef, 2001; Mosley, 2010; Rogers, in press; Souto-Manning, 2010; Wallace, 2001). However, critical literacy in teacher education in the United States is still very much in development. There are some examples (see Table 1.1) but we still know very little about how pre-service and in-service teachers gain the pedagogical knowledge for critical literacy. Indeed, many of us charged with teaching teachers have been faced with the nagging question, who will teach critical literacy teachers? And, what will these educational practices look like?

In our work preparing teachers, we draw on three frameworks of what teachers should know and be able to do: accelerative literacy practices (e.g., Clay, 1993, 1994), critical literacy (e.g., Lewison, Leland, & Harste, 2007), and socio-critical consciousness (e.g., Villegas & Lucas, 2002). In Chapter 2, we illustrate each of these frameworks with a detailed description of our course. Sometimes our emphasis on critical literacy is resisted. Teachers complain, "We need to include critical literacy in addition to everything else we are required to do?" Other times, we hear relief that there is a tradition that matches their beliefs and practices: "I never knew that what I was doing was called critical literacy." Other times, there is ambivalence. Always, there are questions.

When we set the stage for critical literacy in our teacher education classroom, we like to introduce different approaches to critical literacy to underscore our point that there is no one-way of approaching critical literacy. Rather, critical literacy is a stance toward texts, discourses, and social practices. Over the years, as we have made sense out of the scholarship in critical literacy, we have come to think about three major traditions within the field of critical literacy education: genre approaches, multiple literacy approaches, and social justice approaches (Rogers, in press).

We share with the teachers in our classes the different approaches. First, a genre approach to critical literacy focuses on the importance of students acquiring competence in the linguistic structures of dominant discourses through the analysis of the patterns of texts and the ways that these structures carry out social functions. This tradition is influenced by the systemic linguistic theory of Halliday (1994) who points out that the grammatical aspects of texts can be traced to textual formations (mode), social relations (tenor), and ideological representations of the world (field). Advocates of this approach argue for explicit instruction and direct access to genres of power (Cope, 1993; Cope & Kalantzis, 2000; Delpit & Kilgour Dowdy, 2002; Fairclough, 1992a). Examples of this approach in practice might include: the analysis of different advertisements for one product or different websites focused on a topic; reading and analyzing a biography of a person written by several different authors; and viewing and reading fractured fairytales represented in books or movies.

Another approach to critical literacy education is grounded in the concept of multiliteracies (multiple literacies) that sprang from the work of the New London Group (1996). The New London group called for a widening of the field of literacy studies to include those new forms of literacy made possible by digital technologies and globalized communication networks. They pointed out that new literacies should be used, critiqued, and studied. Teachers who embrace a multiple literacies approach to critical literacy education begin by inquiring into the literacies that exist in a learner's life and find ways to integrate these literacies into the curriculum (González, Moll, & Amanti, 2005; New London Group, 1996; Street, 1984). Tools for learning about students' family and community resources might include: inquiring into family stories through interviews, documenting local literacies through community mapping, or inviting parents and community members to share their expertise. Teachers using this approach also find ways to critique the production and interpretation of such texts. This is important because as Luke, O'Brien, and Comber (1994) remind us, "left uninterrupted, everyday texts play major parts in building and reproducing social structures" (p. 113).

Third, a social justice approach to critical literacy is characterized by a "problem-posing, problem-solving" model of education that is rooted in dialogue between the teacher and learners. This approach seeks to move from critical analysis to social action and there is an explicit emphasis on working toward social justice (Comber et al., 2001; Freire, 1973; Purcell-Gates & Waterman, 2000). Teachers who use this approach ask: What issues genuinely motivate and energize my students? Using student issues to drive the curriculum is often a starting point with this approach. We like to use Comber, Thompson, and Wells' (2001, p. 455) questions as the basis of this approach: "What worries you?", "What do you like about your community?", and "What do you want to change?" We add, "Do you think children can change the world? How?" These questions provoke rich discussion around the issues that are interesting and motivating to students. From here, we can develop text sets of literature that explicitly address social issues.

While the instructional designs and emphasis may be different in each approach, there are many points of conceptual overlap:

- Language is infused with values. It is not neutral.
- Learning occurs within sociocultural contexts.
- Dialogue and participation are at the heart of a community of practice.
- Literacy practices hold the power to transform social reality.
- Inquiry and reflection are cornerstones in developing critical literacy.

In our work with teachers, we believe it is important to emphasize multiple traditions of critical literacy because this offers different entry points for teachers as they develop their consciousness about critical literacy education. Regardless of the approach, at the heart of critical literacy education is inquiry into power, language, and identity.

Language: The Heart of Critical Literacy Education

Language is central in any classroom. It is one of the tools through which meanings are made. So, too, are non-verbal modes such as body language, the physical environment and layout of the classroom, proxemics, and gesture. Verbal and non-verbal modes of meaning are the tools through which meanings are made, communicated, understood, challenged, and transformed. All of these tools create the contexts of the classroom. Classrooms have certain structures that pre-exist any group of students and teacher—structures with institutionalized and cultural histories. For instance, the front and back of the room, the design of the space and the furniture that is available all hold institutionalized and cultural histories that mediate interactions that occur within. Other aspects of the classroom context are created among teachers and students such as new ways of interacting around texts that are online or the use of hybrid languages to share knowledge. We see our role as teachers and researchers to break open the contexts that exist and to examine the material and discursive structures of these contexts so that we can be more responsive and responsible to our students, their families, and our communities. On the role of critical language awareness, a process we liken to discourse analysis, Janks (2000) writes:

> Critical language awareness emphasizes the fact that texts are constructed. Anything that has been constructed can be de-constructed. This unmaking or unpacking of the text increases our awareness of the choices that the writer or speaker has made. Every choice foregrounds what was selected and hides, silences or backgrounds what was not selected.
>
> (Janks, 2000, p. 176)

Doing this means attending both to the language bits that circulate in the classroom and also the ways of being, representing, and valuing that are embodied in learning environments. Gee (1996) captures this distinction as discourses (with a lowercase "d") and Discourses" (with a capital "D"). "discourses" are the language bits that comprise communicative events. This includes the hard and soft structures of language—grammar, morphology, intonation, and so on. Discourses—with a capital D—includes the ways of using, being, and representing language. Discourses refer to the systems of meaning that are attached to what we say, or the tools that we use. Discourses draw on and construct larger meta-narratives—narratives about gender, race, and class, for instance. Discourses play many roles in the classroom. They sustain, build, resist, or transform existing narratives and ideologies.

Discourses are both always in existence and are always being constructed and transformed through interactions, especially within learning contexts such as our teacher education classroom. Students come to our classroom with histories of participation with literacy and school. They walk into our classroom and see themselves as particular kinds of teachers of reading and writing. They have semi-sedimented narratives about the role and purpose of literacy education. We want to bring these discourses—those that already exist and those that will be created—to their attention.

The goal of critical literacy teaching is to draw our students' attention to the ways in which discourses circulate, to the ways in which they are constructed, and how they might design practices that lead to more just and equitable social futures. Thus, in our critical literacy classroom one of our primary concerns is to enable students to engage with social struggles in ways that they find meaningful. Through the tools and frames associated with discourse analysis, we demonstrate and provide teachers with ways of slowing down interactions by asking: What happened here? How do we know? What else might have happened? What was meant in this interaction? Could it have been interpreted in a different way? How do we know? We know that important things are said in important ways; or put another way, we recognize not just *what* people say but *how* they say it.

Likewise, our students come to our classrooms with histories as discourse analysts—they just don't know that that is what they are doing. They know, for instance, what their friend means by her tone of voice. They understand sub-plots in movies by what and who are absent as well as what is present. They read Internet texts looking for the fine print or to compare information across sites. They know when they are being duped by and with language. Our role is to draw out of them this inclination to analyze discourses. As discourse analysts, we bring this stance of attending critically to discourses (both verbal and nonverbal) into our work as teachers and researchers. Throughout the book we draw attention to the ways in which our students engaged in discourse analysis to unpack the multiplicity of meanings that resides in any text. We also explain the conditions that we established in our classrooms that made this unpacking of texts more of the norm than the exception.

Discourse Analysis as a Tool for Teachers' Learning

Discourse analysis is gaining popularity as a tool in teacher research. Like other scholars, we believe it is important for teachers to actively study how their own discourse practices shape learning outcomes (Comber et al., 2001; Johnston, 2012). An increasing number of scholars are integrating discourse analysis into their teaching lives (e.g., Schaenen, 2010; Van Sluys, Lewison, & Flint, 2006; Webb, 2005). In this book we share how we used discourse analysis to aid our teaching and how our students did the same. We applied the tools of narrative analysis, the building tasks and inquiry tools, critical discourse analysis (CDA), and multimodal discourse analysis (MDA) in the midst of our teaching. We give examples of this in each chapter. We also returned to more deeply studying artifacts of teaching and learning once the course had ended. Thus, we argue for a layered approach to discourse analysis in teacher research that folds in an ongoing analysis of language but also returns for a closer study. For too long, one of the greatest hindrances to teacher researchers of using discourse analysis as a method in their work has been the time commitments of close study of discourses. Indeed, analyzing interactional patterns, discourse structures, and positionings takes many passes through the data and much time. However, as we show in each chapter, some of this work can be accomplished in the midst of teaching—in fact, it can become the subject of teaching and our feedback to our students. Second, we encourage our students to be discourse analysts as well. In each chapter we focus on a slice of time in our classroom when pre-service teachers were inquiring into their own practices using the tools of discourse analysis.

Literacy Research and Discourse Analysis

Over the past decade there has been much scholarship devoted to the intersection of discourse analysis and literacy research (e.g., Bloome et al., 2008; Burns & Morrell, 2005; Gee, 2002; Janks, 2005; Lewis, 2006; Rex & Schiller, 2009). We believe this is so because of the many areas of commensurability that exist between literacy research and discourse analysis.

First, because literacy practices are considered communicative events, it stands to reason that discourse analysis would be useful to analyze the ways in which texts, talk, and other semiotic interactions are constructed across time and contexts. Second, discourse studies provide a particular way of conceptualizing interactions that are compatible with socio-cultural perspectives in literacy research (Gutiérrez, 2006; Lewis, Enciso, & Moje, 2007; Luke, 2003). A shared assumption is that discourse can be understood as a multimodal social practice. That is, discourse moves back and forth between reflecting and constructing the social world through a range of sign systems. Seen in this way, language cannot be considered neutral, because it is caught up in political, social, racial, economic, religious, and cultural formations (Blommaert, 2005). A third area of commensurability is that discourse studies and literacy research are both traditions that address problems through a range of theoretical perspectives. Many of the problems that are addressed, particularly in a globalized world system, have to do with power and inequality. Discourse analysis provides the tools for addressing the complexity of movement across literacy sites and practices in an increasingly global and digital world. Because of the reflexive tendencies of discourse analysis, it holds the potential for continuing to change and evolve to meet the needs of new questions in literacy research and teacher education.

There are many varieties of discourse analysis. In our work, we draw on approaches that share a critical orientation toward the social world emerging from feminism, critical race theory, critical social theory, and so on. This work shares the assumption that language is a social practice and because social practices are not treated nor created equally, all analyses of language are inherently critical. We refer to this collection of scholarship as critical approaches to discourse analysis (Rogers, 2011). In this book we will demonstrate how we used four varieties of discourse analysis—narrative analysis, building tasks and inquiry tools, critical discourse analysis, and multimodal discourse analysis—as tools in our teaching and research. Table 1.2 is a display of the instructional designs, pedagogical frameworks, and kind of discourse analysis that features in each chapter.

TABLE 1.2. Instructional Designs, Frameworks, and Discourse Analysis

Chapter	Instructional Designs	Frameworks	Discourse Analysis
3	Literacy autobiographies Critical reading of children's literature	Culturally relevant pedagogy	Narrative analysis
4	Student-led inquiry Small group discussions Play	Linguistic diversity	Building tasks: Cultural models, situated identities, and social languages
5	Book clubs Online discussions One-on-one pedagogy	Critical race theory	Critical discourse analysis
6	Teaching elementary students literacy (*Jazz Baby*) Conference presentations	Multimodal literacy	Multimodal discourse analysis

One last note about discourse analysis in literacy research: Scholars of critically oriented discourse analysis have concerned themselves—by and large—with a critique of power, domination, and oppression. By way of contrast, a number of scholars are calling for a focus on the relationship between literacy and productive uses of power (Luke, 2004; Martin, 2004; Scollon & Wong Scollon, 2004). Luke (2004) pointed out the potential for reconstructive versions of discourse analysis, which focus on how liberation, solidarity, and community are constructed. Martin refers to this approach as "positive discourse analysis," which can provide a complementary focus on "how people get together and make room for themselves in the world—in ways that redistribute power without necessarily struggling against it" (2004, p. 183).

In literacy research, much scholarship has examined the ways that literacy events and practices (at individual, classroom, school, or societal levels) reproduce and construct racist, sexist, and classist social relations. Race in literacy research, for example, has most often been discussed in terms of racism and discriminatory practices and policies. However, a positive discourse analysis would examine the discursive composition of anti-racist practices and policies, those that create an alternative to dominant discourses in society (see also Reisigl & Wodak, 2001). Scholarship exists that illustrates how schools can create opportunities for all students by integrating multiple literacies and associated ways of knowing and being into the language arts curriculum (e.g., Maybin, 2007; Richardson, 2007). Yet we know less about the discursive contours of multimodal, multicultural, anti-racist, socially just classrooms, curricula, and literacy policies, areas that we address in this book.

Structure of the Book

Uniquely positioned as teacher researchers, we share an ethnographically informed discourse analysis—rich with details and context—of the instructional designs that characterize critical literacy teaching across the course of a year in our teacher education classroom. The book also functions as a guide for conducting critical discourse analysis. Each chapter refers to a set of appendices, which include a set of tools—theoretical` and methodological—for conducting critical discourse analysis. What results, we hope, is a book with much potential for teacher educators, discourse analysts, and teacher researchers studying the power and potential of language in their classroom.

Chapter 2, "Inside the Design of our Teaching and Research," explores the context and methods of the study. We illustrate how we situated our teacher education work in the community of the school where our course was located. We also introduce the traditions of discourse analysis that will provide a structure for the chapters that follow.

Chapter 3, "Narrating Literacy, Identity and Culture: Narrative Analysis," illustrates how we used cultural narratives—both spoken (autobiographical) and written (literature)—in our classroom to create a community of practice responsive to the diversity of cultures, races, levels of power, and languages. The chapter foregrounds the narratives of a number of our students and demonstrates both how the teacher education students engaged with critical narrative analysis as well as how we more deeply understood their stories through narrative analysis. Throughout the chapter we refer to a set of appendices that guide the reader through the steps of conducting narrative analysis.

Chapter 4, "Inquiry into Linguistic Diversity: Discourse Analysis," focuses on a student-centered inquiry into language variety and assessing oral reading that emerged generatively during our instruction. The students' questions and inquiry morphed into their desire to take action and write a letter to Marie Clay (1994), whose work they drew on when learning to do running records, asking about her thoughts on issues of language diversity, assessment, and power. We demonstrate how the students were engaged in critical language inquiry throughout this process. Likewise, we analysed their inquiry using Gee's (2010) building tasks analysis, which helped us understand how the teacher candidates' positioned themselves as students, pre-service teachers, and future teachers. As this chapter unfolds, we refer the reader to a series of associated appendices that illustrate the process of conducting a building tasks analysis.

Stemming from a problem in our teaching, we decided, mid-year, to include a unit on whiteness studies and racial literacy, the focus of Chapter 5,

"Practicing Racial Literacy: Critical Discourse Analysis." Moving from whiteness studies to anti-racism, the teacher education students explored their own racial histories through the lenses of whiteness studies and critical race theory. Drawing on the traditions of critical discourse analysis, we show the process and product of this work as the teacher education students worked with one another and us to design anti-racist pedagogy. Throughout the chapter we build on the discourse analytic tools presented thus far and refer the reader to a series of appendices that guide the reader through the process of conducting a critical discourse analysis.

Performative literacy practices are the focus of Chapter 6, "Performing Literacy: Multimodal Discourse Analysis." As we moved toward the end of the school year, we noticed that many of our teachers were embodying critical literacy practices in their teaching and professional work as teachers. They called upon the tools of multimodal discourse analysis to make a space for multiple modes of meaning making in their teaching and in their own learning. Multimodal discourse analysis provides us with tools for understanding the relationships between language and action. Likewise, we demonstrate in this chapter how we read their practices through a multimodal lens. At the same time, we refer to the associated appendices that describe the methods of conducting multimodal discourse analysis.

In Chapter 7, "Conclusions," we bring the book to a close by reflecting on the role of discourse analysis in critical literacy education. We acknowledge that the approaches we have advocated for throughout the book are not aligned with the current focus of teacher learning, as defined by federal education reform efforts. And yet we know that we need to reframe the conversation about how knowledge is defined, constructed, and evaluated. We reflect on how teacher research in the context of critical literacy education may lead to better instruction, teacher-initiated educational reforms, and political and social action. As the teachers participated in our community of practice over the course of the year they practiced rehearsing their roles as critically engaged literacy teachers. Likewise, we have set forth an example of collaborative, longitudinal teacher research and in this last chapter we reflect on how this kind of arrangement has benefited our own intellectual lives, which includes our teaching of teachers. We include recommendations for how we might encourage future educators to become discourse analysts of their own practice.

The book is designed as an interactive guide for learning discourse analysis—one that will guide the reader through the process of conducting critical discourse analysis with appendices featuring theory and method, sample transcripts, step-by-step guides for conducting different kinds of critical discourse analysis, and additional readings and resources. Table 1.3 includes an outline of appendices and associated tools for each chapter.

TABLE 1.3. Toolkit for Conducting Critical Discourse Analysis

Chapter 3—Critical Narrative Analysis	
Part I: Preparing for Narrative Analysis	
Choosing a Type of Narrative Analysis	Appendix 3A
Part II: Conducting Narrative Analysis	
How to Identify Themes in a Narrative Analysis	Appendix 3B
Locating Narrative Structure	Appendix 3C
Creating Transcripts	Appendix 3D
Identifying the Clause as the Unit of Analysis	Appendix 3E
Analyzing Positioning	Appendix 3F
Part III: Steps in Conducting a Critical Narrative Analysis	
A Guide to Conducting Critical Narrative Analysis	Appendix 3G
Additional Reading and Resources to Support Narrative Analysis	Appendix 3H
Chapter 4—Discourse Analysis	
Part I: Preparing for the Building Tasks Analysis	
Creating Stanzas	Appendix 4A
Part II: Conducting the Building Tasks Analysis	
Identifying Theoretical Frames and Building Tasks	Appendix 4B
Overview of Theoretical Frames and Building Tasks	Table 4.1
Carrying out a Descriptive Level of Linguistic Analysis	Appendix 4C
Representing the Discourse Analysis	Appendix 4D
Codebook: Survey of Linguistic Resources	Table 4.2
Example of Conducting a Building Tasks Analysis	Table 4.3
Part III: Steps in Conducting a Building Tasks Analysis	
A Guide to Conducting a Building Tasks Analysis	Appendix 4E
Letter from Dr. Marie Clay to Our Class	Appendix 4F
Additional Reading and Resources to Support a Building Tasks Analysis	Appendix 4G
Chapter 5—Critical Discourse Analysis	
Part I: Preparing for the Critical Discourse Analysis	
Developing Research Questions and Segmenting the Text	Appendix 5A
Faircloughian CDA Framework	Table 5.1
Part II: Conducting Critical Discourse Analysis	
Using the Triparte Schema of Genre, Discourse, and Style	Appendix 5B

(Continued)

TABLE 1.3. (*Continued*)

Leslie's Verbal Processes	Table 5.2
Tonya's Verbal Processes	Table 5.3
Looking Across Genre, Discourse, and Style	Table 5.4
Survey of Linguistic Features and Functions Connected to Orders of Discourse	Table 5.5
Part III: Representing the Findings	
Representational Issues to Consider	Appendix 5C
Part IV: Steps in Conducting Critical Discourse Analysis	
A Guide to Conducting Critical Discourse Analysis	Appendix 5D
Additional Reading and Resources to Support Critical Discourse Analysis	Appendix 5E

Chapter 6—Multimodal Discourse Analysis	
Part I: Preparing for the Multimodal Discourse Analysis	
Creating a Multimodal Transcript	Appendix 6A
Still Frame Transcription	Table 6.1
Part II: Conducting the Multimodal Discourse Analysis	
The Descriptive Analysis of Multimodal Transcripts	Appendix 6B
Jonah and Tamara's Use of Verbs	Table 6.2
Examining Modality	Appendix 6C
Part III: Steps in Conducting Multimodal Discourse Analysis	
Guide to Conducting Multimodal Discourse Analysis	Appendix 6D
Example of Multimodal Transcription and Analysis	Table 6.3
Codes for a 30-Second Segment of Transcript	Table 6.4
Jonah and Tamara Segments	Appendix 6E
Jonah and Tamara Segment 1	Table 6.5
Jonah and Tamara Segment 2	Table 6.6
Tonya and CeCe Segments	Appendix 6F
Tonya and CeCe Segment 1	Table 6.7
Tonya and CeCe Segment 2	Table 6.8
Additional Reading and Resources to Support Multimodal Discourse Analysis	Appendix 6G

Part IV: Revisiting Critiques of Critical Approaches to Discourse Analysis

2

INSIDE THE DESIGN OF OUR TEACHING AND RESEARCH

Our Experiment with our Teaching

In this chapter we discuss the design of the inquiry we conducted with our teaching in a pre-service teacher education program. We drew on the tradition of teacher research (Cochran-Smith & Lytle, 2001; Mohr, Rogers, Sanford, Nocerino, & Clawson, 2004; Rogers, Mosley, & Kramer, 2009) to pose problems, collect and analyze data, and refine our practices in the classroom where we were co-teacher researchers. As critical literacy teachers, we placed language in social contexts at the center of our pedagogy and thus drew on the tools of discourse analysis in both our teaching and research.

Context

The teacher education program that is the focus of this project was located at a university in St. Louis. The guiding principles of the teacher education program stated that graduates of this program will be committed to equitable and just education for all students, will know the subjects they teach well, will know how to teach, and will enact the role of inquirer. The program followed a cohort model and the students took three literacy courses together. Two of the literacy courses were located at an urban elementary school and included a practicum component. Every Tuesday from 2 pm until 5 pm (September–May), the teacher education students met at an urban elementary school in an African-American community we call Liddell, about three miles from the university. The university class, held in an unused classroom, included a practicum as well as a seminar. The school was located in a district close to losing accreditation that had adopted a scripted reading program that had all but eliminated culturally responsive literacy instruction in the schools.

We introduced our students to the history of the Liddell community by engaging them in discussions with the senior librarian at the branch of the public library that lies next door to Liddell Elementary School. Throughout our work with these teachers, we encouraged their participation in the community and made ongoing links between their instruction and the community in which they were teaching.

Briefly, we will describe here the history of this community. St. Louis is a city with a history of racial division between African-Americans and Whites (Heaney & Uchitelle, 2004). The Liddell neighborhood was the location of many prominent institutions during the middle of the twentieth century including schools, churches, and community organizations. Homeowners in Liddell took great pride in the neighborhood and worked over time towards renewal. Prior to 1950, Liddell was a primarily White neighborhood with grand houses and many public and private institutions. In 1947, a newspaper reported that the neighborhood was "blighted" and describes the surprise of Liddell residents upon hearing this news (Bliss, 1947). In this particular city, the conditions of African-American communities were not in the interest of White city dwellers in the second half of the twentieth century, and reforms did not center upon creating new jobs for African-Americans. In fact, many of the manufacturing jobs of the city moved to the county and African-American contractors were not hired to perform rehab services and demolition. During a time of racial desegregation in St. Louis schools, neighborhoods, and other institutions, racial tensions led to an exodus of White residents and the city did not support Liddell in maintaining its strength as a community.

The city is characterized as maintaining the status quo with regard to inequities along education, housing, and employment lines despite reform attempts such as school desegregation (Morris & Morris, 2002; Wells & Crain, 1997). Cities and schools within the metropolitan St. Louis area are racially segregated and many primarily African-American neighborhoods, like Liddell, are dilapidated. This urban decline is attributed to a complex set of factors, including access to jobs, White-flight, housing, education, health care, and community organizations (De Souza Briggs, 2005; Jargowsky, 1997; Wilson, 1996).

The period after *Brown v. Board of Education of Topeka* brought changes to the children and families of the Liddell neighborhood (Heaney & Uchitelle, 2004; Wells & Crain, 1997). With desegregation, people began to fight for what they saw as the best interests of the community, and for many White families that meant impeding the integration process. Within or near Liddell's borders, three elementary schools opened in the mid-1960s to accommodate a growing population of African-American students (Wright, 2002). As it became clear that Liddell would have to integrate, resources were systematically drawn away from the Liddell neighborhood and school. In 2002, Rebecca Rogers approached the administration of the school, eager to build a relationship between the school and the university that emphasized the mutually beneficial exchange of knowledge and resources in a context of reciprocity. The administration agreed to host the literacy courses and provide a classroom. In turn, the course provided literacy teaching once per week for students who needed support in reading and writing, professional development for teachers at the school and enrichment programs for students in arts education. The collaboration lasted for three years. However, monetary and human resources continued to be drawn away from this school and dedicated to charter schools, and after the close of this study, despite being a cornerstone of the community, the district closed the elementary school (Rogers & Pole, 2010).

Participants

Our class included four graduate students and 11 undergraduates. Fourteen students were European American. There was one African-American woman enrolled in the class. Thirteen of the students were women and two of the students were men. When we asked the students to write their cultural autobiographies, we learned that they were diverse in terms of their geographic, religious, and socio-economic backgrounds. Although we introduce these focal participants here, throughout the rest of the chapters we will delve further into their stories, focusing on six of the 14 due to the completeness of their data sets. Table 2.1 is a chart that can be used for ease of referencing participants throughout the book.

A graduate student in the class, Jonah, completed his undergraduate work at a public state university in the Midwest (see Chapters 3, 4, 5, and 6). He returned to the city where he was born and raised in order to attend graduate school. During in-class discussions around culturally relevant pedagogy, Jonah often discussed his Jewish heritage. It was his religious and cultural affiliation that positioned him to understand oppression. He described how he was very proud of his grandfather—a former mayor of the city where he grew up—who worked for racial integration. Jonah brought many social justice experiences with him into

TABLE 2.1. Reference Chart of Participants

Participant	Race, Religious, or Ethnic Background	Degree Sought	Geographical Background
Tonya	African-American	Master's degree	West Coast; Urban
Jonah	White; Jewish	Master's degree	Midwest; Racially diverse suburban
Leslie	White; Jewish; Christian	Undergraduate	Midwest; Urban to suburban
Lisa	White; Christian scientist	Undergraduate	Southwestern; Suburban
Chelsey	White; Jewish	Undergraduate	East Coast; Suburban
Rex	White; Christian	Undergraduate	Midwest; Rural

the classroom—from workers' rights to gender rights. He often worked to scaffold his peers' thinking around issues of justice. Jonah seemed to listen to various viewpoints and did not dominate discussions.

Leslie (see Chapter 5) self-identified as a White, middle-class, Christian-Jewish liberal in an interview. Leslie attended public schools in St. Louis. Leslie double-majored in Education and Anthropology. In an autobiography, she described herself as "devoted to teaching practices that promote justice and build community in her classroom." During the course of the study, Leslie participated in several social actions including a living wage campaign and a homeless awareness campaign.

Lisa (see Chapter 4) described herself in a social positioning exercise as female, Caucasian, a "United Statesian," part of the upper middle class, a Christian scientist, and from a Midwestern, suburban, middle-sized city. Lisa also described in her literacy autobiography that reading for pleasure, especially books that were relevant to her life, was replaced by reading to gain information during school, particularly in fifth grade. As Lisa looked back on her history as a reader, she communicated a negative affinity with reading that came from an overwhelming role as a "school reader." Lisa spent a summer at sea in an honors program just before this study began, often hearing world leaders speak on global problems. Lisa's case illustrates inquiry in both literacy teaching and critical reflection practices. She picked up the practice of inquiry and believed that there was not a child too young for critical reflection.

Chelsey (see Chapter 5) is a European American undergraduate student who joined this group during the spring semester. Chelsey struggled with the technical aspects of teaching literacy and often did not adequately prepare for her teaching sessions. She commented several times in class and in her journals that she thought it was not developmentally appropriate to engage young children in discussion around race, racism, and anti-racism.

A White man in his early twenties, Rex (see Chapter 5) was enrolled in the undergraduate teacher education program. He was also a member of the Reserve Officers' Training Corps (ROTC) program and planned on going on active duty in the military after college. Rex described growing up in a small "conservative, rural, Midwest" town and coming from a "very conservative Lutheran family." Rex admits having to unlearn stereotypes about all sorts of people once he arrived at the university. Rex did not resist engaging with issues of culturally relevant and anti-racist instruction. He also, however, had difficulty seeing aspects of White privilege and entered into heated discussions with colleagues in class about these issues. Claiming a balanced perspective, he said, "I am not extremely anything." Rex's teaching suffered because of his lack of preparation for class—he often did not have lesson logs completed and/or had not completed the readings. As instructors, we spent ample time trying to accelerate Rex as a teacher of literacy.

A graduate student in the class, Tonya (see Chapters 3, 4, 5, and 6) received her undergraduate degree from the same university where she pursued her graduate degree. Tonya was the only African-American woman in class. Tonya grew up on the West Coast in a large family. From a very young age, she self-identified as an avid reader participating in literacy activities at home, in school, and in church. Tonya's parents did not attend college. Tonya decided to double-major in Education and African-American studies. During the course of this study, Tonya participated in a Dismantling Racism Institute for Educators (DRIE) weekend workshop with Jonah, another class member. Tonya also taught at an elementary school where she established an academic program for students who participated in the desegregation program. Tonya readily engaged with issues of culturally relevant and anti-racist literacy instruction—in discussions, in journals, and in her teaching.

Researcher Roles

We were both teacher educators in this course. Rebecca routinely taught these courses and initiated the move from the university to the elementary school. Several years later, Melissa, a graduate student at the time, co-taught the course with Rebecca. At the beginning of the year we decided to design a teacher research project around our practices in the courses. We rotated in our roles as teacher researchers. As European-American teacher educators who are committed to integrating anti-racist practices in our professional and personal lives, we also collaborated in a teacher research group called the Literacy for Social Justice Teacher Research Group (LSJTRG) (Rogers, Mosley, & Kramer, 2009). We are both active in community activism and social justice initiatives and have made personal and professional commitments to actively interrogate White privilege and to facilitate anti-racist/pro-justice pedagogy.

We came to this project with different experiences of teaching and of conducting research. Melissa taught for three years in a second grade classroom in St. Louis, near the neighborhood where she was raised. She also attended graduate school in St. Louis. She became interested in classroom research and critical literacy through her experience of LSJTRG. Rebecca collaborated with Melissa in her second grade classroom and, through that project, introduced her to the idea of pursuing educational research. Upon entering the doctoral program, Melissa collaborated as a teacher educator for three years, eventually teaching her own classes at a neighboring university and then taking a university position after earning her doctorate. Rebecca was a university professor of five years when this project commenced. Prior to teaching at the university she was a literacy specialist in an elementary school and also in an adult general education (GED) classroom. She attended public schools kindergarten through graduate school in New York. Our theoretical backgrounds and interests converged around sociocultural theory, critical discourse studies, and race-based pedagogies.

Our Pedagogical Approaches

We situate our study in the tradition of research that has studied effective literacy teacher education practices within methods courses (Assaf, 2005; Assaf & Dooley,

2006; Lewison, Flint, & Van Sluys, 2002). Like others, we focus on the pedagogical approaches that teacher educators use to support pre-service teachers working with diverse groups of children (Ladson-Billings, 1994; Turner, 2006; Xu, 2000). We centralize inquiry into matters of language, identity, and power to cultivate critical pedagogy, an umbrella concept that includes a variety of pedagogical approaches. The foundation of critical pedagogy is the recognition that the classroom can be a microcosm of society, thus seeing the classroom as one of the sites for challenging multiple and intersecting forms of oppression (Apple, 2004). Paulo Freire's work (1970) is also foundational to this perspective because of his use of critical literacy towards inquiry, dialogic learning, and social transformation. In our teaching and research we pivoted between theories and practices of multicultural teaching (e.g., Banks, 1997), culturally relevant/responsive teaching (e.g., Gay, 2002; Ladson-Billings, 1994), and critical race/anti-racist teaching (e.g., Dei, 1996; Giovanni, 1994; bell hooks, 1994; Taylor, Gilborn, & Ladson-Billings, 2009).

We designed a year-long curriculum for our elementary education teacher education majors around issues of equity and justice within the context of literacy education (see Table 2.2).

In the first semester of literacy coursework, the class "Teaching Reading in the Elementary School" had the following objectives for pre-service teachers:

1. Have a working knowledge of the language and practice of emergent language and literacy in the contexts of learning to read and teaching reading.
2. Plan and conduct appropriate instruction based on students' strengths.
3. Explore literacy acquisition and learning from a range of perspectives including the linguistic, cognitive, social, and psychological.
4. Engage in conversations about the political, social, and economic nature and consequences of literacy instruction.
5. Participate in the development of multicultural, multilingual, anti-racist, and pro-justice literacy curriculum.

The second semester, "Practicum: Diagnosis of Reading Difficulties," carried the following objectives:

1. Have a working knowledge of the language of assessment and the assessment of language and literacy.
2. Become sensitive observers of student's literate behaviors.
3. Collect instructionally relevant information about student's literacy development from different sources.
4. Plan and conduct appropriate instruction.
5. Understand the relationship between texts, readers, and contexts.
6. Communicate assessment information clearly and effectively to parents and colleagues.

TABLE 2.2. Outline of Class Readings, Activities, and Data Sources

Date	Topic and Readings	Type of Data	Description
September 7	Course introduction Culturally relevant pedagogy (Ladson–Billings, 1994)	• Artifacts of tutoring (lesson plans, reflective logs) • Artifacts (class assignments)	Journal 1: Response to readings
September 14	Foundations of literacy learning (Clay, 1993; Fountas & Pinnell, 1996; Orellana & Hernández, 1999)	• Artifacts of tutoring (lesson plans, reflective logs) • Artifacts (class assignments)	Journal 2: Response to readings
September 21	Social theories of learning and literacy development (Macedo, 2003)	• Artifacts of tutoring (lesson plans, reflective logs) • Artifacts (class assignments)	Journal 3: Response to readings
September 28	• Creating a literacy program • In-class discussion "Are linguistic variations recorded as errors in a running record?"	• Artifacts of tutoring (lesson plans, reflective logs) • Artifacts (class assignments)	Literacy autobiographies (Florio–Ruane, 2000): Share your narrative of becoming "literate". Be specific. What events were influential?
October 5	Understanding literature (Fountas, Pinnell, & Bird, 1999; Sweeney, 1997)	• Artifacts of tutoring (lesson plans, reflective logs) • Artifacts (class assignments)	Inquiry project 1: Observe a child reading orally. Do they read like they are talking? In which books? Do they re-read? What choices do they make as a reader? What did you learn about the child? Write a reflection on/analysis of the experience.
October 12	Introducing books to readers/Finding a productive level (Clay, 1996; Commeyras, 1994) • Read-aloud *Me & Neesie* (Greenfield, 1984)	• Artifacts of tutoring (lesson plans, reflective logs) • Artifacts (class assignments)	Writing samples from students in tutoring

(Continued)

TABLE 2.2. (*Continued*)

Date	Topic and Readings	Type of Data	Description
October 19	Representation and literacy (Wheeler & Swords, 2004) • Read-aloud *Be Boy Buzz* (hooks, 2002) • Film on linguistic variation	• Artifacts of tutoring (lesson plans, reflective logs) • Artifacts (class assignments) • Videos of Seminar	Videotape of discussion of language variation Inquiry project #2 Book Introduction. Introduce a book to a child. Tape record the book introduction. Then, analyze the way(s) in which you supported the child's engagement with the text. Discuss . . .
October 26	Writing processes (Schneider, 2001) Book club discussions in class begin (Purcell-Gates, 1995)	• Artifacts of tutoring (lesson plans, reflective logs) • Artifacts (class assignments)	Journal 4
November 2	Word study and developmental spelling (Fresche, 2001)	• Artifacts of tutoring (lesson plans, reflective logs) • Artifacts (class assignments)	Inquiry 3: Write with a child The purpose of this assignment is to think about your child as a writer. What purposes do they have for writing in their everyday lives? What genres do they prefer to write in? . . .
November 9	Nonfiction literacy (Grace, 2004) Read-aloud *Lookin' for Bird in the Big City* (Burleigh, 2001)	• Artifacts of tutoring (lesson plans, reflective logs) • Artifacts (class assignments) • Videos of tutoring	Videotape of the "design of the space" including tutoring materials and books that tutors bring to the session.
November 16	Instructional conversations (Clay, 1987) Read-aloud *Fly Away Home* (Bunting, 1991)		
November 23	Assessment (Johnston, 1997)	• Artifacts of tutoring (lesson plans, reflective logs)	In-class discussion: "How do you know that we care" Inquiry 4: Guided reading assignment

TABLE 2.2.

Date	Topic and Readings	Type of Data	Description
		• Artifacts (class assignments) • Videos of tutoring	Develop a guided reading framework for one of the books that you will be reading with your case study student.
November 30	Communicating with parents	• Artifacts of tutoring (lesson plans, reflective logs) • Artifacts (class assignments) • Videos of tutoring • Videos of seminar	Leslie tutoring using baby animals book and *The Best Thing* (pre-culturally responsive pedagogy) Book groups' presentations (multicultural book), that is, Lisa reads *Le Petit Prince*
December 7	Presentation of book club books and final celebration	• Artifacts of tutoring (lesson plans, reflective logs) • Artifacts (class assignments) • Videos of tutoring	Videotapes of final celebration (Jonah, Tonya) Reflective essays
January 20	Assessment in a diverse society: Ladson–Billings (2001) Multicultural children's literature (websites) Read-aloud: *The Big Box* (Morrison & Morrison, 2002)	• Artifacts of tutoring (lesson plans, reflective logs) • Artifacts (class assignments)	Return to literacy autobiography and addendum
January 27	Exploring the contexts of literacy assessment: Clay (1993), Johnston (1997), Fountas and Pinnell (1996)	• Artifacts of tutoring (lesson plans, reflective logs) • Artifacts (class assignments)	Running records
February 3	• Assessing the known: Johnston (1997), Bear et al. (2004); Allington (2002)	• Artifacts of tutoring (lesson plans, reflective logs)	Lesson plans Videos of design of space

(Continued)

TABLE 2.2. (*Continued*)

Date	Topic and Readings	Type of Data	Description
	• Multicultural education	• Artifacts (class assignments) • Videos of tutoring	
February 10	• Critical literacy (Lee, 2010) • Discussing strengths and how students approach texts • Observation survey (Clay, 1993)	• Artifacts of tutoring (lesson plans, reflective logs) • Artifacts (class assignments) • Videos of tutoring	Tonya tutors using *The True Story of the Three Little Pigs* (Schiezka, 1996). Lisa tutors Helena
February 17	Special education and power (Rogers, 2002)	• Artifacts of tutoring (lesson plans, reflective logs) • Artifacts (class assignments) • Videos of seminar	• Two analyzed running records from tutoring sessions with a description of your interpretation and instructional response (including one socially relevant text) • Whiteness discussion using *Mr. Lincoln's Way* (Polacco, 2001)
February 24	• Family literacy • Attending Liddell's black history program	• Artifacts of tutoring (lesson plans, reflective logs) • Artifacts (class assignments) • Videos of tutoring	• Journal: Write a plan of how you will make a meaningful connection with your student's family/guardians • Videotapes of tutoring small group reading instruction • Initial assessment of student
March 2	Assessing word knowledge and the logic of errors (Bear et al., 2004; Johnston, 1997)	• Artifacts of tutoring (lesson plans, reflective logs) • Artifacts (class assignments) • Videos of tutoring	Videotapes of tutoring small group reading instruction (multiple tutors and students working together) and debriefing

TABLE 2.2.

Date	Topic and Readings	Type of Data	Description
March 16	Assessing comprehension (Harvey & Goudvis, 2000)	• Artifacts of tutoring (lesson plans, reflective logs) • Artifacts (class assignments)	An analysis of your student's word knowledge based on the reading and discussions over the last week
March 23	• Observing and writing (Fletcher & Portalupi, 1999) • Read-aloud *Whitewash* (Shange, 1998) • Discussion of worker's rights and literacy as a human right	• Artifacts of tutoring (lesson plans, reflective logs) • Artifacts (class assignments) • Videos of tutoring	Critical literacy assignment
March 30	Assessing writing: systematic responses to student work (Fletcher & Portalupi, 1999)	• Artifacts of tutoring (lesson plans, reflective logs) • Artifacts (class assignments) • Videos of tutoring	Journal: Every person has a range of literacy practices in their homes and communities, which can be used as a place to build "schooled literacy." What are yours? Reflect on critical literacy through your work with your student and readings.
April 6	Guided Reading Read-aloud *Mr. Lincoln's Way* (Polacco, 2001) • Introduce book club books • Mini-lecture on "Anti-racist, pro-justice literacy education" (McIntosh, P., 1989)	• Artifacts of tutoring (lesson plans, reflective logs) • Artifacts (class assignments) • Videos of tutoring	Writing assessment: Choose two writing samples from your student. Your analysis of the writing should attend to the content, fluency, voice, and conventions. Include a plan for instruction and how you will communicate your analysis to the student's parents.
April 13	Book clubs (whiteness in children's literature) Qualitative reading inventory	• Artifacts of tutoring (lesson plans, reflective logs) • Artifacts (class assignments) • Videos of seminar • Videos of tutoring	Book club discussions (video recordings)

(*Continued*)

TABLE 2.2. (*Continued*)

Date	Topic and Readings	Type of Data	Description
April 20	Book clubs (Children's books and accompanying readings) (Blume, 1970; Cooley, 2004; Fuqua, 2006)	• Artifacts of tutoring (lesson plans, reflective logs) • Artifacts (class assignments) • Videos of seminar • Videos of tutoring	Case studies of work with children Book club discussions (video recordings)
April 27	In-class activity: "Moving to Action . . .Strategy session on anti-racism." What can you do to interrupt racism in the lives of children? (Michie, 2003; Peterson, 2003)	• Artifacts of tutoring (lesson plans, reflective logs) • Artifacts (class assignments) • Videos of seminar • Videos of tutoring	Reflective essays
May 3	• Celebration with children—families are invited • Critical pedagogy	• Artifacts (class assignments)	Final case studies

In our design of the curriculum in this classroom, we focused on critical social issues, especially racism, because the study was located in a city with a contested history of race relations. What follows is a description of the approaches we used in our course.

Teaching for literacy acceleration within a critical framework. The teacher education classroom focused on reading and writing instruction using critical literacy and approaches that use assessment-based instruction toward the acceleration of literacy development (Dozier et al., 2006; Dozier & Rutten, 2005–2006; Lewison et al., 2002). We use the term "accelerative" to indicate that teachers use these approaches to support students who are learning to read and write by beginning with what is known, and building on the known. Accelerative approaches, therefore, are intensive and designed to prepare students to be successful in their grade-level classrooms, where materials may be chosen because of grade level rather than because they are appropriate for students.

Teaching for literacy acceleration is intended to support the slowest developing students, through focused literacy instruction, and learning school literacy in a way that accelerates them to their grade-level peers. Along with reading key texts in accelerative instruction (Clay, 1993, 1994; Fountas & Pinnell, 1996), the practicum supported the pre-service teachers in learning how to focus on developing flexible, strategic reading and writing in students' zone of proximal development.

The pre-service teachers became quite familiar with the phrase "within a critical framework." We emphasized throughout the course that teaching for acceleration must be embedded in meaningful, powerful practices of literacy. Critical literacy refers to those approaches to literacy instruction where the emphasis is on helping children (and teachers) develop a sense of agency with literacy so that they can accomplish goals they deem important and also resist coercive ideological effects of literacy and language (Comber et al., 2001; Janks, 2000; Lewison et al., 2007; Luke, 2000; Rogers et al., 2010).

Field Experiences in an African-American School. Part of the intention with moving the literacy courses from the university to Liddell Elementary School was to create first-hand experiences of working in the City schools that would put the pre-service teachers in a better position to critically evaluate narratives of how City schools serve students and the social and political histories of these schools.

Tutoring occurred from 3pm to 4pm each time we met. Each session included re-reading an instructional/independent level book, introducing and reading a new book, word work, and writing. The pre-service teachers were expected to have a lesson plan filled out before coming to class. We observed their teaching as often as possible and, each time, had a debriefing meeting that included feedback on their teaching of reading and writing. Each week the tutor was asked to fill out a reflective journal soon after teaching. The elementary students that were part of the practicum program came from four first and second grade classrooms. Our students had opportunities to meet with the classroom teachers throughout the semester. The teachers invited our students to observe in their classroom in order to get a sense of their classroom curriculum. At that time it was *Open Court Reading©*, an elementary basal reading program for grades K-6 developed by SRA/McGraw-Hill that focused on decoding, comprehension, inquiry, and investigation, and writing in a step-by-step fashion. Often, our students reflected on how the teachers supplemented the literacy curriculum and were knowledgeable and caring—and are what Edwards, McMillon, & Turner (2010) refer to as "classrooms of hope" (p. 154). The principal extended invitations to our class to attend school assemblies and celebrations. At the end of the school year, we held the Educating for Change Curriculum Fair at this school. Many of our students were involved in the fair—either as organizers or as presenters (see Chapter 6 for a description of this event).

Teaching for Sociocritical Awareness. We borrow from Villegas and Lucas (2002) the framework of sociocritical competence or the inclusion of classism, sexism, and racism to change how teachers explore language and culture with children in their classrooms. This framework draws from multicultural teaching (e.g., Banks, 1997), culturally relevant/responsive teaching (e.g., Gay, 2002; Ladson-Billings, 1994), and anti-racist teaching (e.g., Dei, 1996; Giovanni, 1994). What these approaches have in common is their focus on race, culture, language, ethnicity, and a diversity of perspectives (Sleeter, 2000–2001). Throughout the design of the course we sought to integrate course experiences that would make race visible (Greene & Abt-Perkins, 2003) and interrogate how race is constructed in schools and society. Our goal was to examine the workings of White privilege, internalized oppression, and institutionalized racism through theory and practice and provide students with the tools to integrate these approaches into their literacy teaching (Cochran-Smith, 2004; Edwards, McMillon, & Turner, 2010).

We wanted our students to learn about the history and culture of the community in which the school was located. We knew this would be a process that took longer than a year but we hoped to ignite our students' interest in the communities where they would teach. Along with our conversations about Liddell Elementary and its surrounding community, we also asked our students to complete a photograph project in which they and their students take photos of prominent areas in the community and use them as the basis of reading and writing instruction. In class, we modeled an example of a digital story that included resources and local literacies associated with churches, parks, recreational centers, restaurants, and corner stores.

We sensitized our students' attention to the ways in which dominant groups around the world historically have organized their educational systems in ways that reify human difference (e.g., race, gender, class, and language) as deficits. This, in turn, gets represented as the source of students' failure (Greene & Abt-Perkins, 2003). This legacy has continued with veracity in the United States, particularly following *Brown v. Board of Education of Topeka* (1954) because as Ferri and Connor (2006) point out, special education is used as a legitimate way to continue racial segregation in schools achieving what Meier, Stewart, and England (1990) referred to as second generation discrimination. Thus, disability continues to function as a "discursive tool for exercising white privilege and racism" (Blanchett, 2006, p. 24). In this manner, we also spent ample time sensitizing our students to what Crawford and Bartolemé (2010, p. 159) refer to as "the pedagogy of labeling" that occurs through the special education process. A constant through our work was reminding students to frame their representations of students' learning in terms of strengths versus deficits, because of the culturally negative consequences of deficit framing, particularly for linguistically diverse students.

Study of Cultural and Linguistic Diversity. We approached the ongoing exploration of cultural and linguistic diversity through narrative-based pedagogies (Clark & Medina, 2000; Juzwik, 2006; McVee, 2004), in which we asked the pre-service teachers to become familiar with the stories of culturally diverse people. The first book that the class read and discussed was *The Dreamkeepers: Successful Teachers of African-American Children* (Ladson-Billings, 1994). Early in the semester, we arranged for a public librarian to provide a lecture on African-American children's books. This accomplished a two-fold purpose. First, it moved us out of the classroom and into the community where students could learn more about the resources available for their students and their families. Second, they became more familiar with the rich heritage of African-American children's literature. We also immersed our students in multicultural children's literature through our read-alouds and the leveled books and text sets that were available for them to use in their literacy teaching.

At several points in the semester, we asked our students to explore linguistic diversity more systematically. At times, this inquiry arose from a question or issue that surfaced in class. For instance, in October we noticed that many of our students were using the term "slang" to refer to African-American Vernacular English (AAVE). This signaled to us the importance of spending time teaching about the history, culture, and linguistic background of AAVE. We accomplished this through a mini-lecture in class, readings (Perry & Delpit, 1998; Wheeler & Swords, 2004), and student-led inquiry into language variety. Students learned more about African-American Vernacular English, Australian Aboriginal English, and other variations of English spoken around the world (see also Chapter 4).

At other times, this inquiry was built into the design of the course, as was the case with the book clubs. A culminating activity of the first semester was a book club. We asked our students to choose one of four professional books to read, discuss and then share with their colleagues in class. The books all included themes of linguistic and cultural diversity and were: *Other People's Words* (Purcell-Gates, 1995), *Resilient Children* (Barone, 1999), *Noa's Ark: One Child's Voyage into Multiliteracy* (Schwartzer, 2001), and *Of Borders and Dreams* (Carger, 1996).

Throughout the course, we encouraged our students to elicit family stories and funds of knowledge from their students and use these as the basis for literacy instruction (Edwards, 1999; González, Moll, & Amanti, 2005). This happened through the use of photographs as well as through narratives told during the instructional time. Several of the teachers gave their students a disposable camera to take pictures of their family, community, and other important parts of their lives (Allen et al., 2002; Duckworth, 2001; Orellana & Hernández, 1999). The pictures were used as the basis for reading and writing. Other teachers used the prompts detailed in Comber et al.'s (2001) work, which generate much dialogue and discussion, such as: What do you like about your community? What would you like to change? Can children change the world? Such questions opened the door for authentic and meaningful writing.

Another narrative-based approach was the use of literacy and cultural autobiographies. At the beginning of the year, we asked our students to write their literacy autobiography. When we recognized that their autobiographies generally did not include an analysis of culture, power, and race, in January we asked them to revisit their narratives through the lens of culture. We asked them to critically read their original narratives and then to choose three pieces of children's literature where they could locate themselves culturally. We called this an "Addendum" and "Finding Myself in Children's Literature" assignment (see Chapter 3).

While the first semester might be characterized as learning about African-American culture, language, and traditions, in the second semester, we widened the focus to include whiteness and White privilege (see also Chapter 5). This shift happened for two reasons. First, the only African-American student in our class brought to our attention that our focus on African-American culture made her feel marginalized. She expressed that during the first semester, the children's literature read-alouds that focused on African-American culture brought the students' gaze on her as an expert (fieldnotes of read-aloud, *Lookin' for Bird in the Big City* (Burleigh, 2001)). Second, while we wanted our students to learn more about African-American culture, we realized that this became a barrier to more deeply exploring their own racial and cultural positionings. In the second semester, we launched an exploration into whiteness, White privilege, and anti-racism through readings, lectures, read-alouds, book clubs, whole-group discussions, and reflective essays.

Research Design

Our research design was intended to understand learning and inform our teaching. Duckworth (2001) calls this kind of inquiry "teaching/learning research" that is "research on learning that can be done only by someone who is committed to helping someone else to learn" (p. 181). Lytle and Cochran-Smith (1992) describe teacher research as inquiry that occurs from an emic perspective, in which teachers/researchers focus less on interpretation and more on praxis, or the connections between their observations, reflections, and actions in the classroom. Further, they point out that within teacher research, there may be a concern with both the creation of local knowledge and with the creation of public knowledge. In our work, during our teaching, we were focused on local knowledge, placing us in an active role of creating knowledge based on our experiences that reframed our practices. There was a close relationship between this creation of local knowledge and the frameworks of critical literacy instruction. Critical literacy instruction is focused on the ongoing inquiry into language and literacy practices, and how those practices create more just spaces and opportunities for learning. We turn to the details of our data sources and analytic procedures in the next section.

Data Collection

Our participants consented to participate in our research project at the beginning of their first semester with us. Because we were grading the students as well as doing research, we were careful to ask a colleague to collect consent forms and explain the study. She was also present during data collection throughout the year and available to talk to the students if they felt conflicted about participating in the research. For one year, we collected data in the form of video- and audio-recordings, field notes, interviews, and document collection on the following class activities: seminar discussions, tutoring sessions, small group discussions, book club discussions, and pre- and post-interviews. We took ethnographic field notes and recorded one another's teaching and then transcribed, debriefed, and analyzed the data together (Carspecken, 1996). We recorded, using video, more than 20 hours of teaching and learning in our classroom, and because we were conducting teacher research, we used these videos for the dual purpose of teaching and research. For example, we often used video recordings of tutoring sessions to guide students in debriefing about their practices with their colleagues.

Participant Observation. We each took the role of participant/observer in the classroom, rotating roles as classroom teachers and as researchers. Each of us was involved in the ongoing data collection and data analysis over a period of one year. We recorded classroom literacy lessons through ethnographic documentation and fieldnotes (Emerson, Fretz, & Shaw, 1995; Spradley, 1980). We wrote fieldnotes as we were teaching and when the class had ended.

Interviews. We conducted semi-structured interviews with the focal participants twice during the course of the study (in December and in June) (Spradley, 1979). We also interviewed the children who participated in the literacy practicum about their literate lives in and out of school.

Written Documents. As a part of the regular class routine, we asked the teachers to keep an "audit trail" that included their assessments, their reflective notes, their lesson logs, and case studies that documented their students' progress (Harste & Vasquez, 1998). We did the same. We made copies of this "audit trail" throughout the semester and used it as the basis of our teaching decisions. We archived the record of our weekly teaching—including lecture notes, handouts, and reflective journals.

All records of their learning were collected. We also read newspaper articles to help us understand the socio-political-economic context of the community. We gathered census data and historical reports from the town library.

Literacy Lessons. We audio-taped and video recorded multiple literacy lessons of the teacher–student dyads. We also collected the supporting documents for these lessons. These documents included assessments, lesson logs, reflections, and student writing samples. Each day we observed two teachers teaching. After the tutoring session ended, we would spend ten minutes debriefing with each teacher. Additionally, each teacher would videotape their own teaching lesson and share a section of the video with the class. The purpose of the videotape analysis section was to build a community of practice where the teachers are talking about teaching literacy and providing their colleagues with feedback and support, as they would in a school setting.

Seminar. After the literacy lessons, the class would meet to discuss the articles, participate in a mini-lesson, and talk about the advances that their students had made in their literacy learning. Each seminar session lasted approximately one hour. We recorded a number of sessions over the course of the semester. In addition, we took fieldnotes during the seminar time.

Researcher/Teacher Journals. After many lessons, we debriefed and informally analyzed the lesson. Both of us took retrospective fieldnotes at the end of the lesson or at the end of the day (Van Maanen, 1988). This journal guided us in the process of remembering events and experiences, describing the situations, and developing ideas, questions, and goals that were important in the teaching and research.

Analysis

Our inquiry, as teacher researchers, continually influenced classroom practice (Wells, 2001). In the life of a teacher researcher, collecting data and analyzing data are not viewed as separate activities. Rather, our attention is usually brought to moments of crisis and surprise, moments of tension and insights. Perhaps something happened that we did not expect. Or, we might have been surprised by a conversation. Maybe a discussion went really well or maybe it fell apart. These are the moments that often prompt further analysis. We might ask: What happened? Why did this happen? What might it mean? What are the implications for our practice? To more closely understand what happened, we used analytic devices from qualitative research and discourse analysis.

Our analysis occurred both during the course of our teaching and after our teaching. Likewise, we encouraged the pre-service teachers to engage in ongoing analysis of their practices. Some analyses occurred on the spot and impacted our next pedagogical move. We also took the time when we were outside of our classrooms to analyze and reflect on our classroom practice. We were drawn to places where there were tensions, problems, or insights. These were the spaces that we returned to again and again, where we spent time poring over transcript and video data wondering why things went a certain way. Even if they did not impact our practice directly the analysis afforded us insights that helped us think about our praxis for other classes.

Qualitative Analyses. We analyzed the data using an inductive, cross-comparative analysis (Miles & Huberman, 1994). We created vignettes of each of the teachers based on the data set. We also selected segments of the class to analyze, such as book clubs, particular literacy lessons, or a read-aloud. After data collection ended and analysis formally began, we studied each videotape and provided a "thick description" of each tape. We then matched our descriptions of the tape with the rest of the data record (e.g., fieldnotes, writing samples, books, and transcripts) from that session. This process helped us to generate broad categories within and across the case studies.

Discourse Analysis. Throughout the life of the project we drew on the tools of narrative analysis (López-Bonilla, 2010; Wortham, 2001), building tasks and inquiry tools (Gee, 2010), critical discourse analysis (Fairclough, 1995; Rogers, 2011), and multimodal discourse analysis (Jewitt & Kress, 2003). While we did not formally teach our students the theories and methods associated with these approaches we did encourage them to critically analyze language and literacy practices and, what we found, was that they were intuitively using many of the methods associated with discourse analysis. We noticed that in our own analysis, we tended to gravitate toward four major kinds of discourse analysis, varieties that we showcase in each of the chapters that follow. Here we briefly describe each one.

Narrative Analysis. We focused throughout our teaching and research on narratives, the reportable stories that our students told about themselves, their teaching, and their learning as well as the overarching narratives of the class. These narratives were ways of relating to the world and to one another as well as accomplishing social positioning in relation to ideas about literacy development (Bruner & Weisser, 1991; Wortham, 2001). We drew on approaches to narrative analysis that incorporate narrative structure, positioning theory, and discourse analysis (López-Bonilla, 2010; McEwan & Egan, 1995; McVee, 2004).

Narrative analysis focuses on the elements of discourse that do social work. For example, reference and predication work in narratives to point out people and name them as predictable types in the narrative through voicing (Wortham, 2001). Also, context does important work in narratives, as contexts are often named and described in the attempt to construct larger storylines about literacy events. It is interesting to note that the listener's/reader's familiarity with the event (i.e., reading a book, or going to the library) is an element of narrative that contributes to its social power. Looking at the ways that narratives created storylines, identities, and larger ideas about literacy contributed to the social learning that occurred in our teacher education classroom and in our analysis of that learning.

Seven Building Tasks and Inquiry Tools. Starting from his often cited distinction between "discourse" and "Discourse"—distinguishing the language bits from the social practices that surround them—Gee's scholarship (2011a) brings together a social theory of language with theoretical devices for inquiry. Situated meanings, social languages, figured worlds, and Discourses may be thought of as "tools" for discourse analysts to ask specific questions of the data (p. x). These are the social and cultural frameworks for understanding how people use language to accomplish social goals. Gee (2011a) reminds us that anytime we are communicating, we are building social relationships, identities, and figured worlds. The second part of Gee's framework is what he refers to as "building tasks" (Gee, 2011b, p. 29). Building tasks are the kinds of things that are being built or designed as people make and interpret meanings. The building tasks are entry points that aide the analyst in constructing meaning from a network of discourse patterns. Some of the tasks include: significance, activities, identities, relationships, politics, connections, sign systems, and knowledge. It should be emphasized that Gee's approach to discourse analysis asks the analyst to attend to learning—how meanings are built and transformed over time.

Gee reminds us that anytime we are communicating, we are building social relationships, identities, and figured worlds. The question for the discourse analyst is: What sign systems are being used to accomplish these social goals? The "building tasks," the second part of his framework, are the kinds of things that are being built or designed as people make and interpret meanings. The "building tasks" include entry points that aide the analyst in constructing meaning from a network of discourse patterns. Some of the tasks include: significance, activities, identities, relationships, politics, connections, sign systems, and knowledge. It should be noted that Gee (2011a) introduces many more building tasks in his book *How to Do Discourse Analysis: A Toolkit*. We have chosen to represent seven of the building tasks here as he does in his earlier work (2006). Each dimension has a set of associated questions that aides the analyst. For example, within "sign systems," Gee asks the question, "What sign systems are relevant (and irrelevant) in the situation?" In "significance," Gee poses the question, "What are the situated meanings of some of the words and phrases that seem important in the situation?"

Critical Discourse Analysis. Norman Fairclough, most well known for his work in critical discourse analysis, has consistently worked on the following question: How does one move between the textual and the social? The key concepts—and associated analytic tools—that he has consistently used as leverage to study social change are *orders of discourse*, *interdiscursivity*, and *dialectics*. Fairclough (2003) explores the kinds of semiotic resources people draw on as they design and interpret social practices through *ways of interacting* (genres), *ways of representing* (discourse), and *ways of being* (style). Ways of interacting (genre) refers to the kinds of texts that people design and call on (e.g. traditional Initiation-Response-Evaluation (I-R-E) patterns of classroom discourse or historical fiction). "Ways of representing" (discourse) refers to the clusters of meanings that give rise to macro-narratives or cultural models. "Ways of being" refers to the kinds of identity work that people enact as they are using language. This heuristic—or order of discourse—provides a means for understanding the relationships between the textual and the social. A key element of Fairclough's framework is the interdiscursive relationship between and within domains—that is, between and among genres, discourses, and styles and the social world. The analyst attempts to describe, interpret, and explain the relationships between texts and social practices at local, national, macro-regional, and global scales (Fairclough, 1995).

Multimodal Discourse Analysis. A multimodal discourse analysis is concerned with how meanings are made—both in the outward representation and in the inner interpretation of signs (Kress, 2010; Norris, 2004; Wohlwend, 2007). "A mode is a socially shaped and culturally given semiotic resource for making meaning" (Kress, 2010, p. 79). Modes of meaning are complex and include many design elements that designers may draw upon. Audio design includes the elements that constitute music and sound effects. Spatial design includes the elements that constitute the meanings of the space around the interaction (how people arrange the space around them using objects). Gestural design includes how our body moves, such as the way we gesture with our hands, arms, and bodies, our affect as it is expressed through facial expression and posture, and how we stay close to or far away from others and objects. Visual design includes the ways that meaning is made through colors, perspective, and other elements of design. In conducting a multimodal analysis, the goal is to identify which modes are being used and how the designer is using multiple modes effectively to construct meaning.

Moving Forward

As we weave in and out of the praxis in our teacher education classroom, our intention is to demonstrate how discourse analysis aided our teaching in the moment and also gave us additional insights after the fact. As teachers and researchers we moved in and out of our analysis at different points in time and for different reasons. Along the way, we share how our research caused shifts in our curricular design and how we engaged our students in discourse analysis.

3
NARRATING LITERACY, IDENTITY, AND CULTURE

Narrative analysis

In this chapter we take you into our teacher education classroom to experience some of the narratives students told about their early literacy experiences. Sharing literacy narratives has become a fairly routine practice in teacher education classrooms, a practice that provides opportunities for developing critical literacies (Florio-Ruane, 2001; Johnson, 2006; McKinney & Giorgis, 2009; Parker, 2010; Rodriguez & Cho, 2011). We show how we used narrative analysis to understand their experiences, which, in turn, helped us to support them to go more deeply in their own analysis and reflections. Throughout the chapter we guide you through the steps of conducting narrative analysis.

Throughout our teaching and research we focused on narratives, the stories that our students told about themselves, their teaching and their learning as well as the overarching narratives of the class (Ochs & Capps, 2001). Narratives were particularly important in the following contexts.

Assignments: Narratives were often central parts of writing assignments, for example, a Literacy Autobiography (a paper that was written in the fall and revised in the spring); a paper entitled, "Finding Ourselves in Children's Literature;" and Weekly Journal Entries that were responses to readings.

Read-alouds: We chose read-alouds to share with the students, and made spaces throughout for pre-service teachers to share stories of their lives in small groups (see Table 2.2 for titles). In these contexts, pre-service teachers used narratives to connect to stories, build meaning about social issues, and to earn positions and identities in a social space.

Online Forum: Individuals drew on their histories of learning as well as their work with students in the practicum to make sense of readings and course topics. In this online forum, stories functioned in a similar way as in read-alouds, above.

Book Club Discussions: Book clubs around professional literature for teachers and children's literature throughout the year provided opportunities for representation and construction through narratives (Rogers & Mosley, 2008).

Tutoring Debriefing: Narratives were particularly important in making sense of experiences of working with children and reconstructing what occurred in ways that inquired into the literacies of the student. These were also contexts in which pre-service teachers shaped their own identities as teachers as well as positioning their students in relation to their teaching (Mosley & Johnson, 2007).

Making space for narratives in the context of literacy coursework and practicum contexts had several purposes. First, narratives were intended to help the pre-service teacher come to know how literacy learning occurs throughout the lifespan by looking inside his or her own history. Second, narratives provided a context for the pre-service teacher to engage in critically reading his or her own and one another's narratives for ideas that may not have otherwise been examined. Finally, through telling narratives about the students they tutored, the pre-service teacher could construct an identity as a particular kind of teacher (Juzwik, 2006). In all of these ways, the pre-service teacher worked toward building a story of him or herself that could be drawn on in later reflections.

We also found it important to place personal narratives in the public space of the classroom so that we could learn from one another, and through dialogue, build understandings across multiple perspectives, an important part of practicing critical literacy. As Florio-Ruane writes:

> Studying cultural narratives may encourage teachers to examine the lives of persons whose backgrounds differ from their own and simultaneously uncover, in Zeichner's (2002) words, "their own cultural identities and re-examine their attitudes toward and beliefs about different ethnocultural groups".
>
> (Florio-Ruane, 2001, p. 20)

In spaces where narratives are shared, people intuitively do the work of narrative analysis. We listen to stories, correct ourselves when we misrepresent a part of our story, or perhaps return to earlier narratives to build meaning across our stories. Tools of narrative analysis had a central place in our teacher education classroom. Krämer-Dahl (2000), who writes about doing narrative analysis with her pre-service teachers, reflects: "[T]ime and again I have seen that the same students who can intelligently point to the construction of power and positioning in the texts of others find it very difficult to recognize the same aspects in their own writing" (p. 103). While this kind of analysis requires support, we have learned from others who do research in teacher education that teachers can become careful analysts of their own language (Johnston, 2012; Rex & Juzwik, 2011).

Narratives draw us in because they are stories of life, of literacy, and of learning. However, these stories also hold a great deal of information about how our students understand the world. It will be interesting to notice, throughout this chapter, what stories are tellable? What are the ways of positioning oneself and others, taken up in a narrative event? And finally, what can the narrative structure tell us about the pre-service teachers' developing understandings of literacy?

Narrative Analysis

Traditions and Concepts

There is not just one kind of narrative analysis but a range of models that we will demonstrate and draw upon in this chapter. Riessman (2005) suggests that there are four models of narrative analysis that are well suited to the analysis of oral narratives: thematic analyses, structural analyses, interactional, and performative analyses. Appendix 3A: Choosing a Type of Narrative Analysis includes an overview of these approaches.

As people tell narratives, they represent and construct identities and also the world (Gee, 1991; Wortham, 2001). Narrators develop themes as one way to do this, and these themes can be identified through an analysis. Our first pass through the narratives concentrated on the themes. Appendix 3B describes how to identify themes in narratives.

In order to answer our questions about narratives, it is also helpful to know how narratives are put together—the architecture of the story—so that we have a way of talking about how narrative tools accomplish what the teller has intended. We call this a "structural analysis." To determine narrative structure, we first have to parse the story into recognizable parts (see Appendix 3C). Then, we can look across narratives for similarities and differences, or look at how one person's narratives shift over time.

Finally, people always tell narratives within a social context and shape their narratives in relation to the people who are listening. Often, in doing so, narrators further construct the world around them by positioning themselves and others through the narrative. Narrative analysis also helps us to understand the moment-to-moment work that our students are doing when they present stories to one another, otherwise known as an interactive or performative analysis. Through these four methods of analysis, we come to understand how narratives shape both identities and the social spaces of our classroom.

Students' Oral and Written Narratives

When narrating experiences in small groups, class papers, interviews, and peer debriefings, the pre-service teachers had opportunities to explore identity, culture, and literacy. The first kind of narrative is a written narrative. We draw on both the literacy autobiography the teachers wrote, a report of how each teacher found him or herself in children's literature, and a letter that we wrote in response to their narratives. We consider our letter to be a narrative as well—one where we share our thoughts in response to our students' ideas. We also consider a form of oral narrative in this chapter, and that is an event when several students shared their "Finding Ourselves in Children's Literature" papers to a small group by telling stories from their own childhoods about the literature they selected to discuss.

Narratives are often presented through transcripts. Appendix 3D and Appendix 3E describe how we created transcripts for this book and how we segment transcripts using the unit of analysis, the clause. Throughout this book, you will see transcripts of classroom interactions, interviews, and passages of the pre-service teachers' written work presented in clauses, idealized lines, or stanzas (which we discuss in Chapter 4).

As we looked across the narratives told over time, both written and oral, we came to understand patterns in our students' use of narrative tools to construct themselves, one another, and ideas about teaching and learning literacy. We also better understood our own narratives told in class as well as the master narratives that characterized the class.

Early in the year, we asked our students to write their personal literacy autobiographies. After reading the autobiographies, we gave feedback to each student through a letter that invited them to consider their autobiographies as "a living document, something you will revisit in your journey of becoming a teacher" (feedback letter, October 10). We wrote:

> We greatly enjoyed reading your autobiographies. As we read them, we thought about a quote from Plummer (1995), who writes:

> What are the links between stories and the wider social world—the contextual conditions for stories to be told and for stories to be received? What brings people to give voice to a story at a particular historical moment? Once told, what functions might stories serve in the lives of people and societies? How might stories work to perform conservative functions maintaining dominant orders? And how might they be used to resist or transform lives and culture? (p. 25)

> We would like for you to actively reflect on the intersections between your particular literacy autobiography and the way in which your narrative is shaped by the political, cultural, racial, economic, and historical times in which you became literate.

Our analysis of their narratives impacted our teaching, resulting in our asking them to revisit their narratives and to read through the lens of race and culture. We deliberately asked our students to think about the intersections between their narrative and the narrative they tell about their literacy teaching. In our feedback letter we wrote:

In what ways do our literacy autobiographies shape the types of literacy environments we construct for the students we work with? What connections can you make between your narrative and the narratives of the children you work with?

In January and February, when the pre-service teachers came back to school after winter break, and after we had spent more time in class addressing how race, gender, culture, and sexuality are represented and constructed through literacy practices, they wrote two papers. The first was an addendum to their personal literacy autobiography. The second was called "Finding Ourselves in Children's Literature," which included descriptions and interpretations of three examples of children's literature that reflect the individual's culture, and could be books that they experienced as a child or found for the assignment.

Table 3.1 is an overview of the themes we identified during our thematic analysis of these narratives.

The common threads throughout the stories were interesting, such as the influence of struggle on literacy learning and the influence of the family on becoming literate. Another common theme was what was left out of their literacy development, particularly around the books (multicultural) that were not present in their reading lives. In the area of themes about culture, most students wrote about culture as defined by their gender, ethnicity, religion, and social class, but others defined culture as ways of being in the world or geographical region.

We then returned to the narratives and looked more carefully at the composition of themes in the narratives, the structures of narratives, the interactional work of narratives, and finally, the ways that identity construction occurred in the narratives. In the next section, we explain the results of our narrative analysis as well as how the pre-service teachers engaged in analysis of their own stories. We organize these findings into sections based on a key narrative that we analyzed, but then highlight the critical social issues included in their stories that were linked to the process of becoming literate. Throughout, we show how we used narrative analysis to better understand the stories that created our classroom community. We should emphasize that some of our analysis happened while we were teaching and, indeed, informed our teaching. Other parts of the analysis were carried out after the fact.

Examples of Narrative Analysis

When pre-service teachers shared their narratives with one another, they were not simply spectators but they were asked to respond and explore culture alongside their colleagues. They wrote, reflected, and rewrote their narratives within the context of these conversations. In their initial autobiographies, they told stories about literacy as comfort, as familial, as a set of practices that bring people together. As they told stories about schooling, they introduced themes of struggle and conflict between reading, writing, and school-based literacy practices. As the

TABLE 3.1. Thematic Analysis of Narratives

Participant	Themes about Literacy Development	Themes about Culture
Rachel	Influence of home on literacy; role of women in books and in her life on her literacy development; learning/ emotional difficulties of siblings as influences	Culture as family structure; economic class, activities, and religious/ethnic identity
Elizabeth	Influence of class on literacy; places value on high-quality literature; miseducation based on books she was not exposed to	Culture as class, identity, gender, and goals
Leslie	Literacy as a gendered activity, both in terms of choices of books and her relationships with reading; struggles to identify with books; miseduation	Culture as race, class, social activist identity, religious/ ethnic identity, and struggles with learning
Jonah	Literacy as led by interests, by father's influence, by caring teachers. Impacted by culturally responsive literature and experiences. Defined by struggles with literature and reading	Culture as race, social activist identity, religious/ethnic identity, and struggles with learning
Tonya	Influence of mother's reading and writing; church; learning through familial/community relationships; miseducation	Culture as relationships (family, friendships), Black culture
Elena	Literacy as learning to "do it myself"; libraries as influences; struggles with getting along in another country	Culture as ethnic identity (American); race, and ways of doing things
Lisa	Reading to connect with family; connections between reading, dancing, and thinking; miseducation	Culture as race, gender, and ways of seeing the world
Melanie	Family literacy; reader identity as something to struggle for; school as a mirror of home values	Culture as family membership, economic class, and gender
Kelly	Literacy as mediated by access to programs, books, and people; influence of community on literacy	Culture as economic class, privilege, gender, and religion
Nellie	Literacy "comes naturally"; reading as a habitual activity; influence of mother	Culture as white, gender, and religion
Pamela	Family's influence on literacy; school as mirror of home values; reader of popular novels; struggles with reading development	Culture as family practices, social class, and White culture
Sarah	Influence of race, gender, and region on literate identity; literacy and struggle	Culture as gendered performance, region of origin, and ways of competing in school

students revisited their literate autobiographies in relation to children's literature they articulated more clearly how their ideas about themselves and culture were defined by what they read. For example, students pointed out the absence of their racial identity in the picture books they read as a child and the stereotypes of White affluent or middle-class characters that were not necessarily culturally accurate in the books they adored.

Through the written assignment and their tellings in class, our students became more aware of privilege, whiteness, and how they were positioned in society. We think that hearing and analyzing one another's literacy narratives helped to foster the habits that we associate with critical literacy—examining multiple perspectives, interrogating taken for granted assumptions and attending to the social and political aspects of literacy (Lewison et al., 2007). The students applied these critical literacy practices to an exploration of their own identities, as we will illustrate in two examples.

Example 1: Lisa's Narrative of Reading The Giver

Three of our students named *The Giver* (Lowry, 1993) as a novel that reflected their culture. This book is commonly read in upper elementary classrooms and is the first of a trilogy of books about characters discovering cracks in utopian societies (see www.loislowry.com for a description of *The Trilogy*). *The Giver* introduces Jonas, an 11-year-old boy, as he comes to understand more about the world he lives in and what is missing from his experiences in that world. Jonas lives in a world devoid of evil and sadness but also more positive intense emotions. However, he is placed in a series of situations in which he discovers what he and his society is missing and, through these discoveries, takes a series of actions that lead to his separation from his world. He goes through changes in the novel that lead to his growth and development as a social actor.

Lisa, Jonah, and Leslie all named this book as reflecting their culture. Jonah reflected, further, that his reading of *The Giver* was an act of reading his own life and identity and, in fact, he re-read this book periodically to take stock of how he has changed as an activist throughout his life. Leslie and Lisa both identified this as a "coming of age" book for them, as well. Lisa wrote her "Locating Ourselves in Children's Literature" paper in response to reading *The Giver*. This paper is the source of our narrative analysis. In Lisa's narrative it was evident that becoming literate had a lot to do with identity development. In others' narratives about reading this novel, we heard variations on this story but, in each, we heard the teller construct an identity as a reader who critically read his or her own life next to a text.

If you recall from Chapter 2, Lisa was a White, middle-class woman who experienced relative success with schooled literacy. She developed a thirst for multicultural experiences in college and spent a semester at sea, hearing world leaders discuss global problems. She consistently reflected on and inquired into language and literacy practices.

Thematic Analysis. Lisa's entire narrative of reading *The Giver* (Lowry, 1993) is represented in full in Figure 3.1. It was a little over one page long. The themes of the narrative that follow are introduced in the first passage of the complete narrative. Lisa focuses on how children are protected from many aspects of the

This book was about a totally new culture for me, as for anyone. The story is of an idealistically wonderful world where there is no strife from birth to adulthood. At 12 each child is given his or her task in life. Friends of Jonas are given the Assistant Director of Recreation and Caretaker of the Elderly, but Jonas is given to a special man. This man, The Giver, teaches Jonas that all that seems so wonderful is not the beginning or the end of the story. Rather, there are lots of ideas that must be kept and Jonas will have to keep them next. He learns that color exists and feelings of rage and ideas that were unconceivable because they have been protected by the Giver.

I felt awed as I read this book. I did not know what to think of it. It struck me as similar to where I was in life. As children, we can feel that the world is protected for us and that we are allowed to experience mostly good. However, soon reality creeps in, and we are asked to bear it. We learn that there is greatness and horror to reality. That the life that revolves around us contains so much more than we had seen at first. Like Jonas, I felt I was making choices about how to deal with the bad as well as how to deal with the good. As someone who grew up in middle to upper-middle class, I was protected from many of the hardships of the world. I lived in a little town where moms stayed home mostly rather than working, where playgroups were the thing, where trips to the movies were often, where children were given many choices to govern themselves . . . this was seemingly close to the world Jonas had begun for his first 12 years. I could see some of what Jonas was experiencing in my own life. The values that the Giver conveys are some that are helpful to any sixth grader trying to navigate his or he own world.

I read *The Giver* in my sixth grade classroom. My teacher was into books that made his students think slightly out of the box. I remember opening the book and feeling as though I had slipped into another life. This was one of the things I treasured most about reading a good book. We had discussions in class so we could process/construct in a Vygotskian way. We needed to throw ideas out and hear other people in order to make meaning out of the text. Had I read this book at home, I would not have had the other sources from whom I drew conclusions. It would be very interesting to reread this book now to see how it affects me at this stage in my life. Perhaps I can find the time.

This book has powerful implications for discussions on government. The Giver is a knowledgeable source who keeps secret information so that others cannot be hurt by it. Accordingly, he has to keep some good information to himself as well because it has the possibility of leading to bad. I think kids can see the government in this sort of role at sixth grade. They can debate whether or not good and bad should be kept from a society. They can discuss what life must be like for a keeper as opposed to what life must be for the ignorant. It is an inspiring way to look at the power of knowledge in our world. This can easily tie in with issues of social justice. If one pays attention to all that is happening around the world, one has a much broader scope, but one also sees a lot that is saddening and maddening. And there are places to take that sadness and madness in order to turn it into action. [Here, Lisa inserted photo of the cover of *The Giver*.]

The role of the media is somewhat parallel to the role of the Giver. They do not keep all information to themselves, but they are a filter for our society. It would be interesting to do an inquiry into what kinds of media show us what kind of information. One could look at newspapers, magazines, the internet, the tv, the radio, etc. Informed citizens are ones who can know that they don't know everything and then do something about it. This kind of activity would be a good discovery of the process of doing just that.

FIGURE 3.1 Lisa's full narrative of reading *The Giver* (Lowry, 1993)

world, but at the age of 12, or in early adolescence, things begin to change. The second theme is that the process of going through this change is connected with figuring out who you are and how to "navigate your world." The third theme personalizes these ideas, and relates to Lisa's process of learning to "navigate her world" through literature like *The Giver* in the social space of the classroom. The fourth theme was that of socioeconomic class: part of the protection of young children is a class-specific action. The final theme is that of the role of media in both representing reality and also filtering what parts of reality are shared with the world and what is left out.

Structural Analysis. We used stanzas to look more closely at Lisa's talk, an analytic tool to view structure. Stanzas show topically related utterances or clauses (see Appendix 4A). Stanzas help us to see how the various parts of a narrative connect to the whole. The following structural analysis focuses on the second paragraph of Lisa's paper about *The Giver*. In this paragraph, there were six stanzas.

Stanza one

1. I felt awed
2. as I read this book.
3. I did not know

4. what to think of it.
5. It struck me as similar to
6. where I was in life.

Stanza two

7. As children,
8. we can feel
9. that the world is protected for us
10. and that we are allowed
11. to experience mostly good.
12. However,
13. soon reality creeps in,
14. and we are asked to bear it.
15. We learn
16. that there is greatness and horror to reality.
17. That the life that revolves around us
18. contains so much more
19. than we had seen at first.

Stanza three

20. Like Jonas,
21. I felt
22. I was making choices about
23. how to deal with the bad
24. as well as how to deal with the good.
25. As someone who grew up in middle to upper-middle class,
26. I was protected from many of the hardships of the world.

Stanza four

27. I lived in a little town
28. where moms stayed home mostly
29. rather than working,
30. where playgroups were the thing,
31. where trips to the movies were often,
32. where children were given many choices
33. to govern themselves.

Stanza five

34. This was seemingly close to the world
35. Jonas had begun for his first 12 years.
36. I could see
37. some of what Jonas was experiencing
38. in my own life.

Stanza six

39. The values that *The Giver* conveys
40. are some that are helpful
41. to any sixth grader trying to navigate his or her own world.

Stanza one is an orientation to the narrative in which Lisa introduces the theme of the similarity of her life to Jonas's life. The book was a tool for her to analyze what was happening to her as a 12-year-old reader. In stanza two, she uses the pronouns "we" and "us" to indicate a generalization about how young children are protected from reality and then the loss of innocence when children learn more about the world. Stanza three personalizes the narrative as she states specifically how this reality was disrupted in her own life, and identifies herself as a person whose class put her in the same group as Jonas who was protected from hardships. Stanza four expands on the idea of what it means to grow up as a "middle to upper-class" child. Stanza five returns to the idea in stanza three that there are parallels between her life and Jonas's life, and stanza six concludes the narrative by moving back to how the book acted as a tool for her to analyze her life.

Interactional/performative analysis. Lisa draws on many tools to make this narrative tellable. It is important to note here that we assume two audiences for this piece. The course instructors are an audience but also Lisa knows that she will share this work with her peers in a discussion. Therefore, we looked more carefully at how she positions herself and others and makes this narrative "tellable" (Bruner, 1991, p. 12). Lisa uses particular linguistic strategies to build interest for this story. In the first stanza, we noticed her use of the word "awed" (line 1) as a descriptor of how she felt when she read *The Giver*. The book seemed to surprise her because of its similarity to her life. The story is worth telling, to Lisa, because of this similarity (line 5). She goes on in stanza two to elaborate on this point. The book holds a truth about the world, that as children age they come to know that the world is not good, fair, or at all what it seems. She identifies herself in line 7 ("as children") as part of a group and uses the pronoun "we" in lines 8, 10, 14, 15, and 19 and "us" in line 17 to emphasize that this group shares particular ideas as part of coming of age. Coming of age narratives are present in literary works as well as a commonly told story about identity development (Millard, 2007). She characterizes the main aspects of a coming of age narrative in stanza two, including a loss of innocence (line 13) as reality "creeps in" as well as a sense of burden of new knowledge (line 14). Lisa's coming of age narrative includes becoming aware of the limitations of one's knowledge and upbringing.

We can also evaluate how this narrative was tellable in the social context in which it was written: an assigned paper for a course that emphasizes how culture, race, gender, and class are part of identity and literacy learning. In the third stanza, Lisa returns to her story of why this book impacted her. Again, part of the assignment was to choose books that represent not just culture but *your* culture. Here, she reorients the reader to why the book reflects her culture. In line 22, she positions herself as a person who actively "makes choices" about how to deal with her new knowledge. She draws a connection between her background (middle to upper-middle class) in line 25 and the ideas she presented in stanza two about what happens as children come of age. She makes a direct connection between her ideas about how children come to see more of the world as they age and her middle-class to upper-middle-class position. She accomplishes her goal of showing culture in children's literature and locating herself in the books she chose.

What kind of identity work was Lisa doing in the telling of this narrative? We have addressed the themes of the narrative, how the narrative was structured to communicate those themes, and the interactional strategies that she used, but we are still left with the question, "Who is Lisa in this narrative?" Across the papers there was an element of privilege in the histories of our students. Many of them talked about access to great books and to libraries as well as extra help with reading from private tutors, good schools, and other markers of privilege. In the above example, Lisa indicates in stanza three that her economic status (middle to upper-middle class) protected her from "hardships." Her read of her privilege is that at some point in her life, those protections fall short of keeping "reality" from impacting her life. Through positioning, she activates a storyline of herself as a reader, a person whose identity is shaped through reading. That storyline allows for her to attribute particular actions to herself (i.e., being "awed" by a book) as well as take on particular identities (being middle to upper-middle class).

Positioning is a complex narrative tool, as we can see in this example, and includes one's positioning of self as well as others. Appendix 3F summarizes the actions that people take, through language, to position themselves as particular kinds of people, people who are, for example, "middle to upper-middle class" or someone who is a critical type of reader. Positioning is also used to define others as particular types of people. Here, Lisa positions others who are like her through the use of pronouns, as we mentioned earlier, as well as by evoking coming-of-age storylines about how one discovers new knowledge and loses innocence.

We noticed in other narratives we analyzed that gender, family, and privilege were intertwined for many of the pre-service teachers, who used positioning in their written narratives to show, for example, that women take more active roles than men when rearing children and providing early experiences with literacy. For the most part, except in a few narratives, women were present in both the domestic and school contexts as mothers, sisters, librarians, teachers, and grand-mothers who encouraged literacy development. There was also a sense of those women providing choice and encouraging their daughters to use literacy for social purposes. Family involvement in literacy and privilege were often interwoven as the pre-service teachers narrated their experiences. In all cases, the family was positioned as valuing literacy, providing opportunities (trips to the library, home collections of children's literature, or reading tutors) for literacy. The pre-service teacher often mentioned the context of literacy learning that he or she grew up within and implicitly suggests that those contexts shape their ideas about early literacy development.

In many of their narratives, the pre-service teachers stopped short of making a critical appraisal of privilege. In Lisa's talk, above, she mentioned her economic status as a protection but did not explore the ways in which this status privileged her interests over those of others. Several pre-service teachers noted that a lack of exposure to discussions of culture, class, identity, gender, and race in literature was a form of mis-education—a reference to the influential text *The Mis-Education of the Negro* (Woodson, 1990). For example, Tonya pointed out that books available for African-American girls were not available when she was younger. Emily and Rachel noted that their favorite books held stereotypes of White affluent or middle-class characters that were not necessarily culturally accurate. In our feedback to the class we wrote the following:

> Many of you addressed the importance of "good" families who "cared" about and "valued" your education. What do such normative descriptors mean? How are such descriptors race-based and class-based? Does the definition of a "good" family and a family who "values" education shift across cultural contexts? What happens when you compare the types of family structures, living conditions, type of parent involvement, etc. that you had growing up with that of your students? If your students are exposed to different conditions, we are likely to judge them based on what we think is the norm in terms of literacy experiences. We would like to recall an argument made by Donaldo Macedo (2003) who questions the types of reading achievement that we heard constructed in many of the literacy autobiographies.

> The type of reading achievement (one that is defined solely by school measures of achievement) is constructed as a set of practices that function to disempower those who, through an accident of birth, are not part of a class structure where literacy is a fundamental cultural capital. . . . I want to argue that literacy is not a matter of mechanically learning to read in the dominant academic discourse that still informs the vast majority of literacy programs.

> Macedo (and others) argue that our inability to name and locate class and racial structures not only reproduces the false myth that we live in a class-less and non-racist society. This denial continues to privilege white people who benefit from racist structures and continues to exploit people of color.
> (feedback letter, October 10)

Over time, students started to look more closely at privilege in our class discussions, their work with children in the practicum, and in their own lives, as revealed in ongoing interviews we conducted with them. Perhaps this happened because they were drawing on narratives of their upbringing, childhood, and entries into literacy. Perhaps their peers were challenging them to clarify, extend, and analyze those narratives. We discuss the transfer of these discussions about privilege, race, racism, gender, and other social positionings in Chapters 4 through 6.

Example 2: Pamela's Story of Struggles with Literacy

Struggles were also present when pre-service teachers wrote about early experiences with literacy. Struggles included the ability to identify with books, reading, and literacy and the understanding was that these struggles are ongoing in a person's lifetime. Several students were turned off to reading in school and had a tenuous relationship with literacy when the purpose of reading and writing became grade-focused and less personal. Pamela, for example, was a student who had very positive experiences learning to read in her home, in a family where reading was encouraged and young children shared books with one another and parents. Here, we conduct an analysis of Pamela's narrative of her learning disability from her literacy autobiography. We use Labov and Waletzky's (1997) narrative structure (see Appendix 3C) to illustrate the different components of her narrative.

Orientation. I remember one instance when I was trying to read that clearly stands out as a negative event.

Complication. We were given a book and a worksheet one day in class. The teacher told us to read the story and answer the questions after we finished reading. I attempted to read the book, but I could only read a few of the words. Thus, I could not fill the worksheet out since I had not read the story. In an attempt to turn the situation around, I tried to copy another child's answers for the worksheet who was sitting across the table. Obviously I had not grasped the concept that words are read only from left to right when they are positioned upright because I copied the words upside down and in reverse. At this point, I was frustrated and wanted to cry because I did not understand how to read complex words.

Resolution. After this occurrence, I was sent to a resource room during the reading period. I received extra help in a much smaller classroom of children. Thus, I had more one-on-one interactions with the resource teacher when I was reading.

Coda. I went to the resource room and received reading help for less than a year. After first grade, I stayed in the normal classroom for reading lessons.

Thematic Analysis. This narrative is about the construction of Pamela's reading difficulties in school. She begins explaining the trouble she had in school as a young child when reading was the task at hand. There is also a theme present of how reading is taught to young children as if each child is able to read the same text independently. In this narrative, children are asked to read independently and answer questions to bring their attention to details of the story. A worksheet reading activity is an independent event. Pamela also introduces the theme of frustration during reading in the resolution of the narrative and how children respond to frustration by copying. The final theme in this narrative is the hard work Pamela did to learn how to read: She only received help in the resource room for "less than a year." This theme illustrates her identity as a hard worker.

We also looked for what seemed to be missing in this narrative. She named the "resource room" without naming the reading disability (a disability that she does identify with later in her paper). Unnamed were the cultural practices of reading and instruction that normalized particular kinds of reading development—the "normal" classroom she described. Also missing was an articulated evaluation of this incident from her current point of view.

Structural Analysis. In the orientation Pamela orients the reader to an event that occurred many years before, and in the complication of the narrative she constructs a place she assumes will have recognition: a classroom where books and worksheets test students' comprehension. In the complication of the narrative, she reveals that her story was about a young girl making a decision to copy another child's work in order to complete an assignment. The complication is that when reading was expected of her, she was unable to complete the assignment. Even though she "attempted" to read, she was unable to read more than a few words. The teacher's voice was absent in both the complication and the resolution of the story—except for the indication of anger from her teacher—as were the voices of her parents. Pamela does not evaluate the narrative, or provide a perspective on how the environment or ideas about reading in this classroom positioned children who could not read at the same level as their peers. The resolution is more closely tied to her own identity as a hard-working student. Pamela's own emotions were indicated throughout the narrative. She sees now, as an adult, that she was frustrated and passive in this situation. Also passive was her use of verb phrases such as "I was sent" and "I received" in the resolution of the narrative. She was not passive throughout the narrative, however. The coda of the narrative indicated that she did not stay in this resource room but transitioned back into the classroom in less than one year, suggesting success or improvements.

Interactional/Performative Analysis. Pamela did not recall much about this experience but the telling of the narrative was meaningful. The division of the narrative into a structure from Labov and Waletzky (1997) allows us to see how she narrated her identity. The stories of herself as a young reader were told to position her as someone who has succeeded in spite of a disability.

Later in the paper, she describes herself in relation to other students in the class—as a slower, less accurate reader. She also admits, "I have a reading disability which prevents me from processing information like normal students." She attributes the success to her parents' encouragement and also the extra time that she spent on schoolwork. Her identity as a reader is context-specific and flexible. For example, Pamela mentioned in her literacy autobiography the following identifications: being an "average reader compared to other students in my class"; "I read very slowly, but I have defeated this disability by spending extra time on school work"; "I loved the book so much that I decided to create my story book depicting the penguins in *Mr. Popper's Penguins*"; and finally, "I read many multi-cultural books at school. After reading the multicultural books, the teacher would hold a discussion where students could ask questions and express their opinions concerning different cultures. These discussions enabled me to learn about other children all around the world."

Pamela evoked storylines of disability, cheating, and embarrassment in her narrative of struggle. However, because she told this story, she was also able to tell the counter-story, or the story of her perseverance for literacy. Labov and Waletzky's (1997) narrative structure, which we used to understand this longer narrative, allowed us to see how, within a single story, a teller can be different selves—the self of a young, passive child and the self of a hard worker who overcomes a disability. Pamela's narrative of development is tellable because it adds a twist to a familiar storyline: She was a child who struggled but with encouragement and hard work, overcame those struggles.

The notion that learning disabilities led to problems learning literacy was prevalent in several of the pre-service teachers' narratives. For example, we heard narratives that suggested that testing shaped literacy instruction in schools and led to struggles. In our feedback letter to our students' narratives, we asked the class to consider how the narratives they told about their students shaped the kinds of literate identities that are imaginable. We wrote:

> Becoming literate involves learning how to decode and encode meaning. It also involves acquiring particular types of literate identities or "ways of being" with literacy. Our job as teachers, then, also involves setting up the conditions where our students will develop a positive and productive sense of literate identity—much like the ones you all have acquired.
>
> (feedback letter, October 10)

We invited our students to consider the stories they told as living narrations and to think about them in relation to the students they teach. We asked, "In what ways do our literate autobiographies shape the types of literacy environments we construct for the students we work with? What connections can you make between your narrative and the narratives of the children you work with?"

Conclusion

Narratives in the context of our class held great importance, in particular because it was through narratives that the pre-service teachers came to re-read their backgrounds and experiences that may have been previously unexamined. Unexamined narratives of privilege with literacy are often simplified stories of what is present or not present when it comes to literacy in one's history. However, when exploring their histories of literacy, they came to explain the complexities of their own histories. Simplified, unexamined stories potentially limit literacy teaching practices because they lead to unfair comparisons between one's own background and the background of the students who he or she teaches.

The role of narratives in the pre-service teacher classroom reached beyond the act of responding to literature or telling autobiographical stories. Narratives were used as a tool to interpret experiences with teaching young children, to make sense of course readings in an online forum, and also to respond to read-alouds of multicultural literature. In all of these contexts, the pre-service teacher worked towards building a story of him or herself as a literate person who was in the process of becoming literate across his or her lifespan. In pre-service teacher education courses, students are making sense of how they are going to enact the practices of teaching literacy they are exposed to, and envisioning how they will modify those practices based on the students they will teach. It is important that their sense making takes into account their own histories of becoming literate.

Telling stories as class activities encourages students to think critically about their stories. The public telling of narratives opens up the possibility that multiple perspectives will be called on in the interpretation of those stories. Along with opening the story to diverse perspectives, the public telling of narratives requires that the teller provide context, a reason for telling the story, and sometimes, justify why the story is an important one to tell. Adding layers of context to a narrative is another aspect of critically engaging with stories. Through their written and oral tellings, pre-service teachers can extend the meanings of narratives and also the power of those narratives to shape their current and future reflections on their experiences. Appendices 3B–3G bring the tools of narrative analysis together into a concise guide. Appendix 3H "Additional Reading and Resources to Support Narrative Analysis" provides additional resources for conducting narrative analysis.

In the next chapter we explore how our students inquired into linguistic diversity and assessing oral reading, an issue that emerged generatively during our instruction. The students' questions and inquiry morphed into their desire to take action and to write a letter to Marie Clay (1994), asking about her thoughts on issues of language diversity, assessment, and power. We will meet Lisa again, as she leads the committee charged with compiling the letter. We demonstrate how the students were engaged in critical language inquiry using the tools of discourse analysis throughout this process. We draw on Gee's (2010) building tasks and inquiry tools to ask about the storylines and identities they construct for themselves in writing this letter.

4

INQUIRY INTO LINGUISTIC DIVERSITY

Discourse analysis

Critical literacy education focuses on investigations into language and power. Threaded through our course—in the readings, the feedback that we gave to students, the assignments, and the teaching—was attention to language. What we said about our students' learning has a great deal to do with the conditions that we set up for them as learners (Cambourne, 1995). Like other teacher educators we work very hard to support our students as they change the frames—and subsequent language practices—to describe their students. This semester, like all other semesters before, after our students had their first meeting with the elementary students to "roam around the known" (Clay, 1993, p. 12), we reconvened as a group and gave each person a turn describing their students' literate behaviors. Comments focused on what their students *could not do* were far more common than what they *could do*. We heard, "Marcus does not know many sight words,"; "Aleshea cannot read a book on grade level"; and "Sherry only wrote one sentence." Likewise, their descriptions were not very specific. Balancing where they were as learners and where we would like them to be, we coached them to reframe their comments focusing on what literate behaviors their students controlled. This was hard work for our students because they have learned—through their history of participation in school—that a teacher's job is to assess what a student cannot do, diagnose their difficulty and intervene accordingly.

In our written feedback, in one-on-one conferences and during seminars, we continually asked our students to focus on their students' strengths. As the semester moved on, we tightened our criteria of acceptability, especially in written work, expecting that the representational choices made reflect the strengths and evidence-based paradigm we modeled. We did this because we recognized that language not only represents the social world—in this case literacy learning—but also shapes it. We wanted our students to understand that language and literacy can be either oppressive or liberating and how it functions has a great deal to do with their decisions.

In this chapter we focus on a problem that arose early in the semester when we noted that several students used the term "slang" to refer to their student's discourse patterns. We worried about this representation because it reflected a linguistic hegemony where one language variety—in this case standard English—was privileged as the superior variety, with other varieties being marked as slang (Baugh, 1999). It was not enough to bring to our students' attention the fact that using the term "slang" was a pejorative representation of students' language, which we did. We wanted the pre-service teachers to go more deeply in their understandings of linguistic diversity. Indeed, linguistic hegemony signals the linguistic aspects of racism and the racializing function of language that serves to sort and classify students as able and not able. Hopson (2003) writes:

> For colonized persons throughout the world, language plays a key role in either framing and maintaining or challenging and deconstructing dominant themes and ideologies that reproduce global social relations.
>
> (Hopson, 2003, pp. 234–235)

Our intention was to link language to historical and structural contexts, to situate language issues alongside concerns such as domination and conflict and to foreground how these matters are the concern of literacy teachers. Over the course of two months, the students participated in a number of in-class and out-of-class activities designed to deepen their knowledge of linguistic diversity. Students researched multilingualism and presented their learning to peers in class. They formed a language committee charged with crafting a letter to Dr. Marie Clay,[1] a researcher who developed such tools as the *Observation Survey of Early Literacy Development* (Clay, 1993) and the reading intervention *Reading Recovery: A Guide Book for Teachers in Training* (Clay, 1994). They inquired about recording linguistic diversity in running records in their letter. Several of the books the students chose for their end of the semester book clubs focused on multilingualism (e.g., Purcell-Gates, 1995; Schwartzer, 2001). What was particularly exciting about this slice of our classroom life was that, in many ways, our students were leading the charge with inquiry into language and power. This chapter, like all the rest, dually focuses on how they critically analyzed and used language and also our analysis of their learning. Along the way we demonstrate an approach to critical discourse analysis that draws on building tasks and inquiry models to understand social practices (Gee, 2010).

The Building Tasks Analysis

Traditions and Concepts

Gee's tradition of discourse analysis, referred to as a "building tasks" analysis, draws on American anthropological linguistics, social discourse theories, and cognitive psychology. As we discussed in Chapter 1, Gee (2010) introduced the distinction between "discourse"—language bits and "Discourse"—the sociopolitical uses of language. The theory of language buttressing Gee's approach to discourse analysis is that people use language in purposeful ways, situated within social, historical, and political contexts. He brings this theory to life through five related frames and a set of building tasks that illustrate how language ties to the social world.

Theoretical Frames. The theoretical frameworks are situated meanings, cultural/discourse models, social languages, intertextuality, and figured worlds. These are the social and cultural frameworks for understanding how people use language to accomplish social goals. Gee (2011b) writes:

> [S]ituated meanings, social languages, figured worlds, and Discourses move us from the ground of specific uses of language in specific contexts (situated meanings) up to the world of identities and institutions in time and space (Discourses) through varieties of language (social languages) and people's taken-for-granted theories of the world (figured worlds). This progression is, in my view, the point of discourse (or, better d/Discourse) analysis.
>
> (Gee, 2011b, p. 43)

In other words, Gee views these tools/concepts as a bottom-up progression—from situated meanings, through social languages, through figured worlds, to Discourses. As we point out in Appendix 4B, Table 4.1, this model can work both ways. That is, identities and institutions (Discourses) can press back down through figured worlds and social languages to shape all the different ways that individual people use language in context (situated meanings).

Gee's (2011a, p. 151) concept of "situated meanings" evokes Bakhtin's notion of genres and dialogues (1986) and refers to how people make words mean something—and that meaning has historical significance and is connected to other meanings. "Cultural/discourse models" are the storylines, narratives, and explanatory frameworks that circulate in a society (Gee 2011a, p. 177). "Social languages" refer to grammar and the function of language as it allows us to express socially situated identities and relationships (p. 161). "Intertextuality" refers to how texts are drawn upon and re-articulated within or across social practices (p. 166). And "figured worlds" are the kinds of mental models that shape how people make sense of the world (p. 171). We imagine the theoretical frameworks to be the umbrella under which the building tasks operate. Table 4.1 in Appendix 4B is an overview of the theoretical frameworks and building tasks.

Building Tasks. The building tasks are tools that bring the theoretical frame-works to life. The building tasks include: *significance, activities, identities, relation-ships, politics, connections, sign systems*, and *knowledge.*[2] As people interact they are building social relations, identities, activities, identities, and knowledge with and through language. The building tasks aide the analyst in constructing meaning from a network of discourse patterns. For example, the "significance" building task (Gee, 2011a, p. 92) is concerned with the situated meanings that are privi-leged in an interaction. The "relationships" building task (Gee, 2011a, p. 114) refers to how people interact with other people, texts, or Discourses. The "iden-tities" building task recognizes that people use language to create certain roles for themselves and that these roles are differently emphasized in the social space of the interaction.

Each building task has a set of associated questions that guide the analyst. For example, with the significance building task we may ask the question, "What are the situated meanings of some of the words and phrases that seem important in the situation?" With the identities building task we may ask, "What beliefs, values, and positions are relevant to and under construction in this situation?" And with the relationships building task, we may ask, "What sorts of social relationships are visible, relevant, and under construction in this situation?" Each of the building tasks is meant to provide the analyst with some conceptual and analytic lever-age. It is not expected that all of the building tasks will be relevant to all texts, rather that the analyst may try out several of the building tasks to see what can be uncovered. The question for the discourse analyst is: What linguistic resources are being used to accomplish these social goals?

Inquiring into Linguistic Diversity

Literacy teachers need to understand the difference between reading difficul-ties and linguistic differences. Too often, linguistic differences are translated into deficits (Artiles, Rueda, Salazar, & Higareda, 2005). One way we sensitized our students' attention to this issue is through our practice of taking and scoring run-ning records, an assessment technique in which the teacher documents a student's miscues and strategies while they are reading orally (Clay, 1993). During practice running records, one of us would read aloud a running record we had used with a young student. We simulated the reading behaviors of the student as they were re-corded in the record. The pre-service teachers would take a running record of our oral reading and then analyze the miscues and determine an accuracy and self-correction rate. We modeled miscue analysis for the group, thinking aloud about the linguistic resources the student used when they made the miscue (meaning, syntax, and grapho-phonic knowledge).

One practice running record included examples of African-American Ver-nacular English, the term we used to describe the syntactical structures and pro-nunciation patterns used by many of the African-American students at Liddell elementary. This day, the record included the following miscues: "*look*" was read for the word "*looks*," reflecting the deletion of the *s* from third person singular verbs; "*running*" was read as "*runnin*" and "*anything*" was read as "*anythin*," reflecting the deletion of the final consonant in consonant clusters that occur at the end of words; and "*father's*" was read as "*father*," reflecting the deletion of the possessive *s* (Baugh, 1999; DeBose & Faraclas, 1993; Dillard, 1972; Rickford, 1999).[3]

During the miscue analysis, a student asked, "Should linguistic variation be counted as an error in a running record?" Students argued that they needed to know what a student used when reading a book written in Standard English, ostensibly to bridge AAVE to Standard English grammar and phonology. However, the question came up, if AAVE is a rule-governed language, is the use of that language ever an error? Further, if they did not record the linguistic resources their student did call on in their reading, were they ignoring their students' cultural and linguistic identities? The discussion was lively. Clearly this issue piqued their interest. Rather than simply provide an answer to their question, we wanted them to think about the various sides of this issue and what this meant for representing children's literacy learning. We asked them to sort through these language questions in the context of the whole running record with colleagues at their table.

As they did this, we circulated throughout the room and noticed that one group was looking through their copies of *An Observation Survey of Early Literacy Achievement* (Clay, 1993) trying to find a passage where Clay addressed linguistic diversity in assessments.

"I remember reading something about this," Lisa commented.

Kelly found a page where Clay discussed how "childish pronunciations" should not be counted as an error and so their group inferred that linguistic diversity, a more substantive matter, should also not be counted as an error.

As we listened to them make sense out of recording and analyzing linguistic diversity, Rebecca commented, "This is something we could ask Marie Clay about."

Spontaneously, Lisa responded, "We should write her a letter!"

We encouraged their initiative and they asked their colleagues who would like to join a "language committee" that would be charged with writing a letter to Marie Clay. We ended class by giving the students a reflective question to respond to for the following class.

> What are your thoughts about recording and interpreting linguistic variations when you are taking a running record? Outline what you see as the major issues and how you would resolve this in our recording of oral reading. You can draw from as many sources as you would like (e.g. class discussions, online discussions, readings, teaching experiences, etc.) to support your emerging theory.

Between classes, the language committee consulted with Rebecca about the work of their committee. Like Lisa noted above, we knew that Clay had written about linguistic diversity and after class we returned to several of her books, including Clay's (1991a) *Becoming Literate: The Construction of Inner Control*, where we found the following reference to language diversity as a dialect of Standard English. She wrote:

> A good teacher would not destroy the first language that children use so fluently. She would try to add to their speech a dialect for Standard English to be used in some oral situations and to pen the world of books to them. She would leave them their first dialect for friends and family. This poses two real problems for the teacher. She must first establish communication with the child despite the fact that she may speak a strange and unusual dialect. Beyond this, she must help the child to work in the new dialect, knowing that for most of his [*sic*] waking life he is going to live and speak among people who use his home dialect.
>
> (Clay, 1991a, p. 71)

We shared this passage with the language committee. Together we discussed that Clay used the term "dialect" whereas some African-American sociolinguists do not consider AAVE a dialect of English. AAVE is classified as a Niger-Congo language and while the vocabulary of AAVE is English, the syntactical constructions reflect its Niger-Congo lineage (Baugh, 1999). We agreed that Clay clearly valued language diversity but still, the question remained: What was the best way to make sense out of language diversity in the running record? They wanted advice on how to proceed with their committee work. We suggested they collect the responses from the reflective question we distributed the previous week, analyze them, and synthesize the major issues and concerns of their classmates. This could serve as the basis of their letter to Marie Clay.

The committee gathered the responses from their colleagues and met to analyze the documents for patterns and threads they found in their responses. They shared their analysis with the class. Overall, the class agreed that because the miscue was based on a student's primary language and did not obstruct meaning, then it should not be counted as an error. It should, however, be taken note of so a teacher could learn more about their student's linguistic resources. We were pleased to see that the class was thinking deeply about language diversity and the importance not only of the quantitative analysis of the miscues but a qualitative analysis of the kinds of miscues being made. They also raised a number of issues about the politics of language and labeling students, code-switching, the importance of culture, language, and identity and how not only to score the miscue but how to *respond to* the miscue.

The committee also shared their plan for drafting a letter to Marie Clay on behalf of the class. In the meantime, as a class we agreed that linguistic diversity should not be counted as an error in a running record but that strategies be incorporated that help students recognize the pattern of book language so students learn what Delpit (1995) refers to as the "codes of power" (p. 40).

"Who defines a language?"

The following week, we asked the class to break into small groups and teach one another about the linguistic variation they learned about through their online inquiry. We had asked them to visit a website that focuses on language diversity (www.une.edu.au/langnet/index.html) and to focus on one particular language. We circulated throughout the room, listening to their talk. One group was particularly interesting because their discussion was informed by sociolinguistic courses that Leslie and Jamie had taken. Evoking Noam Chomsky, Stephen Krashen, and Robert Williams, they taught their colleagues about the difference between learning and acquisition and between autonomous and social models of grammar. At one point in the discussion, Pamela asked her colleagues (as she was looking at a list of AAVE patterns that we distributed to the group), "Who defines a language?" I (Rebecca) jotted this question down to bring up with the rest of the group.

Moving on to another group, I heard Elena and Tonya discuss how they had taken a course in Black Language in college but as Elena noted, "I hope to bring it into my classroom so my students do not have to wait until they are in college to learn about it."

Jonah discussed a similar experience:

> Though I grew up around African-American Vernacular English throughout the majority of grade school, I never knew it was considered a language. I just thought it was slang and it appeared to me that everyone else at school thought that as well. Though it was never used in my home, when I was around my African-American friends who spoke in AAVE it would immediately enter into my speech. Considering that it is a language, I would then see it as derogatory for a teacher to tell a student to stop speaking that way because that would be like telling a Mexican to stop speaking Spanish.

After each of the groups had shared, we brought together some of the discussion threads. I used Pamela's question, "Who defines a language?" as a springboard to talk about the political and historical lineage of African-American Vernacular English. I explained that "Ebonics" was a term coined in St. Louis at Washington University in 1973 by Robert Williams who convened a group of Black linguists to define their own language (Williams, 1975). I talked about the history and political implications of linguistic discrimination through court cases such as *MLK Jr. Elementary School v. Ann Arbor School District* and the Oakland Resolution.

Each group shared what they had learned about language variety with the whole class. They reported on the history, the social, and political contexts of the language variety and they shared possibilities for integrating language variety into the classroom. They came up with quite a few generative ideas for classroom practice including: using literature, music, and poetry that included language diversity; clearly establishing contexts for language use so that students could learn how to code switch; engaging in contrastive analysis of languages; encouraging exploration and a love of language. I ended class by reading aloud *Be Boy Buzz* written by bell hooks (2002) to provide an example of children's literature written with features of African-American Vernacular English.

After class, we reflected on their presentations. What stood out for us was the importance of providing our students with multiple opportunities to inquire into, explore, and think about language. This is the heart of language arts classrooms where students learn to love language, how it works, what it does, what it does to them, and what they can use it for. We hoped that we provided a model that they would, in turn, use with their students. Further, we know that it may be teachers' perceptions and attitudes toward language diversity that is the most detrimental in learning to read (Compton-Lilly, 2005; Solorzano & Yossi, 2001). Our intention was to provide the pre-service teachers with multiple opportunities to reflect on their assumptions about language diversity and to build new knowledge.

Positioning Themselves as Teachers: The Letter to Marie Clay

The language committee wrote a letter to Dr. Marie Clay based on the feedback they received from their colleagues. In this section, using the building tasks and related theoretical frames (Gee, 2010), we focus on the storylines and identities that they fashioned for themselves in this letter. As we discussed in Chapter 3, there are different ways to segment a text—by clauses, lines, or stanzas. Segmentation allows us to represent how speakers organize meaning but such representations are always our theories about how meaning is shaped through the text. Dividing texts into smaller units helps us to see patterns in the text that may be missed by viewing an un-segmented text. In this example, we chose to segment the letter by complete sentences because it was a written text that lent itself to segmentation by complete sentences (versus oral language where breaks in sentences are often less clear). We also segmented the letter into stanzas that included lines devoted to a single topic, perspective, or theme (Gee, 1985; Hymes, 1996; Scollon & Scollon, 1981). We segmented the letter into seven stanzas with a total of 28 lines. See Appendix 4A for a description of how to segment a text into stanzas.

Stanza one: Introduction and Context

1. Dear Dr. Clay:
2. Greetings from St. Louis!
3. We are pre-service teachers in Dr. Rebecca Rogers' and Melissa Mosley's course *Teaching Reading in the Elementary School.*
4. Our literacy instruction program relies strongly on your techniques as outlined in your work *An Observation Survey of Early Literacy Achievement* (2006).
5. Throughout the course of our semester we have become more familiar with your methods of literacy instruction through both a careful reading of your text as well as Fountas and Pinnell's (1996) work *Guided Reading: Good First Teaching for all Children.*
6. In addition, we are learning to effectively implement your techniques by working one-on-one with first and second grade students in the St. Louis City public school district.

Stanza two: The Troubling Event

7. We are writing to you in the hopes of gaining your insight on a key question concerning linguistic variation that has surfaced through our discussions on running records.
8. It was during a practice running record in which the "g" was left off of the word "running" and "anything" that the question first arose.
9. We discussed this miscue in terms of possible evidence of African-American Language or African-American Vernacular English.
10. We were unsure whether or not to mark it as an error, as it was a deviation from the text.
11. This led to class discussions in great length, centering on topics such as the relationship between language and power in a democracy, the difference between "slang" and rule-governed language, and the different contexts in which language is used.
12. Specifically, our discussion has focused on important questions concerning what variety of language is appropriate in what context and why, and if we privilege one variety of language in the classroom over another, whose voices are we allowing to be heard, and whose voices are we silencing.

Stanza three: Why this Matters in our Work as Pre-service Teachers

13. As pre-service teachers of literacy, these questions carry particular weight with their ability to influence the future design and implementation of our literacy curriculum.
14. Our effort to resolve some of these questions as they pertain to literacy instruction led us back to a discussion about the place of linguistic

variations in running records, most notably African-American English in our experiences in tutoring.

15. Specifically, we discussed our thoughts about recording and interpreting linguistic variations when taking running records.

16. As a class we have identified some over-arching themes from our discussion, which we briefly outline below.

Stanza four: Themes from our Class Discussions

17. First, the focus of our literacy instruction is centered on the belief that reading is a meaning making activity.

18. Furthermore, we recognize that linguistic variations when reading a text do not obstruct meaning, and therefore should not be counted as errors.

19. A specific concern we have identified is that counting linguistic variations as errors would hinder our ability to accurately diagnose our students' reading levels.

20. On the other hand, if we fail to record linguistic variations at all, then we are missing an important piece of what defines our students as readers.

Stanza five: Guiding Assumptions

21. Moreover, we believe that how we record our students' linguistic variations affects our view of the place of culture and language in our classroom.

22. Thus, we are concerned that by not including linguistic variations in running records at all we are somehow discounting our students' cultural and linguistic identities.

23. All of this considered, while we don't think linguistic variation should be counted as errors, we are struggling with defining their place in running records.

Stanza six: The Question

24. We recognize that our exposure to your work is limited, given that we have not read all of your writings.

25. This being said, we would greatly appreciate your insight on this issue.

26. Specifically, we are interested in knowing what you see as the role of linguistic variation in running records.

27. That is, how do you record, interpret, and analyze linguistic variations?

Stanza seven: Closing & Signature

28. We thank you for your time and consideration in this matter, and look forward to your response.

Sincerely,
The Students of Teaching Reading in the Elementary School

What Does this Narrative Mean? Using the Building Tasks

In a first read of the letter, a couple of things are noteworthy. First, we heard the pre-service teachers' voice, agency, and positioning of themselves as analysts of their own practices. The students interrupted—or were critical of the usual order of discourse—that relegated them to the role of reader and student. They had questions and wanted answers from one of the premiere experts in the field. This letter marks the teacher candidates as people who were simultaneously wrestling with their identities as learners, as teachers-in-practice, and as future teachers.

After the class had ended, we more closely analyzed the letter to better understand the learning that occurred. As we segmented the text into stanzas, we heard more of the salient threads in this text—threads that have to do with how they used language to design their social world. As noted above, we chose three "theoretical frameworks" (situated meanings, social languages, and intertextuality) and associated "building tasks" to bring to the text (significance, identities, and relationships). We could have chosen others but these were the building tasks that seemed the most relevant for our questions. Next, we crafted three guiding questions to unpack the letter. First, what meanings are represented in the letter? Second, what storylines are the pre-service teachers constructing about themselves or about the field of literacy education? Third, what situated meanings, discourse models, and social languages do they call on?

We worked from some hunches we had about what was significant about the letter and then used the building tasks and associated questions to more carefully analyze the text. (See Gee (2006, pp. 110–115) for a list of questions to bring to the analysis.) Next, we approached the text by describing the linguistic features in the letter to get a sense of the overall organization, flow, and coherence of the text. If we were analyzing an oral text, we may have begun by analyzing the turn-taking structure. Here, we used the simple method of circling and underlining parts of speech, tenses, pronouns, types of statements, verbs, cohesive markers, intertextuality, lexicalization, and so forth. Appendix 4C includes a survey of linguistic features we identified at this stage in our analysis and describes our analytic procedures.

In line three we noted that the statement is an orientation that uses the collective pronoun "we" and is written in the present text. The students assigned ownership of the course to their professors, rather than, for instance, naming the course and saying, "Taught by . . ." We wondered: What may these linguistic devices—use of pronouns and tense—have to do with their identities and social languages? Line by line we analyzed the linguistic resources being used and we began to identify patterns across the lines and stanzas. For instance, in line 4 we noticed the choice of the adverb "strongly" that was used to modify the verb "rely." This is similar to the adverb "careful" (careful reading) in line 5 and "effectively" (effectively implement) in line 6. It appeared that the pre-service teachers chose strong adverbs to modify the verbs. Were they trying to build an image of themselves as particular kinds of students and future teachers, as students who do not passively receive information and take tests but who are diligent and who inquire into their own learning? We continued analyzing the linguistic resources used in each line to see if this emerging pattern held up or if there was counter-evidence.

We also noticed that they situated their learning within several well-known experts in the field, an example of intertextuality that signaled they were part of the literacy education community and were calling on ideas and readings that have particular, situated meanings. Interestingly, in stanza one we also heard how they positioned themselves as both students (diligent students) and as teachers (working with first and second grade students). This dual positioning struck us as interesting because they were enacting particular kinds of identities through this variety of language use. We made a note to see how and if it surfaced throughout the rest of the text. We also noted that they used the present progressive tense in this stanza (see line 6: "we are learning to effectively implement your techniques"). This led us to ask the question: What storylines are the pre-service teachers constructing about themselves?

In the second stanza, we noted that they shifted from the present progressive to the past tense as they explained their question—"Was this an error or deviation from the text?" As discourse analysts, we were interested in both the existence of linguistic devices and how they function. We see that their story presented a picture of themselves, again, as diligent students and as pre-service teachers, wrestling with significant issues such as linguistic variation, language, and power. In stanzas two and three, the tense shifted to the future with the use of a conditional, "if we privilege one variety of language in the classroom over another . . ." (line 12) and the infinitive verb "to influence the future design and implementation of our literacy curriculum" (line 13). This tense was coupled with their projected identities as future teachers, teachers who were concerned with linguistic difference and their students' "cultural and linguistic identities" (line 22).

They called on specific, situated meanings that conjured up identities as literacy teachers (e.g., lines 4 and 6). At the same time, they also positioned themselves as apprentices and learners (careful reading, pre-service teachers, have not read all of your writings—anticipating their future practices as teachers). They were taking responsibility for their teaching in an imagined future. Line 13, for instance, noted, "influence the future design and implementation of our literacy curriculum." It is interesting to note that although the gulf between these students' cultural and linguistic backgrounds and those of the students who they taught at Liddell elementary was wide, they continued to position themselves as inquirers into their own practice. Using the tools of discourse analysis, they inquired into culture, language, power, and identities in ways that anticipated bridging the gulf separating them from their students and their students from schooled literacy. Note that in line 22 they pluralized their students' identities, stating, "we are concerned that by not including linguistic variations in running records at all we are somehow discounting our students' cultural and linguistic identities." By evoking the situated meanings associated with identities, they demonstrate their understanding that students acquire not only literacy and language practices but ways of being in the world through those practices.

This line-by-line analysis attended to the relationship between the linguistic resources and the building tasks/our research questions.

Representing our Interpretations

We ultimately arrived at the following interpretations. First, the teachers positioned themselves both as learners (lines 6, 8, 23, and 24) and as teachers (lines 6, 13, 19, 20, and 21). Their writing demonstrated the flux in their identities as university learners and as future teachers. Within this flux was a relationship they were creating between themselves and Dr. Clay, one that balanced deference and agency, certainty and uncertainty.

The letter is peppered with deference to her—admission to carefully reading her text (line 4), the studious nature of their inquiry (lines 4 and 5), building an argument that they are teachers who care about linguistic and cultural diversity (lines 12–15), and admitting that their exposure to her work is somewhat limited (line 24).

However, there was also a great deal of agency built into the text. The writing of the letter itself suggested that the students saw themselves as having a problem significant enough to write to one of the leading experts in early literacy. Rebecca prompted them in class saying, "This is something we could ask Marie Clay about." However, we have offered similar invitations to other classes to which no one has responded. Thus, it could be argued that the letter itself was an example of an agentic stance. The entire letter was devoted to an explanation of the context and assertions of their principles. While the intended focus was to get her feedback on a question, there is but one question in the letter that appears, buried in the letter, in line 27: "How do you record, analyze and interpret linguistic variations?" It was interesting to note that they had already posed their answer to this question. It seems as if what they were really asking Dr. Clay was, "What do you think about our theory?"

Throughout the letter, they clearly represented themselves as teachers who wanted to take charge of how cultural and linguistic diversity is integrated into their classroom (lines 13 and lines 21–23). They knew that their teaching and their decision making matters (lines 22–23). More than a place to ask Marie Clay how to record, analyze, and interpret linguistic diversity in the running record, this letter serves as a place for them to rehearse a narrative about who they are becoming as culturally responsive teachers.

Their use of certainty and uncertainty signaled their shifting status between apprentice teachers and future teachers. Stanza five is a clear example of their certainty as they outline their guiding assumptions and principles that guide their teaching. They wrote, "we believe that how we record our students' linguistic variations affects our view of the place of culture and language in our classroom" (line 21). Yet, they also admitted that they were "struggling with defining their place in running records" (line 21) and "we were unsure whether or not to mark it as an error, as it was a deviation from the text" (line 11). Table 4.3, located in Appendix 4D, is a visual display of our analysis and interpretations using the theoretical frameworks and associated building tasks.

Here, it is important for us to take a step back and note what we see as the discourse processes associated with agency that were apparent in their process of writing the letter. The students discursively construct the worlds they do and will inhabit, bringing them to life in this letter. We think this movement across time, space, and identity is an important part of agency work, reflecting an understanding of the power of language to create different figured worlds. Their use of collective pronouns signals that they are part of a community of educators. This at once positions them as educators and draws people into the storyline of their letter. While they position themselves as agentic, they are careful to balance deference with this authority, a discursive move we found to be important for them to build their expertise. Talking possible selves into being is an important discursive resource for educators working toward social change. They demonstrate control over the topic of linguistic diversity evidenced by their discussion of dominant frames that devalue linguistic diversity and their posing of an alternative, asset-based, model of teaching that seeks to integrate and build on linguistic diversity. Their letter is richly intertextual, drawing on scholarship, discussions, and their personal experiences. Over time, these discourse processes accumulate into narratives that people tell themselves about what they can accomplish, propelling them toward future actions.

We have included Marie Clay's response to our students (see Appendix 4F). We received her response after class had ended and emailed it to our students to read. If we were still meeting as a group, we would have revisited our discussion in light of her response. We invite you to analyze her response using the discourse analysis tools we have outlined in this chapter or the last. We have provided additional resources for carrying out this kind of analysis in Appendix 4G.

Conclusion

When the language committee began working on the project outside of class time, it was clear to us that our students' interest in analyzing language and power was ignited. When they made an appointment to speak with us about their project, we could see how they were critically analyzing language—both how students' language should be represented and how teachers may best represent language diversity in their assessments. It was also clear to us that they were using the tools of discourse analysis to put into practice key concepts of critical literacy education. They *disrupted the commonplace* position of a student as a receiver of knowledge, and became inquirers instead. They considered *multiple perspectives*, drawing on their classmates' responses to compiling a letter that included many voices. They focused on a *sociopolitical issue*: language variation and power, acting on the notion that language is constitutive—it both represents and reflects the social world. In this case, they were troubled by the idea of misrepresenting their students' cultural and linguistic resources. Finally, they *took action* by using their inquiries to build a conversation beyond their classroom space. Embedded in their inquiry was the notion that education is about problem posing and problem solving in ways that question dominant assumptions and prevailing ideologies. These are four dimensions of critical literacy put forward by Lewison, Leland, and Harste (2007). Implicit in their decision to write to Marie Clay was the idea that they were members of a literacy education community and could ask an expert her thoughts on this problem.

In an interview at the end of the semester, Lisa reflected on this learning experience. She described the process of her committee work in a journal as "doing research on our own practices" (Journal, November 2010). Lisa presented literacy teaching as a collaborative practice around inquiry and a solution that centered upon inquiry rather than one right answer. She exclaimed, "This is what learning in higher education should be like." Lisa said that studying AAVE as a process of inquiry *with* students rather than *about* students should include the following questions, "Okay, so there are these differences, why are there these differences? Where do these differences exist? Why is it important to use one kind of language in one place and another kind of language in another place?" Lisa reminds us that the analysis of discourse practices opens spaces to interrupt, re-build, and reflect on our language and literacy practices, the practice of critical literacy. In the next chapter we demonstrate how we and our students practiced racial literacy drawing on the tools of critical discourse analysis in the context of a book club discussion.

5

PRACTICING RACIAL LITERACY

Critical discourse analysis

In this chapter, we illustrate the complex ways in which we sought to make meaning around issues of race, racism, and anti-racism and in doing so we demonstrate how we drew on the tools of critical discourse analysis both during and after our teaching/learning. As we alluded to earlier, we found that our students tended to focus their cultural analysis on people of color and did not interrogate whiteness as a racialized identity. In Chapter 3, we described how we provided contexts for pre-service teachers to narrate their experiences to further explore the relationship of literacy to gender, family, privilege, interests, emotions, culture, and struggles. In a deliberate pedagogical move, we designed a book club with children's literature that included White people grappling with racism, White privilege, and anti-racism. We selected four books: *Iggie's House* (Blume, 1970), *Maniac Magee* (Spinelli, 1990), *Darby* (Fuqua, 2006), and *The Jacket* (Clements, 2003) because they represented a range of genres, covered multiple points in U.S. history, presented young children as racialized protagonists, and were written for children in the third and fourth grades. They all related to the theme, "Struggle for Equity: Anti-Racism from History to the Present Day." Students were asked to sign up for the first and second choice books. They were placed in book clubs based on their choices (see Rogers & Christian, 2007 for a detailed analysis of the children's literature). We discussed the books before class. During the book club discussions, we rotated between the groups, listening and noting themes and issues that would make for provocative discussions when the whole class came together. The book club, which we focus on in this chapter, had four components: reading, discussion, reflecting in journals, and a whole class discussion (Florio-Ruane, 2001; Raphael, Florio-Ruane, & George, 2001).

Across the contexts of the book club discussions, the students' written records, and whole class discussions, we asked the following research questions: What does racial literacy look and sound like in this teacher education book club? How are meanings made around race, racism, and anti-racism? How may critical discourse analysis be a useful tool for teaching, learning and research? Before heading into our classroom, we will describe how we used critical discourse analysis to more deeply understand our teaching and our students' learning.

Critical Discourse Analysis

Thus far, we have illustrated our use of narrative analysis (Chapter 3) and discourse analysis à la Gee's (2010) "building tasks" (Chapter 4) within the context of our teaching and research. In this chapter, we turn our attention to critical discourse analysis as the set of frameworks and tools that we gravitated toward in learning from the book club discussions (Fairclough, 1993; Gee, 2010). While we did not give our students any formal training in critical discourse analysis, we found that they intuitively drew on the resources as they discussed each of the books. Thus, we focus on how their discussions focused on critical language awareness and a critical reading of the visuals of the book *Iggie's House*. Likewise, when we turned our attention back to the book club data for a deeper analysis, we used CDA.

Traditions and Concepts

CDA focuses on how discourses are constructed as well as how they enact social relationships and social identities, with particular attention paid to dominance/oppression and liberation/justice (Bartlett, 2012; Chouliaraki & Fairclough, 1999; Fairclough, 1992b; Wodak & Meyer, 2001). The CDA framework we use draws most strongly on Fairclough (1993).

Fairclough's version of CDA is rooted in systemic functional linguistics (Halliday, 1994). It should be noted that Hallidayian linguistics has had a much broader impact in Europe and Australia than in North America. Systemic functional linguistics as a theory of language is oriented toward choice and privileges meaning makers (language users) as agents making decisions about the social functions of their language use. This social semiotic theory operates on the understanding that meanings are always being invented (versus being inherited)—that people are actively creating meanings and have choices among representational systems from which to make meanings. As people create meanings, they draw on three semiotic resources. In Hallidayian (1978) terms, these are the textual, ideational, and interpersonal. The textual organizes discourse into recognizable patterns or social practices. The ideational enacts ideas about the world from a particular perspective. The interpersonal enacts experiences of reality. Fairclough's (2011, p. 121) translation of these resources is genre, discourse, and style or "ways of interacting," "ways of representing," and "ways of being," respectively. This is the language we use in our critical discourse analysis (see Table 5.1 in Appendix 5B). We have found this triparte schema useful as a way of making sense out of our own teaching and our students' learning as well as how teaching and learning connect to larger social practices such as justice, liberation, oppression, and freedom.

We use Chouliaraki and Fairclough's (1999) definition of genre as "the sort of language (and other semiosis) tied to a particular social activity such as an interview" (p. 63). Genres may be viewed as "ways of interacting" and include the organizational threads of interacting such as turn-taking structures, cohesive devices, parallel structure, politeness conventions, revoicing, and narrative sequencing. Analysis of the organizational threads of a particular genre allows us to see the *type* of genre that is being constructed. For instance, an interview can be described as a genre but depending on the linguistic realization of the interview (e.g., turn-taking structure or politeness conventions) the genre of the interview can be described in different ways (e.g., formal or informal).

Each utterance both raises possibilities and precludes other possibilities that signify meta-narratives, or *discourses*. Discourses are "ways of representing" ideas and include what Luke (2000) referred to as "systematic clusters of themes, statements, ideas and ideologies" (p. 456). Discourses embody tensions and contradictions. Meta-narratives are identified through idea units. They are also identified through the "ways of representing" that include values, emotions, beliefs, and bodily positions. For instance, an interview about race may evoke various themes (e.g., White privilege and affirmative action). "Discourses" are materialized through circulating statements and idea units—or "discourses". At the grammatical level, "discourses" are evoked through an analysis of the information focus of the text, the lexical choices used, the pronouns chosen, and the exclusion of information or silences.

Finally, communication always involves position taking, so we look at ways of being, or *style*. Styles are "ways of being" and represent interpersonal choice (tenor in Halliday, 1978). An analysis of style includes an analysis of the linguistic realizations such as voice (active or passive), modality (tense and affinity), mood (questions, statements, and demands), transitivity of verbs (e.g., action, affective, ability, and cognitive processes), and systems of appraisal (affect, judgment, and appreciation) (Christie, 2002; Fairclough, 1993; Martin & Rose, 2007) as well as the social identities and positions that are constructed through these realizations. For instance, during an interview with a teacher about anti-racism, the teacher may use the linguistic resources (e.g., modality and pronoun use) to position herself as a certain type of teacher (e.g., an anti-racist teacher or a colorblind teacher). See Table 5.5 in Appendix 5B for a survey of linguistic resources connected to each order of discourse.

Another way of conceptualizing this framework is to return to Gee's (2010) well-known distinction between "discourse" and "Discourse" that signifies the relationship between the "language bits" an individual uses—the grammatical, syntactical, semantic, and non-verbal choices made ("d" discourse) and the social practices they construct or evoke through their language use ("D" Discourse). In our analysis, the relationship between the language bits ("d") and the ways of valuing, believing, and acting that comprise social practices ("D") are actualized through the elements of genre, discourse, and style (Fairclough, 1993; Halliday, 1978) or "ways of interacting," "ways of representing," and "ways of being."

For the kind of on-the-fly analysis that we as teacher researchers carry out in the midst of our teaching, it is sufficient, we think, to keep in mind that every utterance functions in three manners—it represents and reflects a way of interacting, a way of representing, and a way of being. This framework can help a teacher researcher ask and answer questions not only about *what* is being said in a book club or guided reading lesson but also to think more carefully about *how* it is said. For returning to the data after the teaching event has passed, we advocate a closer linguistic analysis that helps to reveal patterns that may otherwise go unnoticed, to which we now turn (see Appendix 5 for a Guide for Conducting Critical Discourse Analysis).

Read Aloud: Anti-Racism

To introduce the book clubs and the theme of anti-racism that would unite the books together under the theme of "Anti-racism from History to Present Day," I (Rebecca) read a children's book, *Mr. Lincoln's Way* (Polacco, 2001) to our class in an interactive read-aloud. Sitting at round tables, our students swiveled in their chairs to listen to the read-aloud. In this book Eugene, a White boy, who is also the school bully, is caught calling an African-American first grader a racist name. Mr. Lincoln, the African-American principal, is determined to reach Eugene through his passion for birds. Mr. Lincoln enlists Eugene's help in attracting birds to the school's atrium. Along the way, Eugene reveals that he is learning his racism from home when he states, "My old man calls you real bad names, Mr. Lincoln. He's got an ugly name for just about everybody that's different from us." Mr. Lincoln continues to teach about tolerance and diversity through the diversity of birds in the atrium. He reaches out to Eugene's grandfather for support from home to overcome Eugene's intolerance.

I defined the concept of White allies as part of my introduction to the book. Sitting on a desk, facing the whole class, I stated:

> White allies are people who are systematically working to dismantle racism by denying the privileges associated with being white. These people are also working in struggle with people of color to undermine racist relations. We don't have very many experiences of white allies. . . . We need examples of white allies and people who are doing anti-racist work. I'd like you to think about that as I read *Mr. Lincoln's Way* and think about the different roles that are available to people in this book.
>
> (read-aloud and discussion, February 15, 2005)

During the reading, I stopped to ask questions such as, "What do you think Polacco is trying to communicate with this illustration?" I asked the students to talk at their tables about parts of the story. Throughout the reading, I asked the students to engage in reflective reading practices as I provided constructs for the concepts of White allies, White privilege, internalized oppression, and stages of White identity development.

Jonah pointed out that at the end of the story Eugene has support for his anti-racist work from both school and home. I named this support and stated, "Eugene has an ally in his grandfather." I also recognized the limits of this alliance, "Of course we can critique the extent to which he is an ally . . . but I think Polacco is giving us useful insight into White racial identity here . . . I would encourage you to think about the ways in which White people are represented in literature." I went on to say, "One of the greatest privileges associated with whiteness is not talking about racism. White people can go days, months, years, and a lifetime without thinking about race. When was the last time you thought about what it meant to be White?" The inevitable answer to this question, especially for an almost all White student body, is "not recently." In retrospect, we realized that this short lecture on White privilege asked the White students to publicly admit their compliance with White privilege, a step many of them were not ready to take. Rather than respond directly to the mainly rhetorical question, a student raised her hand and asked, "How do you dismantle White privilege?" I responded by turning the question back to the small groups and asked them to discuss this together.

During the small group discussions, Melissa rested the camera on Jonah and Tonya's small group (refer to Table 2.1 for more on participants). Jonah started the discussion about how to dismantle White privilege.

> Jonah: I guess part of it is recognizing the habit of how you are participating in it. We can find ways to alter, for instance, how we teach history so we do not white wash history.
>
> Tonya: White privilege runs throughout society. It has to do with White people benefiting from other people's misfortunes. It also is rejecting White privilege which is why . . .
>
> Rex: What are all the instances of White privilege? Where are all of the instances where White privilege exists?
>
> Jonah: Well, that's one of the big issues.
>
> Tonya: Well let's deconstruct that, Rex. What do you think?
>
> (small group segment of whiteness discussion, February 15, 2005)

Jonah and Tonya are both engaged in the work of critically analyzing discourses—those they are representing and those being represented by others. Jonah finds a way to open the discussion about White privilege through using the collective pronoun "we," which includes himself as part of the problem and as part of the solution. He also attempts to interrupt Rex's "White talk" by not directly answering Rex's question about naming all of the places where White privilege exists. He knows, drawing on his experience from the Dismantling Racism Institute for Educators, that someone cannot simply be told about White privilege but that they need to discover it for themselves. Related is Tonya's statement, "Let's deconstruct that, Rex." She is asking Rex to look critically at his question and how the question itself presupposes White privilege.

Rex responded, "Well do it. I'd like you to."

In a rapid-fire manner, Tonya responded to Rex, "I think we should. I don't know either. I don't know either." The tone of her voice was raised.

At this point, Jonah placed his hand on Tonya's shoulder, perhaps to calm her down or to assure her that he is working with her and stated, "I know."

Tonya reiterated, "He's really serious. I don't know either."

Jonah responded again with a sympathetic, "I know."

Tonya turned her comment back to Rex and stated, "I don't know either. What do you think?" The irony of a White man asking a woman of color to explain White privilege to him is not lost on Jonah or others in the group. One of the women in the group attempted to talk about a research article she read and Jonah laughed and covered his face with his hand. After a few seconds of discomfort at the table with overlapping talk and an awkward pause, Tonya shared the following narrative:

> Ok, well maybe that there are years of Whites being educated where people of color were denied that education. (As she talks, her hand is outstretched.) So that has built up like she said (referring to Rebecca). A lot of people who go to (our university) whose parents are professionals, doctors, lawyers, whatever which is a form of White privilege because I am the first generation (hand goes to her chest) to go to college whereas I am sure that many of you guys (hand pans the table) had parents who went to college. I mean that is more common in White people than in Black people.

Here, Tonya used a personal narrative to demonstrate how, as a person of color, she has a different experience of "being educated." The discourse of White privilege is made concrete through this narrative about the legacy of education across generations (discourse). She uses a contrastive structure (genre) in the first line to establish the different educational experiences that people of color and White people have access to (discourse). Her level of certainty (style) adds to the overall effect of her point. Her stance of certainty (style) is created through the use of the definitive statement "I am sure . . ." (style). Further, her reference to research (that she doesn't explicitly cite) but implies in her statement "a lot of people" (style) completes the emphasis. This narrative opens up space for several people at the table to comment on their observations about the nature of institutional racism as it is reflected in the differential resources available at schools in the city versus those more well-funded schools in the county.

The range of genres (e.g., narratives and questioning), discourses (e.g., discourse of White privilege and discourse of asking for examples of White privilege), and styles (e.g., stances as "race expert," or "tell me how to do it") represented in this brief set of interactions are part of the history of racial literacy in this classroom. These ways of interacting, representing, and being are part of the shared language of the classroom and follow the participants into their book clubs, as we will see. This whole-class read-aloud and discussion, along with the reading of two articles on anti-racist teaching (e.g., Cooley, 2004/2005; Fondrie, 2001) and Whiteness and handouts on White privilege were dialogically part of the book club conversations (see also Rogers & Mosley, 2010).

Our challenge as teacher researchers was to be present for the kinds of exchanges that would lead toward productive, anti-racist literacy teaching, so that we could scaffold the conversations and address issues. This was no easy feat with 14 students in the class and many opportunities for exploring issues of racism and anti-racism. It was made easier, however, that we were co-teaching, so there were two of us and, in the case of the book clubs, four book clubs.

Practicing Racial Literacy through Book Clubs

One of the dilemmas of our praxis was that we wanted to turn the lens to Whiteness for an exploration of White racial identity, the role of White people in dismantling racism, and how White privilege shapes literacy teaching and learning. However, as an unintended consequence, we found ourselves re-centering Whiteness by choosing books with White protagonists. This focus on Whiteness forced Tonya (the only African-American woman in class) to do even more work of explaining White privilege to her White colleagues.

During the time of this project, we were both reading a great deal of scholarship in racial studies—from critical race theory to Whiteness studies (e.g., Giroux, 1997; Harris, 1993; Ladson-Billings, 1999). We had also attended the Dismantling Racism Institute for Educators and conference sessions on whiteness and critical race theory. We were amply engaged in the theoretical literature and our challenge was translating what we knew in theory into our practice. We found that the focus on institutional racism foregrounded in critical race theory did not help us as we addressed the needs of individuals—either White or people of color—in their journey toward becoming anti-racist educators. We leaned on a framework for understanding racism as held up by both institutions and people and attempted to unravel internalized oppression (for people of color) and White privilege (for White people). Both pillars, we knew, needed to be addressed in our work as anti-racist educators.

We gravitated toward Guinier's (2004) work where she defines racial literacy as an interactive *process* in which the framework of race is used as a lens to explore social and legal practices, explicating the relationship between race and power, and examining mitigating variables such as gender, class, and geography. Racial literacy recognizes the historical meaning of race—that race is a socially constructed category that functions to maintain social hierarchies—as well as the economic outcomes that race creates. Although a perspective and not a solution, racial literacy recognizes the tangible and intangible outcomes of race as a social construct and racism as a mechanism for powerful groups to maintain social, political, and economic advantage. Guinier's conceptualization of racial literacy relies on historical, economic, and institutional practices and locates racial literacy at the institutional level, rather than at the individual level, an absence we found that Twine (2004) from whiteness studies addresses. We were hopeful that book clubs could function as a space for students to engage in discussions about texts for extended periods of time, especially around questions of racism and anti-racism (Flood et al., 1994; Florio-Ruane, 2001; Fondrie, 2001; Glazier, 2003; Lewis & Ketter, 2011; McVee, 2004).

A Critical Discourse Analysis of the Iggie's House Discussion

We returned to one book club discussion for closer analysis because the participants engaged with critical analysis of the representational practices of the author and illustrator and because we knew that a closer analysis would help us learn more about the complexity of their learning. Our focus here is on just one book club conversation, taken from our larger classroom curriculum. To capture both the micro-analysis and the larger context, we looked for overarching ideas about racial literacy in book clubs while keeping the findings from the whole-class discussions in mind. Using the tools of critical discourse analysis we describe, interpret, and offer a set of explanations for the ways in which the teacher education students construct meaning, paying particular attention to shifts and connections between genres of talk, discourses around race, racism, and anti-racism and the stances or kinds of racialized identities constructed throughout the discussion. As we share our interpretations, we note the configuration of genre, discourses, and styles. Table 5.4 in Appendix 5B is a snapshot of the codebook we developed to illustrate the semiotic resources drawn on across the participants in the book club discussion.

Iggie's House, originally published in 1970, focuses on how an inter-racial group of children in suburban New Jersey negotiate an era characterized by struggles over racial desegregation. Winnie, the book's White protagonist, lamenting over the move of her friend Iggie, spies the new family moving into Iggie's old house. She notices immediately that the family has three children and that they are Black. In an effort to be neighborly, Winnie extends her friendship to the Garber children. Their relationship is not without its problems, however. Neighbors sign a petition to force the family to move out of fear of desegregation. When the petition doesn't force the family to move, a sign is posted in the Garber's front yard telling them to "GO BACK WHERE YOU BELONG. WE DON'T WANT YOUR KIND AROUND HERE!!!!!" (Blume, 1970, front cover). This further exacerbates the tenuous relationship between Winnie and the Garber children. Through letters written to the absent Iggie, we see Winnie's White racial development. At the end of the text Winnie recognizes and admits that she knows less about racial relations than she once thought.

One of the first things we noticed about Tonya, Leslie, and Jenna's discussion about this book was the different interpretations of how the protagonist enacted racial literacy. At the level of genre, we examined the turn-taking structure to understand the "ways of interacting" within the book club. Who took the most turns? What kinds of turns were taken? We found it interesting that while Leslie had 98 turns throughout the 17 minutes' discussion, 48 of them are overlapping, back-channeling comments such as "uh huh" and "right," which function to co-construct ideas alongside of her book club colleagues. Given this distribution of kinds of turns, we next examined the ideas (discourses) and stances (styles) represented in the discussion.

Antiracism: Can Talk be Considered Action?

Tonya's primary critique of *Iggie's House* focused on the lack of action in the book, the shallow representation of the Garbers (the African-American family in the book), and the predominance of the privileging effect (where White people's emotions are foregrounded over the material realities of people of color). In the book, *The Garbers*, a Black family, buy a home in the suburbs of New Jersey, where they meet Mrs. Landon, a White woman, who circulates a petition against the Garbers and puts a "go away" sign in the Garbers' yard. Tonya wrote the following in her journal:

> It seems to me that nothing was solved in this book. It was just a story about a 12-year-old White girl and her one to two week encounter with the new Negro neighbors, or colored people as they were referred to by the other White characters in the story, and how their "coloredness" affected the lovely neighborhood on Grove Street.

Chelsey, a White woman in the group, challenged Tonya's perspective that "nothing happened" in the book, arguing that a number of actions occurred. Chelsey called on the following examples to make her point. She mentioned Winnie's survey of the community's attitudes toward the Garbers; Winnie's parents' discussion of racism; the Landons' move out of the community, which demonstrated that they lost the battle with racism in the community; and that Blume wrote following the civil rights movement, which meant that writing the book itself could be viewed as a form of social action. The discourse about anti-racism here is that the actions of anti-racism can occur through talking, thinking, and relating to people in certain ways and learning—actions that have traditionally been considered to be in the cognitive domain rather than the material. Tonya, on the other hand, looked for evidence of material changes to determine if anti-racism is present.

Chelsey, Leslie, and Tonya discussed the question of whether anything happened in the book during their book club meeting. Rex was absent from class. Leslie began the discussion by making a personal connection to the main character: "I feel like I am . . . this little girl." She then offered an explanation for her identification with Winnie.

> (9) Well, (10) because I feel like, um, (12) when she when she talks about like, like um, ok, (13) when she talks about things (14) like people aren't supporting her (15) when she has these ideas (16) and they're not the same as her parents, (17) I feel like that situation (18) is really similar to me sometimes (19) if I try to talk to my parents (20) or like friends, (21) like that aren't in the education program (22) about different like social justice type things (23) they don't really understand it. (24) Especially, like I remember reading, (25) when Dr. Rogers read it [a section of *Iggie's House* aloud], (26) I felt like (27) "oh, I feel like we're alike," (28) you know, so . . .

Leslie explained that she and the character in the book engage with "social justice type things" and most people in her life "don't really understand it." For Leslie, "social justice type things" are represented through verbal, mental/cognitive, and relational verbs—verbal (e.g., lines 11, 13, and 19 "talks"), mental/cognitive (e.g., line 15 "ideas," line 23 "understand," and line 24 "remember"), and relational (e.g., line 14 "supporting," and line 27 "feel"). Leslie's discussion of anti-racism focuses mainly on the psychological and individual domains, carried out through talk and feelings. See Table 5.2 in Appendix 5B.

There was a notable absence of material verbs in this excerpt of Leslie's talk. Further, anti-racism is an unmarked term. She referred to anti-racist actions as, "social justice type things" and used distancing pronouns such as "these ideas" (discourse). She took a stance, identifying herself with the main character who, she believed, engaged with social justice. We hear her affinity in lines 17–18 and in lines 26–27 where she compared herself to Winnie (style). Tonya, however, questioned the limits of Leslie's affinity with Winnie.

> (29) Tonya: I think that's interesting. (30) Um, I think I can see how (31) maybe you could feel that (32) but I didn't feel that at all. (33) Leslie: You didn't? What did you feel from the book? (34) I definitely didn't feel like I was in the book. (35) Leslie: What did you feel like? (36) Tonya: This little, this book made me upset. (37) I don't like to read books (36) where nothing happens. (38) Leslie: Ohhhhh (39) Tonya: Well, ok. (40) Leslie: No, I don't care, I don't care.

At this moment, the participants seemed to agree to explore the group's divergent viewpoints together. I (Rebecca) made a note to ask the group to discuss these viewpoints when we reconvened with the other book clubs. Next, Tonya presented her primary critique of the book, what she saw as a privileging effect, which operates when White people reframe racism (and measures to redress racism) in a manner that privileges the feelings of White people at the expense of the material realities of people of color. Tonya's point was that the African-American voices were deliberately silenced in the book so Winnie's racial identity development could be explored. She stated:

> (72) Tonya: Like you didn't hear voices of um, the Garbers, really (73) And that (74) Leslie: ohhh, mmm (75) Tonya: That made me upset. (76) Because it's all about, (77) this whole issue (78) is centered around them, (79) but the focus of the book (80) is Winnie. (81) Leslie: mmm (82) Tonya: And she doesn't do anything. (83) She's just going through emotions (84) and so . . .

In the book, Winnie's struggle *to talk* with the adults in her life about racism was exactly the point that Leslie identified with. Tonya does not recognize Winnie's White racial identity development if it remains in the mental, cognitive, and emotional realms and does not move toward material actions. In this excerpt, Tonya called on a range of verbs to make her point: mental (e.g., line 72 "hear"), affective/relational (e.g. line 75 "upset," line 83 "going through emotions"), and material (e.g., line 82 "do anything"). See Table 5.3 in Appendix 5B for a display of verbs that Tonya used in this excerpt. Her point about the division between *talk* and *action* is emphasized by her repetition of this argument (genre, discourse) and that she calls on multiple genres (e.g., narrative and comedy) to provide examples for her position that "nothing happened" (line 72) (stance). In this way, we see how genre, discourse, and style are patterned together.

Tonya also argued that Winnie's status as a child prohibited her from exhibiting agency. She stated: "[I]t didn't matter what she wanted to say, or what she wanted to happen, it didn't happen. And like she couldn't really say, you're not going to tell your parents off." In the book, Winnie's mother learns that people are moving into the empty house in their neighborhood. She tells Winnie she will make brownies for the new neighbors. When she finds out the family is African-American, she "forgets" to bake the brownies. Tonya drew on this excerpt from the book (genre and intertextuality) and created what she saw as an unlikely scenario where Winnie directly confronted her mother's racism (discourse).

> (61) Tonya: You're not going to say, (62) 'Mom, I know you didn't forget (63) to bake those brownies (64) are you playin'?' (65) Leslie: Yeah really. *Leslie laughs.* Yeah. (66) Tonya: "Are you racist?" (67) You're not going to say (68) anything like that. (69) It just seems like (70) she was learning a lot too

(71) so I guess if I was like, 12, (72) I would be like, (73) "oh, this is great" (74) but, at this age, (75) I'm just like, (76) nothing happened. (77) Like it just frustrates me.

In Tonya's imaginary scenario, Winnie interrupted her mother's passive racism with a direct confrontation, naming racism: "I know you didn't forget to bake those brownies, are you playin'? . . . Are you racist?" Tonya's point here is that Blume chose a character that, by virtue of being a child, is without agency and not able to directly confront racism. In this passage we also hear a shift in Tonya's understanding of the boundaries of anti-racism (discourse). In line 70 she called on the mental verb *learning* when she stated, "[S]he [Winnie] was learning a lot, too." This statement indicates the possibility for Tonya that learning about racism and anti-racism may be considered an action (discourse, style). Similarly, later in the discussion she stated, "[S]he's like a growing activist but she can't do anything right now," expanding her previous idea to include "right now" (discourse, style). This temporal marker suggests Tonya's openness to the idea that Winnie holds the ability to develop into the kind of anti-racist ally Tonya expects, one that engages in actions.

Listening closely to how meanings around race were constructed in the book club helped us to see how each participant tried out new ideas, the heart of critical literacy education. Toward the end of their discussion, Leslie demonstrates that she has really been thinking about Tonya's point that nothing happened in the book. She offers a theory of why this may have been the case.

(800) She didn't really have any other allies. (801) She had no like, social relationships (802) or connections that could allow her to do anything. (803) Cause she had no power. (804) Just like, with her parents, (805) she couldn't like tell them off. (806) She I mean, she couldn't do anything. (807) But, and so I guess just how like, (808) Iggie's family were the ones that made her feel like she had power, (809) and was able to give her new ideas (810) that clearly no one else had on her block, (811) or at least no one was willing to talk about . . . (812) I think that's why she wasn't able to do anything?

Leslie adopts the discourse of anti-racism and argues that the absence of "allies" in Winnie's life may have prohibited the range of actions she took (discourse). We hear how Leslie is closely analyzing the relationships in the book—between Winnie and her parents and with Iggie's family—through a lens of power (lines 803–811). She seems to concede Tonya's point that Winnie's anti-racism stops at the level of personal development and does not include any substantive action, a point she repeats twice (lines 803 and 806, genre). She ends with a rhetorical question, which demonstrates her willingness to adopt a new perspective and to stand in the uncertainty associated with racial literacy (line 812) (discourse, style).

In their book club discussion the following week, Tonya drew on the genre of comedy to draw the group's attention back to the limitation of Winnie's anti-racism work. She says:

> (30) It kind of reminded me of like (31) a lot of times, you know, (32) if you watch comedy shows or something (33) and if you watch (34) Black comics talking about White people (35) and they will say, (36) "oh, I'm not racist, (37) I have a Black friend. (38) They come over to my house. (39) I have three Black friends."
>
> Leslie: (40) uh-huh
>
> Tonya: (41) That's like the comic jokes (42) because White people will say (43) that they have Black friends to prove (44) that they are not racist or // exclusive
>
> Jenna: (45) uh-huh
>
> Tonya: (46) But they'll always know (47) how many they have (48) or how many times they have seen them (49) or exactly what they have talked to them about. (50) So it is just like (51) "come on, now, (52) that's not your friend."

Tonya aligns herself with "Black comics" who talk about "White people" who "will say that they have Black friends to prove that they are not racist" (lines 30–39). Her basic argument is that there is often a disjuncture between the talk and actions of White people. She brings the conversation about racism into the present context, drawing on a contemporary example, one that her White colleagues can relate to. Her point evokes a telling laugh from the White participants in the book club.

The humor functions to soften her critique (genre, style) of the discourse of anti-racism as it is presented in the book and, perhaps, the underlying theme of the book clubs and the social relationships in the class itself. That is, knowing a Black person and calling them a friend does not make someone anti-racist. She explicitly critiques this position and with a slight laugh and ironic tone says, "So it is just like come on, now, that's not your friend" (lines 50–51). The others in the group laugh along with her. Using a combination of direct and indirect modes (humor as indirect/verbal mode) and direct (eye contact), Tonya makes her point about the limits of the friendship between Winnie and the Garbers. We learned that this was a common configuration of interactional moves for Tonya in this set of book clubs. Looking closely at the configuration of genre, discourse, and style also enabled us to notice movement in the discourses that Tonya used to represent action in the book. See Table 5.4 in Appendix 5B for an example of how we analyzed each line of this excerpt using genre, discourse, and style.

As the group continued their discussion, the topic turned from the characters' actions to the responsibility of the authors and the designers of the book covers in representing race. This multimodal analysis of the ideas and images represented on the book covers provided Chelsea with a way to dig more deeply into her racial analysis. She critiqued the narrow representation of racialized identities offered in the book, pointing out that the illustrator's use of colors for the book covers communicates social values and metaphors about race.

As we listened to the book club conversations, it became clearer to us that becoming racially literate is an interactive process that includes both support and challenge. Indeed, the participants supported one another in becoming racially literate, modeling discourses, racial vocabularies, and conceptual models for further inter-racial understandings. They also demonstrated how racial literacy includes disagreement, challenges, and multiple perspectives. The multi-perspectival space of the book club offered a window to see ideas and viewpoints different from their own which, in turn, shed relief on their own constructs around race.

Tonya continued in the discussion and in her written work to struggle with the work that people of color do to dismantle racism both in the children's books and in their class discussions. However, perhaps because of interactions with her classmates such as these, she became more open to the racial literacy work of the group. Tonya wrote the following in her journal in response to an article called "Gentle Doses of Racism: Whiteness in Children's Literature" written by Fondrie (2001).

> I understand that change is not going to happen unless White people work, too, but is it necessary for books to exist where White people are positioned as the main character? Don't these books silence the voices of the oppressed? At first read, I felt the author's sentiments were the polar opposites of my own. Fondrie (2001) states, "I always place the burden of acting or speaking on the characters who represent other groups. They are the ones who must act and speak and think appropriately in my estimation." *Then, I realized something interesting . . . I have been doing the same thing! I criticize society for placing the burden of racism on people of color, yet I also criticize books like* Iggie's House *for attempting to shift some of the burden to White people and how they deal with racism.* I realize that I have issues that I need to sort out about how I feel about discussions and literature centered on whiteness, White privilege and White allies before I make a conclusion about the validity of these topics. I have to come to understanding on the significance of each of these topics in discussions on racial issues and whether or not I feel that they are necessary and helpful or just another indirect tool of oppression.

In this journal, Tonya evoked the materiality of anti-racism through her choice of the linguistic units "burden" and "deal with." In a reflexive move, she recognized how her critique of the White characters in *Iggie's House* minimized the anti-racist efforts of other White authors and of her White colleagues who were trying to enter into the work of anti-racism. Tonya seemed to recognize that, for White people, a stage in "dealing with racism" may be synonymous with talking about racism and anti-racism. She is left wondering about the possibilities and constraints of discussions and literature in the struggle for anti-racism. We encourage you to look more closely at Tonya's reflection using the analytic guide for CDA found in Appendix 5.

Conclusion

When we sat next to our students during this book club, we heard aspects of racial literacy practiced in the moment-to-moment interactions. We took note of participation structures, discourses of racism and anti-racism, and different positions taken. We tried to attend to what aspects of the book they discussed and what was ignored. When we brought the book clubs back together, we often framed our discussion points around "ways of interacting," "ways of representing," and "ways of being." As teacher researchers and also discourse analysts, it is a way of thinking and making sense of the world. We may, for example, ask the groups to focus on the major themes (discourses) that were discussed and debated during the book club. If we noted an interactional pattern that was troublesome—some students dominating the discussion, for instance—we may address this as well (genre). Because we were particularly interested in multiple positions taken on the concept of anti-racism, we were sure to draw these out of the discussion as well (style). In this way, we used the tools of critical discourse analysis to build our critical literacy classroom.

Our students conducted their own critical analysis of the characters' words and actions—scrutinizing the intentions and consequences. In doing so, they engaged their racial imaginations about what is and should be considered anti-racism. The space of the children's literature provided a support for the students to engage with the motives, intentions, dispositions, words, and actions of the characters. That is, as they re-interpret Winnie, they also re-interpret themselves and their relation to one another in a way that they may not be able to without the presence of fiction. Winnie's fictional character allowed the pre-service teachers the space to rehearse their critiques and praises around anti-racism that they may not have the courage (yet) to do with people. This rehearsal adds to each person's stock of discursive resources that they may call on in their next set of interactions.

As we moved toward the end of the school year, we noticed that many of our teachers were embodying critical literacy practices in their teaching and professional work as teachers. As we saw briefly with the multimodal critique of the book covers in this chapter, the pre-service teachers increasingly called upon the tools of multimodal discourse analysis to make a space for multiple modes of meaning making in their teaching and in their own learning. Multimodal discourse analysis (MDA) provides us with tools for understanding the relationships between language and action. Likewise, we demonstrate in this next chapter how we read their practices through a MDA lens.

6

PERFORMING LITERACY

Multimodal discourse analysis

At the end of the year, a number of teachers in our class experimented with the book *Jazz Baby* (Weatherford, 2002) in their teaching with second graders in the tutoring practicum at Liddell Elementary. *Jazz Baby* is a book from a series called *BeBop Books*, published by Lee & Low as a multicultural leveled text collection. Leveled text collections are produced for teachers who match books to readers by selecting texts along a gradient of difficulty that challenges students to learn new strategies without overwhelming them with text features they do not yet control (Fountas, Pinnell, & Bird, 1999). Recall from Chapter 2 that our work with pre-service teachers was situated in a classroom in an urban elementary school. Their students were African-American, and the surrounding community was both historically and presently shaped by events in which race played a role, for example, historical and systemic segregation and discrimination. There was also a strong history of cultural practices in this community, such as music linked to the African-American community—jazz and blues—as well as visual arts, literature, and theater. In this chapter, you will read about our analysis of two pre-service teachers' literacy lessons with the book *Jazz Baby*. The book is an example of a text that teachers use when teaching for literacy acceleration because of its familiar content and appealing illustrations and language (see Chapter 2 for a discussion of accelerative frameworks).

The focus of this chapter is the ways in which our pre-service teachers drew on their deepened understanding of pedagogy and literacy teaching conventions in order to improvise within the structure of the literacy lesson in ways that were responsive to students' ways of interacting with narratives and texts (Ladson-Billings, 1994). Not coincidentally, the data from this chapter brings us to the close of the school year. At this point in the semester most of our students were procedurally comfortable with their knowledge of ways to accelerate literacy development including introducing texts using supportive book introductions (Clay, 1991b; Labadie, Mosley Wetzel, & Rogers, 2013), following the student's lead using assessment strategies and choice words (Johnston, 2004), and teaching for problem solving (Johnston, 1997). We noticed that as teachers became comfortable with literacy teaching, they were more in-synch with their students, drawing on culturally relevant pedagogy and multimodality to connect on multiple levels with their students.

Jazz Baby (Weatherford, 2002) was an important book in our collection because it displays children who appear to have different races and ethnicities playing musical instruments in the style of jazz. The text is predictable based on the illustrations, which are brightly colored and appealing. In the lessons we will draw on to talk about multimodality and multimodal discourse analysis, verbal exchanges mimicked the action of the book. The book is full of rhythm and allows the reader to anticipate the words on the page as they follow the movement of the images and rhyme. On each page, the repeated words, "Jazz baby, jazz baby," are printed in a wave shape, calling the reader to sway with the words. The characters make gestures that respond to the music, like clapping, snapping, and moving their shoulders. The characters are full of action and movement as they move and play to the beat. In their planning, the teachers may not have anticipated how these illustrations would shape the students' readings of the text, but instead, drew on these resources and modalities in the moment to shape the interactions.

Using critical discourse analysis, we demonstrate how we read practices of literacy teaching and learning through a multimodal lens. First, we provide an example of how we carried out multimodal analysis—moving from the construction of a multimodal transcript, a review of key concepts, a guide to conducting the kind of multimodal critical discourse analysis we used, and finally, how we interpret and represent patterns of multimodal interaction. Second, we make an argument that the teachers were teaching literacy in a creative and improvisational way that is, itself, multimodal, and invited students to actively construct literate understandings through multimodal designs.

Along the way, we demonstrate how our students supported their students to critically read texts through multimodal analysis. We will illustrate multiple ways that the pre-service teachers prepared and supported students to "read themselves" as part of the story. To understand this work, we draw on Freire's (1983) notion of the role of a teacher in teaching reading. He is speaking about teaching adults, and writes:

> Nor could I reduce learning to read and write merely to learning words, syllables, or letters, a process of teaching in which the teacher fills the supposedly empty heads of the learners with his or her words. On the contrary, the student is the subject of the process of learning to read and write as an act of knowing and a creative act. The fact that he or she needs the teacher's

help, as in any pedagogical situation, does not mean that the teacher's help annuls the student's creativity and responsibility for constructing his or her own written language and reading this language.

(Freire, 1983, p. 10)

We observed that literacy teaching in the practicum was becoming more learner-centered, as our pre-service teachers learned ways to respond to their students' creativity.

Throughout the chapter we draw on the metaphor of improvisation to illustrate the creative way in which the teachers and students collaboratively designed meanings across modes. Jurow and Creighton (2005) write:

> [I]mprovisation, in music and in social life, involves creatively using the resources at hand to devise an action or response that allows one to develop new possibilities for participation and understanding. Improvisation is not unrestrained freedom ... it involves a productive tension between individuality and tradition, innovation and structure.
>
> (Jurow & Creighton, 2005, pp. 275–276)

As Sawyer (2004) points out, improvisational teaching is disciplined. It is purposeful but not predetermined. This kind of teaching does not just value students' ideas but draws on them as a resource for furthering their learning.

Multimodal Discourse Analysis

The tools of narrative research, critical discourse analysis, and multimodal social semiotic approaches analysis come together in this chapter. Discourse analysis has been critiqued for its emphasis on written and spoken texts as the source of meaning, often at the neglect of meanings made in other modalities (Linnell, 2005; Street, 1984). In many cases, the reach of language is insufficient for the representational work that needs to be accomplished. Yet, in Western societies, written and spoken language have been privileged or naturalized as "the tools" of representation.

Traditions and Concepts

Teaching is an embodied act of "designing" as teachers draw on an array of modalities, including verbal conversation, gestures, emotions, movement, rhythm, music, and composition in order to make meaning with students in interactions. Students, too, draw on this array to bring together new ideas and concepts with their own identities and ways of seeing the world (New London Group, 2000). A theory of multiliteracies, drawn from the New Literacy studies, suggests that designing occurs every day, in every moment of classroom life, and is part of a social practice of meaning construction. This body of work includes ethnographic work on local practices of literacy in and out of schools (i.e., Gee, 2000; Heath, 1983; Hull & Schultz, 2002; Street, 1993). Researchers focus on how local literacies within any context shape interactions around literacy, such as how students draw on storytelling or ways of talking in and out of school. Researchers also focus on how practices for doing literacy are shaped by the institution of school, such as parents reading to their children at night. Finally, researchers focus on the political nature of literacy, asking how local and school-type literacies are viewed, valued, and encouraged both in moment-to-moment interactions as well as historically in communities (Finders, 1997; Hicks, 2002; Jones, 2006). Research on multiple literacies (multiliteracies) has, for the most part, fallen short of interrogating what happens when teachers (or in our case, pre-service teachers) expand their practices to include multiple literacies. Often, teachers may incorporate multiple literacies without critically examining how those literacies are either transformative or oppressive for students (Heller, 2008).

In the sense that we are interested then in not only the multimodal design of practices but also the ways in which designers position themselves and are positioned by others, we need a theory and method of analysis that again, as we discussed in Chapters 3 to 5, interrogates the form and function of discourse and action. A multimodal discourse analysis focuses on designing as ways of interacting, ways of representing, and ways of being as not just verbal acts but as multimodal activities (Rogers, 2011). Appendix 6A describes how we create a multimodal transcript.

In our analyses, teachers and students are designers who draw on available designs (i.e., a guided reading lesson format, a book, or a way of sitting next to a student) as well as construct new designs (i.e., composing blues texts from one's life in response to reading a book that has rhyming language). In doing so, they draw on multiple modes to make meaning in the interaction. Representation is always an interpretation, always partial, and always signifies choices the sign maker is using to construct reality. All signs are metaphors, newly made, displaying the interests of the sign maker and the interpreter as new meanings are made. Kress (2003) writes:

> The sign—a complex message of words, of letters, of colour and font-types with all of their cultural resonances—reflects the interests of its designer as much as the designer's imagined sense of those who will see and "read" the sign. The sign is based on a specific rhetorical purpose, and intent to persuade with all means possible those who pass by and notice it.
>
> (Kress, 2003, p. 2)

Designs are made using five modes of meaning (audio design, spatial design, gestural design, visual design, and linguistic design) (New London Group, 2000).

"A mode is a socially shaped and culturally given semiotic resource for making meaning" (Kress, 2010, p. 79). Modes of meaning are complex and include many design elements that designers may draw upon. Audio design includes the elements that constitute music and sound effects. Spatial design includes the elements that constitute the meanings of the space around the interaction (how people arrange the space around them using objects). Gestural design includes the elements of the ways our body moves in space, such as the way we gesture with our hands, arms, and bodies, our affect as it is expressed through facial expression and posture, how we stay close to or far away from others and objects, or how we move our body through a space. Visual design includes the ways that meaning is made through colors, perspective, and other elements of design. Finally, linguistic design includes the ways that language is used to make meaning, which corresponds with much of what we discussed in Chapter 5 as the ways in which language functions in an interaction (drawing on genres of interacting, ways of representing or discourses, and styles or ways of being). Within each of these meaning units, there are particular semiotic modes we may choose to focus on or not focus on based on our questions and our framework for interpretation of the event.

Appendix 6B illustrates the steps involved in conducting MDA including a descriptive analysis, conducting lexical counts, and examining modality. We provide examples and guides for looking at "ensembles" of modes and for conducting a critical discourse analysis of a multimodal discourse analysis.

Jazz Baby, Jazz Baby: An Analysis of Multimodality in Two Reading Lessons

We turn our attention to two scenes from two lessons in which tutors and their students interact with *Jazz Baby* (Weatherford, 2002), a book about children enjoying music. The scenes demonstrate how the teachers provide the structure and flexibility for improvisational discourse to occur which, in turn, leads to expanded learning opportunities for teachers and students. Both lessons loosely followed a book introduction format (Clay, 1991b) in which the tutor and student "walk through" the book, paying attention to the print and action represented in the illustrations in order to support the student in his or her later reading of the text.

We have chosen the first few pages of the book and their associated interactions to exemplify what we see as the variations in multimodal teaching across the lessons. The book begins, "Jazz baby, jazz baby, join the band. You've got music in your hands." As the story unfolds we are introduced to various instruments as the children "join the band," a rhyming pattern and the familiar refrain of "jazz baby, jazz baby." The author adds to the narrative snapping fingers and other ways to make music with the body, moves like a shake and a shimmy, instruments like a piano and a bass—each introduced through the sounds they make and the refrain "jazz baby, jazz baby." The last page reads, "Jazz baby, jazz baby, hum a song. Let it rock you all night long." See Appendix 6E and Appendix 6F for the interactions we focus on here, as well as a multimodal description of the pages from the book. These appendices represent our verbal and nonverbal transcripts with still frame images. We have not included our tables of descriptive analyses or critical discourse analysis of the transcript in these appendices but we have woven our analysis into our writing about the events. Appendix 6D is a summary of steps that we take when conducting MDA.

Multimodality in Jonah and Tamara's Lesson

As we discuss the interactions that occurred around this text, you can reference Appendix 6E for the transcript. As Jonah conducted his book introduction, he and Tamara constructed meanings around the text, each drawing on multiple modes to do so. In this lesson, Jonah and Tamara improvise in the style of jazz and Jonah enacts his purposes as a literacy teacher by drawing on what Tamara brings to the lesson. We will illustrate how each of these meanings is made multimodally.

Jonah and Tamara's Improvisation. The improvisation in this interaction occurred through multiple modes including movement and gesture, linguistic choices (verbs), and singing. Jonah shows Tamara that the reading of this book is something they are doing together, a very supportive model for a book introduction. For example, Jonah introduces the repeated line, "Jazz baby, jazz baby" (line 8) and suggests, "Want to try that together?" as he gazes at Tamara. Jonah's gaze is a supportive sign that indicates that they are in this "together." Tamara accepts his invitation and begins, "Jazz baby" (line 9) and Jonah joins in with her to read. Through line 10, their shared gaze is on the book and their attention is on the rhythm and the text. As Tamara accepts Jonah's invitation and reads with him, her body sways to keep the rhythm of the book. As she begins to say, "You've got the music," she improvises a sing-song tone, stretching out "haaa-and" (line 11). Tamara improvises with the word "hand," a common discursive move for Tamara—riffing off the print in the text to create new words. We also noted this move later in the transcript, when she riffed, "sh-sh-sh-shake it" (not included in Appendix 6B).

Jonah, continuing to follow Tamara's lead, picks up Tamara's riff and asks, "Where's the music?" (line 12), drawing Tamara into her moment of singing again. The movement of his fist is an iconic gesture, in which the mode resembles what it represents, and emphasizes the word "hand" that also appears on the page. Here, Jonah calls Tamara to attend to the joy of holding music in one's hand. His gesture—a closed fist—compliments the concept in the book.

Tamara responds in line 13, "haa-and," a repetition of her riff, and accompanies her response with a smile, indicating that she is enjoying this play with words. Tamara then extends the ideas represented on the page—that of having the "music in your hands"—through her representation of the action "snapping" in verbal and gestural modes. She independently reads the image of a young girl snapping her hands above her head and says, "I can snap like that" (line 15). She draws on use of a simile "like that" to represent the action in the image. Through her words and actions she demonstrates an affinity with the characters in the book. This strong affiliation is accompanied by her use of multiple modes at once and, in particular, she indicates to Jonah that she is "like" the characters in the book.

As in jazz improvisation, two players, Jonah and Tamara, play off of each other's contributions to create a creative variation of the original theme of the lesson. Throughout we see how one individual introduced ideas that were expanded on by another. The back-and-forth exchange of ideas and the in-synch reading functioned to keep the interaction light and full of motion.

Jonah Enacts His Goals as a Literacy Teacher. Along with playing with this improvisation, Jonah also orchestrates the lesson with purposes and goals in mind. One of these goals is introducing the book so that Tamara will be able to read it independently. Jonah does this by both focusing on the rhyming pattern of the book and also drawing on what Tamara brings as prior experience to the text.

To introduce rhyming, Jonah uses a pointing gesture as he says, "This actually has a little rhyme to it" (line 3), drawing Tamara's attention to the words on the page. He reads, "Jazz baby, jazz baby, join the band. You've got music in your hands." At this point, Tamara leans in (see line 4) and shows through her gaze and her close distance from Jonah that she is interested in the rhyming in the book. His reading of the passage is quickly paced and suggested that he may have been modeling fluent reading. He looks directly at Tamara (line 5) but Tamara's gaze indicates that she is not looking at the text. Perhaps Tamara is listening or thinking about the rhyme.

Seconds later, Jonah gazes towards her as he asks, "Do you hear the rhyme?" and points to the page (line 6). He uses multimodal verbs but his pointing gesture allows him to also stay close to the feature of print on the page. Here, he is enacting a goal he has as a literacy teacher, checking for understanding of a concept that he has introduced. He is asking for her attention to the sound of a rhyme, rather than to a feature of the print on the page. His use of the verb "hear" versus "see" emphasizes and draws on her preferred mode—auditory—as we saw in the section above. Tamara's gaze moves to Jonah as she agrees, "yeah," and in line 8, Jonah builds on her agreement by asking her, "Want to try that together?" His gaze holds this interaction together, and allows him to kindly make a request for reading. One second later, they began to read, and Tamara sways as she remembers the lyrics to the text she had been practicing.

Jonah also supports her as a reader by connecting the book to her experiences. Early in the lesson, Jonah asks, "Remember we talked about jazz the last time," to which Tamara recalls, "Smooth jazz." Once he has reminded Tamara of the genre, he opens spaces for her to bring a love of music into the literacy lesson. He does so by listening carefully to the language that she uses to interact with the book and then uses that language as a bridge to the language of the book. For example, when she sings in line 11, "You've got the music in your haaa–and," Jonah picks up on her use of music, asking in line 12 as he laughs (see image), "Where's the music?" When she suggests that the characters are "shaking their behinds," he links her talk to the text of the book, which reads, "shake and shimmy."

Jonah enacts his goals as a literacy teacher by closely attending to Tamara's preferred ways of making meaning of this text. In a segment before the interaction represented in Appendix 6E, when Tamara and Jonah are looking at the cover of the book, it becomes clear to Jonah that she is trying to figure out what the book is about. Tamara suggests, "It's like a baby at the end," looking off into the distance. Jonah asks her to clarify, and she reads, "Jazz and the baby." Here, she notices that there is possibly a baby represented in the book or that the book is about a baby that makes jazz. Jonah points out that "jazz baby" is a phrase. When he does so, he looks directly at Tamara but makes his hand move in a motion of a wave towards the book cover. This wave motion, accompanied by a slight pause between the words "jazz" and baby," functions to let Tamara hear the rhythm of the language of the text. Knowing what "jazz baby" sounds like is critical, for Jonah, to making meaning from this text. In a multimodal signal that she is on the same page, she begins to hum and sway back and forth.

Next, we will see the differences between the ways that Tonya and CeCe interacted around the text using multimodal literacy practices. In both cases, improvisation was important. Whereas Jonah's lesson was improvisational in the sense of the music they created together while reading, Tonya's lesson drew on improvisation in the sense that she changed a "picture walk" to a "character walk" in order to construct an opening for CeCe to become part of the story.

Multimodality in Tonya and CeCe's Lesson

As we discuss the interactions that occurred around this text for Tonya and CeCe, reference Appendix 6F for the transcript of the two pages of each interaction we focus on in this chapter. There were three themes we identified in this lesson: Tonya's lesson brought CeCe into the book as a character; Tonya's language created the conditions of possibility; and CeCe was engaged in practicing critical literacy in this event.

"So Let's Act Like We're Her": Bringing CeCe into the Book as a Character. Tonya improvises on the usual structure and genre of the "picture walk" by turning it into a "character walk." For instance, as they read the first page together, Tonya engages CeCe as a character in the story, a person she can follow along with. Like Jonah, Tonya reads to give CeCe a sense of the rhythm of the language in the text: "It says *Jazz Baby Jazz Baby in the band, you've got music in your hands*" (line 3).

However, before doing so, she asks CeCe, "OK, tell me what you're doing in this picture?" (line 1), to which CeCe responds, "Dancing." As Tonya makes these choices, CeCe is invited into a narrative of being a jazz baby, and enjoying the music. Rather than walk through the book asking what the characters are doing, Tonya uses her book introduction to ask CeCe what she is doing. In line 5, for example, she asks, "So CeCe is dancing to the music. Kind of feelin' it huh?" Out of Tonya's 69 turns, 23 of them are open-ended questions, asking CeCe to come along with her and construct the story.

Tonya co-constructs this narrative around the text with CeCe. There are elements of narrative structure in the lesson. For instance, in line 15, Tonya introduces a crisis into the narrative when she asks, "Where are you?" Her repetitive question, "What is she doing right now?" builds an ongoing narrative around the text in which CeCe must attend to the illustrations. Perhaps her purpose is to support CeCe as she makes meaning from the book and to build excitement and interest when reading a difficult text. In an interaction not included in Appendix 6F, for example, Tonya exclaims, "There she is!" Throughout the event, Tonya uses present-tense verbs to move the narrative along, such as when she comments, "It's just those people and they are dancing. So I guess she isn't dancing, she's making the music."

In many places in the lesson it is as if Tonya and CeCe are having a dialogue and the text is there to facilitate their dialogue, versus the other way around. Tonya reads the text from the book but does not draw CeCe's attention directly to it. In this way, the text of the book fills in their dialogue and acts like background music or a cohesive device throughout the lesson. What is also interesting in terms of this dialogue is the ways that Tonya uses African-American language patterns within the interactions around the book to make it clear that the conversation is in the foreground and the text is the background. For example, in line 5 she uses the final /n/ when saying "feeling."

Tonya and CeCe draw on less movement and more attention to the imagined narrative of CeCe's action in the story. Turning their preview of the book into a character walk invited CeCe into the text by affiliating with a character and then traveling with her throughout the story.

Language of Possibility. Tonya's work in this interaction is aligned with what culturally relevant pedagogy scholars have suggested about successful teachers of African-American students. Tonya suggests through her language that CeCe should explore all of the possibilities open for her as she reads this book (Perry, 2003). Striking is the repetition of the modal verb phrases—"could" and "would" throughout the lesson. This construction invites CeCe to explore possible interpretations and to use her social imagination as she negotiates the text. As Tonya invited her to choose a character to follow throughout the story she asked questions such as: "Who can you be?", "Who would you be?", "Why would you want to be her?", and "What could you be doing right now?" Across the lesson, she and CeCe use the modal verb construction that includes "could" or "would" eight times.

When Tonya proposes, "So let's act like we're her," she points to the character in the book who is snapping her fingers. The use of "let's" suggests a collaborative activity in which the narrative will be built between the two. This use of collective verb and object suggests that reading is a collaborative activity. Tonya uses this expression eight times throughout the lesson, indicating the power of this phrase in her plans as a literacy teacher. However, unlike Jonah and Tamara's lesson, they do not "act like we're her" using actions but, instead, use language to pretend that CeCe is in the book. Perhaps Tonya is following CeCe's lead, because CeCe was less active using her body than Tamara was in the lesson below. She sits close to Tonya but her body position and hands are closed together (see line 2).

Tonya's language reminds CeCe that she will be guided and supported, and the use of "act" in the phrase, "So let's act like we're her," as well as Tonya's choice of verbs of doing (i.e., "doing," "dancing," and "blowing") from lines 1–11 calls on the action-packed nature of the book and keeps CeCe's engagement in the story. For example, in line 5, CeCe nods, smiling, when Tonya suggests, "So CeCe is dancing to the music. Kind of feelin' it."

Their shared gaze on the book, which leads to CeCe peering into the book between lines 1 and 2, brings attention to the illustrations. Tonya's direct question, "OK, tell me what you're doing in the picture," (line 1) asks CeCe to construct a new story without very much information about what the author of the text intends. However, the shared gaze on the book supports CeCe in looking into the action, the illustrations, and perhaps, scaffolds her future reading by focusing on the meaning of the story. In line 3, Tonya reminds her that there is text to support meaning making, as well, stating, "[I]t says . . ." and reading the page to CeCe. She makes a similar move in line 13, "Let's see, tapping their feet and snapping their fingers," introducing vocabulary that will show up on the page of the text where a girl danced by herself in deep connection with the music.

Throughout the interaction, Tonya's questions and their shared gaze hold the interaction together as cohesive devices as she makes pedagogical moves to support CeCe's future reading. CeCe is supported in her reading by Tonya's language but also this shared focus. When Tonya wants CeCe to take a risk and engage with the text, she supports her through her use of multiple modes. However, overall, it is clear throughout the character walk that CeCe's role is to imagine herself as a jazz baby, which leads her to practice critical literacy.

Practicing Critical Literacy in this Event. Towards the end of the interaction, in reference to the page that depicts a boy blowing a horn, Tonya shifts her language to prompt CeCe's use of critical literacy. She moves away from the text and introduces a new narrative that moves outside of the illustrations and into CeCe's own life. In line 10, Tonya asks CeCe, "What could you be doing right now?" The question asks CeCe to make a prediction although she is not pictured on the page. This move allows Tonya to find out how CeCe sees herself in this story.

When CeCe answers, "dancing" (line 11), Tonya can tell from her smile and her answer that CeCe has imagined herself in the story. This pattern repeats in lines 13 to 16. In this episode in the book, CeCe's character (the character they have decided to "act like") was not represented on the page. Thus, Tonya asks CeCe to generate a theory about an absence, practicing an aspect of critical literacy that requires CeCe to use her social imagination and think beyond the text.

As we unpacked the interactions that Tonya and CeCe constructed, multimodally, we noted that Tonya encourages CeCe to become part of the story and, in doing so, opens spaces for her to practice critical literacy. Tonya drew on the language of critical literacy in other ways as well. The majority of Tonya's turns are open-ended questions (23, in total). A common question she asks of CeCe is, "Why . . .?" For example, "Why do you want to be her?" and "Why do you like her better?" Tonya also makes seemingly intentional choices in terms of modality (verbs of doing) and questions that probed CeCe's social imagination. In doing so, Tonya draws on the features of the text that were present—the action in the illustrations and in the print—but also on the missing features of the text. CeCe participates by imagining her role in the narrative they created.

Looking Across the Teaching Lessons

The interactions of these teacher–student dyads showed the very different ways in which the teachers entered into multimodal teaching with the same book. For Jonah and Tamara, the improvisation across modes and in and out of the book shaped the interaction. For Tonya and CeCe there is less improvisation (although she is very creative with the structure of the lesson, turning the picture walk into a character walk) and more teacher guidance across the text. Tonya's use of open-ended, thought-provoking, and exploratory critical literacy questions are notable. Her lesson, too, is multimodal but the multimodality occurs more within their verbal exchange whereas in the case of Jonah and Tamara the multimodality was particularly dense in the nonverbal exchanges.

In both cases, the pairs interacted in ways that mimicked the book, which, for the students, was a supportive way to introduce the story. For Tonya and CeCe, their verbal exchanges mimic the action of the book through their use of multimodal verbs and language. Jonah and Tamara used embodied modes as well, including gestures and movement along with music and rhythm in an improvisational jazz manner. The nature of movements that both teachers and students make with their bodies and hands highlight the motion of being in a jazz band. It seems that both groups are drawing on this genre in the rhythm of the performance as well as the genre of jazz as it is represented in the book. Rather than focusing only on the printed words, each tutor emphasized the narrative of the text, asking the students to read and analyze visual images in order to build print literacy.

In much of the research on culturally responsive instruction using literature, it is argued that literature that reflects students' understandings of the world, language, and positive images of life in communities allows students to make meaning when reading texts. The nature of discussions around the illustrations in *Jazz Baby* (Weatherford, 2002) allow both Tamara and CeCe to draw on their lived experiences making music and hearing music. In this sense, it appears that Jonah and Tonya are drawing on what they have learned about their students, the neighborhood where the school is located, and perhaps the familial literacy practices of these students. They provide moment-to-moment feedback that draws on and extends their students' ways of reading texts. From Tamara's use of swaying and snapping to CeCe's imagined use of things that go "click clack, click clack" we can see that through multimodality they are able to establish a connection.

There are several cohesive devises—links that hold an interaction together and give it meaning—that contribute to our understanding of multimodality in these interactions. The book itself is a cohesive devise, and shared attention in both dyads suggests that the book illustrations and text are key in the meaning making that occurs in each interaction. The illustrations lend themselves to the performative nature of the compositions that each pair has created. There is little sense of a teacher or a student following the others' lead, instead the teachers only find it necessary to provide some indications as to how one might interact with this book.

There were other nonverbal and verbal cohesive devices that function to hold the lesson together. Gaze is an important one across both lessons. Jonah and Tonya both use gaze to indicate attention to the written text of the interaction, especially when they notice their students attending to the illustrations. Perhaps this is an example of following the students' lead and using their attention on the meaning of the story to bridge them to new vocabulary and print knowledge. When it comes to reading the text, this cohesive device of gaze alongside the device of reading the text is a modally dense way of interacting that we see from both teachers.

Throughout our analysis, we have demonstrated how meanings around the text were jointly created between the teacher and student. Jonah and Tonya were able to navigate the demands of teaching for literacy acceleration within a culturally relevant and multimodal context because, at this point in the semester, they know the structure and flow of the literacy lesson as well as have pedagogical knowledge to follow the child's lead within this literacy event. Of course, we would be remiss if we did not answer the question: How did this lesson support Tamara and CeCe as readers? For both students, their instructional reading levels were several levels below the Guided Reading level of the book *Jazz Baby* (a Level G). Tamara's instructional reading level was a D-E and CeCe's was reading at a level E with support. However, both Tonya and Jonah noted how the lesson supported their students as readers. Jonah explained that the rhythm of the book supported Tamara's fluency as a reader. Further, she was able to make connections between the book and her life because her aunt had introduced jazz music to her (case study, 5/05). Tonya described how using a higher level book such as *Jazz Baby* (Weatherford, 2002) helped to support and extend CeCe's comprehension, which was above her skills in problem solving words. Tonya wrote in her case study, "the character analysis in *Jazz Baby* asked CeCe to assume the position of one of the characters in the story and retell the story from their point of view." CeCe had reported that her mother listened to jazz and would let her act as a drummer of a band, beating on pots and pans in the kitchen. Tonya wrote, "making connections between her life and the text extended CeCe's comprehension of the story" (case study, 5/05).

Both Tonya and Jonah extended their professional learning by presenting their teaching at a conference during the Spring semester. Tonya's portion of the presentation focused on her enactments of critical literacy and was called "Critical Literacy: Theory and Practice." Jonah focused on the importance of culturally relevant literature in the literacy curriculum. In this way, the teachers, as well as the students, were embodying literacy practices. For the teachers, they were taking on the identities of literacy leaders—those who can teach competently and proficiently and can teach others to do the same.

As part of this presentation, Tonya said the following about critical literacy:

> It [critical literacy] gets them to challenge whose perspective is included, to draw their own conclusions and to construct their own meanings. Because if they only get fed one story they are just going to take it at face value and not question it. But if they get two stories with different perspectives then they are cross-checking and are like "well this makes sense to me, but this doesn't make sense to me." Critical literacy allows them to construct their own meaning and maybe they can make their own story.

Inviting our students—whether they are adults or children—to make their own stories is part and parcel of a critical literacy curriculum.

Conclusion

To conclude, Tonya and Jonah accomplished the work of preparing students to read an increasingly difficult text. They did so through responsive teaching but also through the analysis of multimodality that their students were drawing on. Jonah had to watch Tamara's nonverbal moves very closely in order to build on her preferred ways of constructing a narrative around the text. Similarly, Tonya knew that CeCe was not experiencing this book using her body, but was prepared to create a narrative through her imagination as a way into reading the text. As they learned to read their students, multimodally, the pre-service teachers were also learning to respond to and guide their students. Specifically, the ways that each tutor co-constructed the reading of the text was evident in our analysis. It was a great accomplishment for these teachers to extend and build on what they knew were their students' interests, to attend to their students' more complex ways of experiencing the texts they read, and most of all, to collaborate with them in making meanings in those ways.

We can argue that this kind of relationship between teacher and student is an entry point into the scaffolding of critical literacy practices. In critical literacy teaching, students and teachers are often performing inquiries around topics that have many sides and perspectives. This is difficult work, but teachers may be able to draw on their knowledge about how students construct meanings multimodally to support them as they are exploring new ideas. Also, as we have seen in our other research, it is often evident that in discussions of critical social issues, there are often silences and other nonverbal clues that students are experiencing discomfort or confusion. The close attention of a teacher to multimodal interactions can bring these students' responses to a teacher's attention (Rogers & Mosley, 2010). Multimodal analysis of one's own teaching would also be useful to add to the reflective work we ask pre-service teachers to do.

A multimodal discourse analysis allowed us to explore the ways that pre-service teachers were learning to read their students' ways of interacting with texts. Returning to our guide to MDA, we notice that the most critical part of our work in this exploration is the multimodal transcription of language, gesture, gaze, and other modalities and the extraction of telling frames. These charts help us to hold still a moment in time in which multimodal interactions are working for students and teachers. These transcriptions help us to describe, for example, Tonya's creativity with a structure of a book introduction, an indication that she is reshaping tools we provide for her rather than focusing on procedures. As we engage in a critical analysis of multimodality in these lessons, we see the growth and development of our pre-service teachers as they develop the practices of critical literacy teaching.

7

CONCLUSIONS

In this book we have shared our story about how we, alongside our students, made sense out of matters of language, literacy, diversity, and power. Creating the time for critical literacy can be daunting, given the continued focus on standards, high stakes testing, and accountability. And yet, for us, critical literacy is what breathes life into our teaching and provides hope in this era of standardization. In this conclusion, we return to our original proposition—critical literacy is not possible with discourse analysis—and share examples from each of the chapters to illustrate how we have shown this to be the case. We also reflect on the role of discourse analysis in our lives as teacher educators and offer some reflections for others interested in the critical analysis of discourse.

Critical Literacy is/as Discourse Analysis

Critical literacy education holds the potential to deepen our awareness of language and power and cultivate the valuing of diversity that, in turn, supports the development of culturally and linguistically diverse pedagogies. And because language is never neutral, teachers and teacher educators can work to examine the material and discursive structures of social practices through discourse analysis so that we might be more responsive and responsible to our students, their families, and our communities. Across the book, we have shown how both critical literacy education and discourse analysis hinge on inquiry into language, power, and identities.

Here, we return to the four dimensions of critical literacy we used throughout the book to make the case that critical literacy and discourse analysis are inextricably linked. That is, aiming for multiple perspectives, disrupting the commonplace, focusing on the socio-political, and taking action (Lewison, Flint & Van Sluys,

2002) require a critical analysis of discourse practices. We'll begin with the notion of *multiple perspectives*. Part of developing a critical stance is recognizing the partiality of perspective. Perspectives—ways of viewing the world—are represented through discourse practices (both verbally and nonverbally). But perspectives also shape the world. What we see depends on where we stand. We saw this vividly in Chapter 5 when Leslie was enamored with the book *Iggie's House* (Blume, 1970) because she identified with the anti-racism of the White protagonist. This deep identification was suspended when Tonya shared her critique, based on her analysis of the character's lack of action in the book. This moment of experiencing the partiality of perspective is at the heart of critical literacy education and is roused by attending to discourse practices. As teachers have the opportunities to hear diverse stories, they intuitively call on the work of narrative analysis: listening attentively for themes and finding connections and disharmony among the stories. We used narrative analysis in the midst of our teaching by analyzing the themes, the perspectives, and the structure of their stories. Our analysis was represented in a letter we wrote to our students asking them to more critically analyze their language choices, silenced themes, and representational choices. Our students wrote, shared, reflected, and rewrote their literacy autobiographies. This cyclical process helped them to ask difficult questions of themselves and make important choices in how to represent their stories. As teacher educators we want our students to anticipate the partiality of representations and actively seek out multiple perspectives before they settle on one. Critical discourse analysts, too, recognize the partiality of their analysis and often seek to develop multiple interpretations of an interaction before they make the case for one explanation.

Disrupting the Commonplace is another dimension of critical literacy that is actualized through discourse analysis. The commonplace is constructed when certain meanings are stabilized and privileged over others. At the core of unsettling the taken for granted is a deep exploration into how meanings are made and positionings offered. When our students are reading an article, for example, we explore the different places where meaning may reside. We ask our students about authorial intention: What did Clay mean when she wrote about linguistic diversity? We can turn to interviews with Clay or other scholarship she has written to answer this question. We also ask them to examine the text itself: What does the text say about linguistic diversity? What words are used? What ideas are excluded? And, finally, we ask them to consider the meanings that are created in the interaction between themselves and the text. Given your backgrounds, how do you make sense out of this text? Like perspective, meanings are always partial.

Many people privilege spoken and written language over other modalities, which, in turn, creates a biased worldview. We know from multimodal studies that knowledge is constructed through many different modes. As the pre-service teachers started to experiment with multimodal pedagogy, they found that they had to question everything, from the books that they used with their students to the ways that they arranged their materials and bodies at the table, in order to create new ways of doing reading and writing with their students. For example, in Chapter 6, we saw how Jonah used the book *Jazz Baby* (Weatherford, 2002) and made space for Tamara to improvise as a reader, inviting her to engage with a book in a very different way. In doing so, he made schooled literacy different for Tamara. In turn, multimodal discourse analysis provided us with tools for understanding how meanings were made through verbal and nonverbal communication, helping us to think about how various modes position us differently.

Another dimension of critical literacy practice, *focusing on the sociopolitical*, can be brought to life through discourse analysis. Discourse—whether it is spoken or written—is a social practice, intended to accomplish certain social goals. We encourage our students to consider the social, historical, and political contexts in which discourse practices emerge, circulate, and are transformed. In addition, we support their analysis of how some meanings are privileged over others, garnering intellectual leverage over other ideas. Analyzing discourse practices—whether during or after an interaction—can help draw attention to the privileging of some meanings over others, an issue of power. As we continued to explore language, culture, power, and literacy with our students, we became aware of the many ways that our students were focused on the sociopolitical issues of language diversity. Chapter 4, for example, focused on a student-centered inquiry into language variety and assessing oral reading that emerged generatively during our instruction. The students' questions and inquiry morphed into their desire to take action and write a letter to Marie Clay whose work they drew on when learning to do running records, asking about her thoughts on issues of language diversity, assessment, and power. We demonstrate how the students were engaged in critical language inquiry throughout this process. They interrogated links between language and power and we, in turn, looked more closely at how situated meanings, cultural models, and figured worlds were constructed through their practices. This helped us to understand how the teacher candidates' positioned themselves as students, pre-service teachers, and future teachers. Ultimately, rather than construct assessments as evaluating what students do not know how to do, our teachers learned to think of assessments as an inquiry tool. We are sure that their close analysis of language diversity had something to do with this framing.

Finally, considering *social action* is an area of concern for both critical literacy practitioners and discourse analysts. Critical forms of discourse analysis address social problems. So, too, does critical literacy. A provocative issue for teacher researchers engaged with critically oriented forms of discourse analysis is how their research promotes or leads to justice, advocacy, and social change. For us, critical discourse analysis helped us to read and write texts differently and supported our students to do the same. We would argue that if our project helps others in the field to try out a new discourse analysis framework to help them think differently about a social problem, this too, is a form of social action. There are other, more outward forms of social action. We created space for our students to take action—through writing a letter to Dr. Clay, presenting at an Educating for

Change Curriculum Fair, and advocating for best literacy practices for the students with whom they worked. In the spirit of teacher research, we embedded action within the design of our study. As a result of our analysis we changed our teaching practices and asked the pre-service teachers to do the same. In essence, we sought to make discourse analysis relevant in the midst of our teaching and learning, not after the fact.

Reflections on Critical Discourse Analysis as a Tool for Educators

For too long, one of the greatest hindrances for educators using discourse analysis as a method in their work has been the time commitments of close study of discourses. Indeed, analyzing interactional patterns, discourse structures and positionings takes many passes through the data and much time. However, as we have shown in each chapter, some of this work can be accomplished in the midst of teaching—in fact, it can be the subject of our teaching and our feedback to our students. This is important because teachers who inquire into their own practice are likely to continue to grow and learn about the complexities of teaching and learning. And we think that this sparks a spirit of inquiry among the learners in our classroom. We noticed our students, themselves, were drawn to following unanticipated questions, looking for alternate theories, and searching for counter-narratives.

Where and when, however, do we actually engage in discourse analysis? In our classroom, where teacher research was occurring at every moment, we learned to pay more attention to both our own language practices and the language of the group as we learned about our students' critical literacy practices. As critical literacy teachers, we placed language in social contexts at the center of our pedagogy and thus drew on the tools of discourse analysis throughout the inquiry. We relied on pedagogical approaches that centered critical inquiry into language, power, and identity throughout the semester. Thus, we were continually adopting the stance of discourse analysts and asking our students to do the same. We modeled this critical stance toward language in our lectures, in the readings, and in our responses to their written work. Often times, discourse analysis was modeled in quick, teachable moments. For instance, we may say to a student reporting on his student's assessment data: "How can you reframe that statement to focus on her strengths as a writer?" In an attempt to make sure a diversity of perspectives were included in the discussion we may say: "We'd like to make sure that all voices are in the room. Who has not offered their perspective?"

Indeed, the discourse analysis frameworks we have presented throughout this book are standpoints from which we pivot from in our work as discourse analysts and educators of literacy teachers. We place great value in the power of narratives, layering the study of narratives into our curricular design. Attending to how specific language uses (situated meanings) create identities and institutions (discourses and cultural models), which, in turn, create theories of the world (figured worlds) is quite relevant in our work as teacher educators. Indeed, our word choices shape the kinds of identities available for our students, which then shape the kinds of literacy practices that are available to them. We routinely use the framework associated with CDA—"ways of interacting," "representing," and "being"—as a guide for understanding our teaching and our students' learning. We may ask: Are the interactional patterns allowing for diverse voices to be heard? What ideas are being represented? Excluded? And, because we know knowledge is constructed through multiple modes, we not only incorporate multimodality in our teaching but encourage our students to do the same. We find instances where our students are intuitively carrying out multimodal analysis and support them in this work. While they did not formally learn nor carry out any one approach to discourse analysis (narrative analysis, critical discourse analysis, multimodal discourse analysis), they did intuitively draw on these frameworks throughout the class.

However, the question of where discourse analysis is located in a teacher research project depends, to a certain extent, on the issues approached and the questions asked. At one end of the continuum, discourse analysis may be employed as part of the curricular design. That is, ongoing analysis of interactional patterns and narratives would influence the emerging pedagogical design. At the other end of the continuum it might reside in the practice of teacher research where discourse analysis is used for a closer, granular look after the project is complete. Finding a way into the discourse analysis can be challenging. We often use moments of tension, surprise, or liberation—something that is analytically significant—as a starting point in our analysis. We became particularly interested in the areas where our students critically engaged with the representation of learning, identity, culture, and race as well as the places that remained a-critical. These became the places that we returned to for closer analysis, even after our chance for pedagogical interventions with this group had passed. In this way, dilemmas in our teaching became the subject for further investigation using discourse analysis (Mosley & Rogers, 2011; Rogers & Mosley, 2008).

We believe there are great possibilities for exploring with teachers the micro-interactions of discussions as we have presented here. Pedagogically it also seems important to build in opportunities for the participants to reflect on the participant structures, topics, and positions that kept the conversation moving along. Similarly, reflecting on the moments where there was a fissure in the dialogue may also prove instructive. Teacher educators and teachers may use critical literacy and critical discourse analysis practices using video recordings and transcripts of discussions about literature and anti-racism as texts. Our awareness of the patterns with which pre-service teachers engage with critical literacy comes from such analysis of text as evidence of learning, and we are convinced that conversations like the ones had around the literature in our teacher education class help to build a discursive history, which, in turn, supports the development of critical literacy. For starters, we would encourage people to try out a stance as discourse analyst, adopt one of the discourse analysis frameworks we have highlighted in this book, and pay close attention to an interaction or a writing sample with the intention of using your analysis to inform your practice. Or, you may "freeze an interaction" in your teaching and ask your students to help unpack the moment, teaching them about situated meanings, cultural models, and figured worlds as you go.

At the end of the day, we believe discourse analysis is a useful set of theories and methods for understanding learning and transformation, over time (Fairclough, 2011; Lewis & Ketter, 2011). Unlike research that focuses on a unit or a semester, our inquiry extended over the course of a year and afforded us the opportunity to watch learning and development unfold across time. Thus, our portrait of a year in the life of our teacher education classroom affords us the long-term perspective of seeing how people *become* critical literacy teachers. This is important because as, Leland et al. (2001) remind us, "building a political consciousness takes time" (p. 391). So, too, does learning the art and science of teaching literacy.

We need to recognize that, to a certain extent, the students in this study were inclined to personal and intellectual growth because of their status as students in a teacher education program. However, we also need to recognize the additional conditions that make such critical literacy work possible. We designed the course to be an ongoing curricular conversation around justice and equity. Through a combination of seminar discussions, readings, online discussions, journal reflections, teaching experiences, debriefing with colleagues about teaching, and book club discussions the pre-service teachers in this study had a variety of opportunities to not only learn about but to learn how to interact with others around critical literacy. Over the course of a year they had built up relationships and trust necessary to overcome ruptures in discussions and different points of view. We acknowledge that the community that was built may not be possible with the time constraints of a traditional semester course.

A shared assumption among those who align themselves with critical discourse analysis is that noticing and naming the language patterns and practices that represent and construct inequitable social arrangements can help others understand their root sources and puncture holes in "regimes of truth." Rather than only resisting, critiquing, and reacting to domination, those inspired by critical social theory, seek, in addition, to design and forge alternative ways of representing, being, and interacting in the world with the goal of creating a society free of oppression and domination, the goal of critical literacy education. Gunther Kress (2011) calls us to think about curricular design in service to the needs of students for future social practices. How may critical discourse analysis contribute to courses of study in different contexts? What kinds of questions can teachers and scholars pose that will help to build the kinds of agentic stances and actions needed in this era of education?

It has been argued that critical discourse analysis has, for too long, studied how oppression is discursively constructed. By way of contrast, a number of scholars are calling for a focus on productive uses of power (Janks, 2005; Macgilchrist,

2007; Mosley & Rogers, 2011; Scollon & Wong Scollon, 2004). Luke (2004) points out the potential for reconstructive versions of discourse analysis that focus on how liberation, solidarity, and community are constructed. Martin (2004) refers to this approach as "positive discourse analysis," which can provide a complementary focus on "how people get together and make room for themselves in the world—in ways that redistribute power without necessarily struggling against it" (p. 183). We believe that teacher researchers are uniquely poised to contribute to the development of positive discourse analysis because of the nature of the questions we ask and the immediacy with which we put our analysis "to work" in our classrooms. More so, our orientation toward learning, transformation, and change are theoretically aligned with a reconstructive approach to discourse analysis. Moving forward, we encourage other researchers to experiment with positive discourse analysis. And we think that there is a great deal of potential in public consultative discourse analysis (PCDA), which aims to use ongoing discourse analysis to inform public policy (Scollon, 2010). PCDA seeks to put the analysis to work in the policy-making process, making the results of the discourse analysis immediately relevant to the interpretation and implementation of educational policies.

Conclusion

One of the responsibilities of literacy teacher educators is to set up the conditions where teachers can become confident and competent with critical literacy education, their own and the students with whom they work. As we have shown, we think critically oriented forms of discourse analysis can help us become better educators, especially when situated within a teacher-research framework. Critical literacy, as practiced by the teachers in this study, has the potential to break open the range of positions offered to teachers and students so that they may see themselves not as consumers of discourses but as producers and designers of social futures. A fundamental problem we face is that too often teachers and students are positioned and position themselves as receivers and consumers of information/directives. When it comes down to it, the teacher will be asked to adhere to local and state assessment procedures and practices to stay in a job. So rather than simply prepare them to question and use critical literacy to interrogate their power, language, and position, we have to reframe conversations about the purposes and goals of teacher education.

Teachers struggle to move beyond subtractive views of themselves and the profession (Valenzuela, 1999) to more powerful and equitable conceptualizations of themselves as learners. In other words, these times for teachers are ripe with tension. Part of our goal in sharing our stories of designing and researching critical literacy pedagogy is to convince you of the critical role of discourses (and discourse analysis) in literacy education and how such a framework may be useful as teachers position themselves as authorities of their practice.

APPENDICES

Appendices to Chapter 3

Guide to Conducting Critical Narrative Analysis

Part I: Preparing for Narrative Analysis

Appendix 3A: Choosing a Type of Narrative Analysis

There are four basic models of narrative analysis (Riessman, 2005). The first is **thematic analysis** and includes a focus on the content of the narrative, or what the narrator "told" in the story. This approach is often useful to examine the variation between narratives among a group of narratives about the same topic.

The second model is a **structural analysis,** which has a stronger focus on how the story is told, rather than what is told. Examples of structural analysis vary depending on the form of the narrative. For example, many narratives fit a temporal story form and can be analyzed by Labov and Waletzky's (1997) method of identifying clauses and their functions (see Appendix 3E) but others do not fit this temporal form and need different frameworks based on how the narrative is constructed through the linguistic choices of the teller (see Gee, 1991).

An **interactional analysis** focuses squarely on the interaction between the teller and the listener, and along with theme and structure, the collaborative nature of the telling is also a point of interest to the analyst. An example of this approach is found in Wortham's (2001) approach to narrative analysis, in which the ways that the speaker positions him or herself as well as the teller is of particular interest (see Appendix 3F).

Finally, Riessman identifies an approach called **performative analysis**, an approach that sees the interactional nature of narrative tellings as a performance of identity. The analytic tools associated with this approach are the identification of characters in a story and their positions, dialogue as it is enacted in speech (revoicing of characters), and the setting of the narrative telling. The objective of these narrative theorists is to understand how the properties of narratives are used (or function) in the creation of self and identity (see also Holland et al., 1998). There are similarities between how people use terms like "interactional" and "performative" to describe analyses. For example, Wortham (2001) would not distinguish between these two approaches but he combines tools to examine the interactional positioning of the self and others within a narrative. We have taken the approach of combining our interactional and performative analyses in this chapter.

Across narrative traditions, there is a common belief that narrative is "a fundamental genre in that it is universal and emerges early in the communicative development of children" (Ochs & Capps, 2001, p. 19). From early on, humans say who they are in the world through the use of stories. Bruner and Weisser (1991) wrote: "[W]e organize our experience and our memory of human happenings mainly in the form of narrative—stories, excuses, myths, reasons for doing and not doing, and so on" (p. 4). Narratives can be oral or written and can take the form of a variety of genres such as letters, legal testimony, dance, and memoir (Ochs & Capps, 2001). In daily life, we narrate our experiences, choosing protagonists, listeners, and readers and situating ourselves at the nexus of the past, present, and future.

Approaches to narrative analysis are concerned with how, through narratives, people represent their goals, stances, and ideas and, in turn, construct the world. These representations have been said to be historically and culturally composed. Holland et al. (1998) explain that across cultures there are different ways that people represent the concept of self, and one of these ways is through particular kinds of narratives. Narratives are representations of self with particular frameworks that vary according to social context, the history of the institutions within which the stories are told, and the cultural norms and values of the people who tell those stories.

Stories impact those around us and often create spaces for dialogue, questioning, and the development of new understandings. Every story shapes the listener, and the teller often uses particular discursive strategies to do so.

Part II: Conducting Narrative Analysis

Appendix 3B: How to Identify Themes in a Narrative Analysis

Themes are related to the research questions of the analyst—you may enter into a thematic analysis with a general sense of the ideas you are interested in. For example, in our research, we were interested in *literacy* and *culture*, so we looked for ways that each of these topics were referenced and constructed. In reading or listening to narratives, there are questions the analyst may ask to determine the themes. Here are a few of those questions that the analyst may ask, related to his or her research questions.

1. What is the story about?

    List the topics that come up in the narrative. (e.g., literacy learning).

2. How does the teller describe each topic? Does s/he draw on ways of talking about the topic that are recognizable to the analyst? These are possible themes of the narrative (e.g., literacy begins in the home and reading came easy to me).

    Keep a running list of these possible themes, organized by their topic.

3. Look for repetition of possible themes and variations. Does the theme seem to emerge as prevalent throughout the narrative? Do possible themes seem to group together? Is there variation in those themes?

    Refine possible themes, collapsing similar themes and distinguishing between themes with important differences.

4. Within the narrative, are there unfinished ideas or missing parts that indicate that a theme is unstable or under construction?

    Identify absences in your list of themes and make analytic notes about what these absences may mean.

The importance of conducting a thematic analysis, beyond identifying the themes of a narrative, is that it can offer the analyst a way to look across narratives. Particular narratives share common themes and the analyst may be able to identify important similarities and variations within the group of narratives (see Table 3.1). It is important to return to individual narratives a second time after completing a comparative thematic analysis of multiple narratives. Upon a second pass through the data, the analyst may see new, important elements of individual narratives because of the work of comparing and contrasting the larger group.

Appendix 3C: Locating Narrative Structure

The form and function of narratives can be uncovered by looking closely at the tools the narrator uses during the narrative event (i.e., positioning) but we also need some organizational ways of understanding narrative structure to be able to look across narratives and at how narratives shift and change over time. Oral narrative events follow typical structures (although as many, such as Gee (1985) have pointed out, these structures differ for speakers from different cultural backgrounds). We can talk about a **narrative structure** as follows:

Orientation

*   Orients the reader/listener in terms of person, place, time, and behavioral situation.
*   Composed of the free clauses that occur before the first narrative clause. Free clauses could come anywhere in the narrative because they are not defined by time.

- Analyst's general focus: context of the story; participants, setting and so forth of the narrated event.

Complication

- Introduces a troubling event and an evaluative commentary on the events represented in the narrative, the conflicts, and the themes.
- Composed of narrative clauses that are related to one another by *temporal junctures*—ordered in a particular way to recapitulate an event.
- Tellability (Bruner & Weisser, 1991) is often introduced in the complication of the narrative.
- Analyst's general focus: Familiar storylines made unfamiliar; tellability.

Evaluation

- Necessary in order for the narrative to have a point, according to Labov and Waletzky (1997): "Narratives are usually told in answer to some stimulus from outside and to establish some point of personal interest" (p. 29).
- Analyst's general focus: Speaker's position in relation to storyline; positioning of audience.

Resolution

- Describes the outcomes of the story or conflict.
- In some narratives, the resolution and the evaluation occur at the same time.
- Analyst's general focus: Speaker's position in relation to storyline; positioning of audience.

Coda

- Returns the verbal perspective to the present moment.
- *Deixis* is one device used in a coda. It points to a referent instead of naming it explicitly, i.e., "and that was that" (Labov & Waletzky, 1997, p. 36).
- Analyst's general focus: Relationship of story to present moment.

Locating the narrative structure in a narrative event allows us to understand what storylines are drawn upon, how they are drawn upon, and how they were naturalized (i.e., taken for granted that they are shared, common stories).

Appendix 3D: Creating Transcripts

A transcript is a written way of representing discourse. In most cases, we will include only the verbal content of discourse in our transcripts, but transcripts can also represent nonverbal action as well as details about how people use intonation, pauses, simultaneous talk, and increases and decreases in speed. In interactional transcripts, you will see the speaker's name before the talk represented:

> Leslie: I think, I feel like, especially when the other day, and while I was reading it, I almost feel like I am this little girl.

Each time a new speaker is introduced, or a speaker begins to talk, we will mark that turn with the participant's name. We write the speaker's talk as if it is prose, using commas to help the reader understand the speaker's meaning, and periods to mark the end of a thought. We call this an "utterance." If we are not conducting a close analysis of the discourse, but instead portraying a longer conversation or interaction, we often will represent discourse this way.

There are also many ways to segment an utterance in transcripts for closer analysis. There are two common ways to segment talk. The first is to number each line and break the talk where the speaker takes a breath, called an "intonation unit" (Rex & Schiller, 2009). However, we take the second approach that segments the talk by the clause.

Appendix 3E: Identifying the Clause as the Unit of Analysis

The most crucial unit when we speak and write is the clause. A clause is made up of a verb and a set of participants. Participants are the noun phrases that name people and things playing roles in the action, event, process, or state of affairs named by the verb.

Here is a short passage of talk segmented by clause. In each line, the participant of the clause is **emboldened** and the action/event/process/state of affairs is *italicized*.

1 Leslie: **I** *think,*
2 **I** *feel like,*
3 Especially when
4 the other day,
5 and while **I** *was reading* it,
6 **I** *almost feel* like
7 **I** *am* this little girl.

When we come across a line like line 3 or 4, we consider the line an "incomplete thought" because it does not include both a participant and an action/event/process/state of affairs. Sometimes these are false starts, in which the speaker does not finish a thought. Other times, they are clues to the setting of the narrative. Here, line 3 is a false start, and line 4 orients the reader to a time—although Leslie does not complete her thought.

The clause is the basic unit of analysis in narratives, and they are organized to recapitulate an event that actually occurred. Clauses can be *narrative clauses* that are locked into certain positions in the narrative because of a feature of narratives called *temporal sequence.* This means that clauses, if rearranged in the narrative, would change the inferred sequence of events. Clauses can also be *free clauses* that can range freely through the narrative sequence (Labov & Waletzky, 1997).

A clause is defined both by its form (it is a phrase with a subject and action) and its function (it carries out an action or communicative purpose) (Gee, 2010). One reason to do this is that our ideas about discourse are that the form and function of each clause are meaningful in terms of how they relate to one another, and a numbered transcript allows us to discuss each clause as evidence or an example of meaning making.

Lines 1–2 and lines 5–7 were easy to segment into clauses because there is a subject (I) and action in each clause. Leslie attributed an action to herself in each clause (e.g., "think" in line 1) and sometimes modifies that action (e.g., "almost feel like" in line 7). Each clause in lines 1 to 2 and in lines 5–7 also contains additional information. For example in line 7, she is identifying with a character in the story who is a "little girl," and in line 5 she is thinking about her identification "while" she was reading the book. This information helps us to understand her narrative by providing context and bringing us into the narrative. Lines 3 and 4 are more complicated because they are clauses that are incomplete. Leslie hesitated during her turn twice, and each time appears to be referencing a time when she was reading the book. However, she does not complete the thought, which might sound like "especially when I was reading it." We still treat this as a clause but note that the subject or action is missing.

Appendix 3F: Analyzing Positioning

Positioning is a theoretical construct for understanding discursive choices within stories (Harre & Moghaddam, 2003; Wortham, 2001). Positioning happens when narratives take the following actions:

- *Voicing* characters (and themselves) as particular types of people by quoting things that were said.
- *Referencing* particular ways of interacting and assigning those ways to the character (i.e., "she was so angry when she called.").
- *Predicating* characters (i.e., "the angry woman").
- Evoking *storylines* that allow those characters to take actions that are consistent with the narrator's way of seeing the world.
- *Positioning* his or her audience in the narrative event by assuming agreement or understanding of a particular *storyline* or *predication*.

Part III: Steps in Conducting a Critical Narrative Analysis

Appendix 3G: A Guide to Conducting Critical Narrative Analysis

Narrative analysis includes a description, interpretation, and explanation of how narratives organize interactions and experiences. Through narrative analysis, we look critically at the stories told in our classroom through thematic, structural, and interactional/performative analyses. We begin by asking questions like: What does this narrative *mean* in terms of literacy, culture, identity, and so forth? And we consider how the narrative is structured to accomplish such meaning. We also ask questions about how authors position themselves and others in those stories, and how they construct identities within public spaces and shape the community within those spaces.

We recommend practicing narrative analysis using this transcript and the following methodology:

1. Create a transcript of the narrative. The transcription allows you to look closely at the narrative, particularly when you look at the unit of the clause throughout the narrative (see Appendix 3D and Appendix 3E).
2. Segment the text into a narrative structure. Think about the structure of the narrative, or how it is organized to understand what this narrative means (see Appendix 3C).
3. Conduct a thematic analysis of the narrative. What is the story about? How does the teller describe each topic? Does s/he draw on ways of talking about the topic that are recognizable to the analyst? (See Appendix 3B).
4. Then, attend to the structural aspects of the narrative. *Questions to ask about narrative sequence during analysis:*

    a. Which clauses are part of each element of narrative structure?
    b. How did the speaker represent experience in each part of the structure (length, arrangement of *narrative*, and *free* clauses), and across each part of the structure?
    c. *To address the following questions, see Appendix 3C: Locating Narrative Structure.*

        i.   In the *orientation* of the narrative, what context and characters are evoked?
        ii.   In the *complication* of the narrative, what seems to be the "trouble" or reason for telling the story?
        iii. In the *evaluation* of the narrative, what point does the teller seem to make? What makes this story "tellable"?
        iv.   In the *resolution* of the narrative, how does the teller describe the outcome of the story? What actions occurred throughout the story that led to this outcome for the characters or teller?
        v.   In the *coda*, how does the author summarize or extend the story to the present moment?
        vi.   What parts of this narrative structure are not represented in the story? Why?

5. Examine closely the ways that positioning works within the narrative—the positioning of identity, family, struggle, and so forth—and provide opportunities for the pre-service teachers to ask similar critical questions. *Questions to ask about positioning during analysis:*

    a. What characters are voiced in the narrative? In what ways?
    b. How are characters referenced and predicated?

    c.   What storylines are evoked through tools of positioning?

    d.   How do those storylines position the audience?

Appendix 3H: Additional Reading and Resources to Support Narrative Analysis

Transcription

Baum, W.K. 1991. *Transcribing and editing oral history.* Nashville, TN: American Association for State and Local History.

Bucholtz, M. (2007). Variation in transcription. *Discourse & Society, 9(6),* 784–808.

Green, J., Franquiz, M., & Dixon, C. (1997). The myth of the objective transcript: Transcribing as a situated act. *TESOL Quarterly, 31(1),* 172–176.

Norris, S. (2002). The implications of visual research for discourse analysis: Transcription beyond language. *Visual Communication, 1(1),* 97–121.

Ochs, E. (1999). Transcription as theory. In Jaworski, A. & Coupland, N. (Eds.), *The discourse reader* (pp. 167–182). New York, NY: Routledge.

Narratives

Connelly, M. & Clandinin, J. (1990). Stories of experience and narrative inquiry. *Educational Researcher, 19(5),* 2–14.

Ochs, E., & Capps, L. (2001). *Living narrative: Creating lives in everyday storytelling.* Cambridge, MA: Harvard University Press.

Florio-Ruane, S. (2001). *Teacher education and the cultural imagination: Autobiography, conversation, and narrative.* Malwah, NJ: Lawrence Erlbaum Associates.

Juzwik, M. (2006). "Performing curriculum": Building ethos through narratives in pedagogical discourse. *Teachers College Record, 108(4),* 489–528.

Mischler, E. (1995). Models of narrative analysis: A Typology. *Journal of Narrative and Life History, 5(2),* 87–123.

Peterson, E.E. & Langellier, K.M. (1997). The politics of personal narrative methodology. *Text and Performance Quarterly, 17(2),* 135–152.

Rex, L. & Juzwik, M. (Eds.) (2011). *Narrative discourse for teacher educators: Managing cultural differences in classrooms.* New York, NY: Hampton Press.

Segmentation of Texts

Gee, J.P. (1985). The narrativization of experience in the oral style. *Journal of Education, 167(1),* 9–35.

Labov, W., & Waletzky, J. (1997). Narrative analysis: Oral versions of personal experience. *Journal of Narrative and Life History, 7(1),* 3–38.

Positioning

Harre, R., & Moghaddam, F.M. (2003). *The self and others: Positioning individuals and groups in personal, political, and cultural contexts.* Westport, CT: Praeger.

Wortham, S. (2000). Interactional positioning and narrative self-construction. *Narrative Inquiry, 10(1),* 157–184.

Wortham, S. (2001). *Narratives in action: A strategy for research and analysis.* New York, NY: Teachers College Press.

Appendices to Chapter 4

Guide to Conducting a Building Tasks Analysis

Part I: Preparing for the Building Tasks Analysis

Appendix 4A: Creating Stanzas

We developed research questions to guide our analysis of the letter our students wrote to Dr. Clay. We asked: What storylines are the pre-service teachers constructing about themselves and the field of literacy education? What situated meanings, cultural models, and figured worlds do they call on in this letter? Next, we segmented the transcript into stanzas to show topically utterances or clauses. Stanzas are a poetic structure that have been used in various approaches to discourse analysis (Gee, 1985). Because we were working with a written text, we used complete sentences to form the basis of the stanzas. If we were working with spoken or digital texts, we might have chosen to segment using clauses, as we discussed in Chapter 3. We asked the following questions about stanzas during our analysis:

> How are individual stanzas constructed (their length, the number of ideas in a stanza, and how they are organized by the speaker)?
>
> How do stanzas relate to one another? Are they parallel in structure and do they relate to one another in content or topic?
>
> Do the stanzas "sound" like they got together, in terms of rate and pauses between?
>
> Does the organization of clauses into stanzas, or stanzas into narratives, reflect something about the teller's identity or culture?

Part II: Conducting the Building Tasks Analysis

Appendix 4B: Identifying Theoretical Frames and Building Tasks

Using our research questions as a guide, we selected the theoretical frames and associated building tasks that we thought may lead to generative insights about the kinds of storylines our students constructed about themselves and the field of literacy education. We decided to work with the theoretical frames of social languages, intertextuality, and situated meanings. For our building tasks analysis, we chose identities, relationships, and significance to work with. The task for the discourse analyst is to connect the theoretical frames with the building tasks

TABLE 4.1. Overview of Theoretical Frames and Building Tasks

Theoretical Frames	Linguistic Resources	"Building Tasks"
The frameworks for understanding how people use language to accomplish social goals.	What linguistic patterns indicate these relations?	Aspects of the social world that we use to build or design meanings.
Situated Meanings What does this word mean in this context? How is it linked to other meanings, intertextually and historically?	**Verbs:** What kinds of verbs are being used? (finite/tenses, infinite, and modal) (mental, verbal, material, and relational)	**Significance:** What different things mean is an aspect of every situation.
Cultural/Discourse Models What are the storylines, images, narratives, or explanatory frameworks that are held, communicated, and understood?	**Sequencing:** How is the text ordered? How are the clauses arranged? What information is foregrounded? Backgrounded?	**Activities:** Any situation is made up of a series of actions.
	Cohesion: How does the text "hang" together? (e.g. pronouns, determiners, tenses, lexical cohesion, perspective, and repetition)	**Identities:** Every event is made up of the enactment and recognition of certain kinds of identities.
Social Languages The grammar and function of language. Varieties of language that allow us to express *socially situated identities* through the relationships between grammar and identities. (d/Discourse "collocational patterns")	**Voice:** Passive or active.	**Relationships:** As people participate in events, they enact relationships with other people, texts, and Discourses.
	Intertextuality: Manifest or constitutive. How does this text draw on other voices, texts, and genres?	**Politics:** Every event and interaction involves the distribution of social goods (social, cultural, material, and linguistic capital).
Intertextuality How does this text refer to other texts?		**Sign Systems and Knowledge:** Ways of knowing and communicating are valued differently in different contexts.
Figured Worlds Frames that people have about how the world works. What does this person assume about the way things operate to have said things the way they were said?		

through an analysis of the linguistic features of a discourse practice. Table 4.1 is an overview of theoretical frames and building tasks.

See Gee, 2006: pp. 110–115 for specific questions to ask while using each building task.

Appendix 4C

Carrying out a Descriptive Level of Linguistic Analysis

With the letter to Dr. Clay in front of us, we were faced with the decision of where to begin analysis. This is one of the most daunting parts of conducting discourse analysis. Should we describe the linguistic composition of the letter, moving line by line? Or, might we start with a slightly more deductive process of investigating how certain patterns that we have already noticed—say different identities being constructed at different points in the letter—are linguistically constructed? Discourse analysts are routinely faced with this choice and there is no one correct route. We think it is important to keep in mind that there are differences between discourse analysis and content analysis. Content analyses focus on the themes or topics that constitute a particular text. Discourse analysis moves beyond identifying the theme to describing, interpreting, and explaining how discourse practices and processes create those themes. So, in reality analysts often merge inductive and deductive approaches, moving line by line through their text describing linguistic features and then looking for patterns or a more deductive approach where they have identified a social practice and seek to look more closely at how that is discursively constructed. Table 4.2 includes a survey of linguistic resources that analysts may begin to identify in their data. This table has been culled from Fairclough (1995), Gee (2006), and Janks (2005). This is by no means an exhaustive list of features but it is one that will help the analyst get started in their building tasks analysis.

Appendix 4D: Representing the Discourse Analysis

Creating charts and tables throughout this process helps to visually organize our developing interpretations. Table 4.3 is a visual display of the interpretations we culled from our building tasks analysis. Our guiding questions were:

- What meanings are constructed through this letter?
- What storylines are the pre-service teachers constructing about themselves? About the field of literacy education?
- What situated meanings and social languages do they call on?

Moving from left to right, the first column represents each stanza. Notice that we have included the line numbers that correspond with each stanza. This helps
(*continued on page 125*)

TABLE 4.2. Codebook: Survey of Linguistic Resources

Discursive Feature	Description	Questions to Ask of the Text
Turn Taking	Description of the structure, sequence, and ordering of an interaction.	• What is the sequence of turns? • What is happening in each turn? • How many turns are taken? • How long are the turns? • How many new ideas are introduced?
Topics and Episodes	The focus on the content of the text; or what the text is "about."	• How are topics taken up, appropriated, or dropped? • How topics are introduced, developed, and closed?
Role of the Speakers in the Conversation	Speakers try out different roles/identities/performances in an interaction. This contributes to the overall meaning of the interaction.	• How does he/she attempt to expose and test their understandings in conversations? • How are roles taken up or abandoned in the conversational exchange? • How are roles constructed in the exchange?
Construction of Meaning	The ultimate purpose of interaction is to construct meanings.	• What contextualization cues seem relevant to the meaning? (e.g. back channeling, repeating, uh-huhs) • How is meaning constructed through multiple modes? • What inferences are made?
Lexicalization Relexicalization Cohesion	The selection of wordings. Renaming/re-voicing. Parallel structure, metaphors, and repetition.	• How are ideas represented through word choice? • What words or phrases show up again and again in the transcript? • How is the text made cohesive through wording choices?

Transitivity: Processes in verbs	Verbs of doing (material, behavioral) Verbs of sensing/saying (mental) Verbs of being (relational) Existential verbs ("There is. . .")	• What verbs are drawn upon in the interaction?
Theme/Rheme	Themes are represented in the first part of the clause and are generally the known information. Rhemes include the new information and are generally included in the last part of the clause.	• What information is foregrounded in the clause by being in the theme position? What is backgrounded?
Tense	Tense sets up when an event occurs in time.	• When is this process occurring?
Voice	Active and passive voice.	• Is the agent represented? Are participants agents or recipients of actions?
Pronouns	First/second/third person. Inclusive/exclusive pronouns. Sexist/Non-sexist pronouns.	• Which pronouns are used and where?
Intertextuality	*Manifest intertextuality:* Intertextual features such as: quoted speech; irony; parody; negation; presupposition; scare quotes. *Constitutive intertextuality:* Interdiscursive features between texts such as: structure, form, and genre.	• How does this text draw on other voices, texts, and genres? Which aspects are explicit (manifest) and which are implicitly referenced through the structure of the text (constitutive)?

TABLE 4.3. Example of Conducting a Building Tasks Analysis

Stanza	Description of Linguistic Features	Interpretations using the Building Tasks / Associated Theoretical Frame	Connections / Patterns across the Letter
Stanza one (lines 1–6) *Introduction & Context*	**Pronouns** "We are pre-service teachers" (line 1) "Our literacy instruction" (line 2) "our semester" (line 5) "we have become" (line 5) "we are learning" (line 6)	Their use of collective pronouns situates them as part of a community of practice of literacy education (identities/social languages).	
	Intertextuality *An observation survey of early literacy* (line 4) *Guided reading: Good first teaching* (line 5)	Explicit links to readings in literacy education (relationships/ intertextuality; significance/situated meanings).	See also line 24
	Verbs/Tense "learning to effectively" (line 6) "working one on one" (line 6)	Present progressive tense positions them as learners and becoming teachers (identities/social languages).	Verb tense shifts throughout the letter from present progressive (stanza one); past tense (stanza two); future (stanza five). This signals that they are trying out various identities.
	Adverbs "relies strongly" (line 4) "careful reading" (line 5) "effectively implement" (line 6)	Positioning themselves as particular kinds of students and practicing teachers (dual identities/social languages).	See lines eight, 23, and 24 for examples of where they position themselves dually as learners and as future teachers developing expertise. See line 13 where they position themselves as future teachers.

Stanza two (lines 7–12) *The Troubling Event: Error or Deviation from the Text?*	**Lexicalization** "a practice running record" (line 8) "this miscue" (line 9) "mark it as an error, as it was a deviation from the text" (line 10)	Their word choice signals membership in a community of literacy educators (significance/situated meanings; identities/social languages)	See also lines 26–27
	"African-American Language or African-American Vernacular English" (line 9) "variety of language" (line 12) "the difference between 'slang' and rule-governed language" (line 11)	Signals their knowledge about linguistic diversity (significance/situated meanings) and stance as discourse analysts (identities/social languages).	See also lines 18–20, 21–23
	Verbs/Tense "was left off ..." (line 8) "We discussed" (line 9) "We were unsure" (line 10) "This led" (line 11)	The verb tense shifts to the past tense as the letter narrates the sequence of events that led to their writing the letter.	
	Mood/Tense "what variety of language is appropriate in what context and why, and if we privilege one variety of language in the classroom over another, whose voices are we allowing to be heard ..." (line 12)	Rhetorical questions stated as ideas. Conditional tense projects into an imagined figurative world (identities/social languages). They are teachers who understand the power of language as it relates to privilege and oppression (significance/situated meanings, identities/social languages).	Verb tense shifts throughout the letter from present progressive (stanza one); past tense (stanza two); and future (stanza five). This signals that they are trying out various identities.

(Continued)

TABLE 4.3. (*Continued*)

Stanza	Description of Linguistic Features	Interpretations using the Building Tasks / Associated Theoretical Frame	Connections/Patterns across the Letter
Stanza three (lines 13–16) *Why this Matters in our Work as Preservice Teachers*	**Thematization** "As preservice teachers of literacy . . . carry particular weight with their ability to influence the future design and implementation" (line 13)	The first part of the clause is called the theme and sets up known information. Here, they position themselves as teachers "in training" and, later in the sentence, they project an imagined future as teachers (identities/social languages).	See also lines 6, 19, 20, and 21
	Lexicalization/Voice "linguistic variations in running records, most notably African-American English" (line 14)	Their word choice signals knowledge about linguistic diversity (significance/situated meanings; identities/social languages).	See also lines 9, 11, and 12
	"Our effort to resolve some of these questions" (line 14) "We identified some over-arching themes" (line 16)	Their word choice signals a particular kind of teachers/students; those who inquire into their practice and carry out discourse analyses of their practices. Active voice constructs them as agents of practice (identities/ social languages).	See also lines 11–12
Stanza four (lines 17–20) *Themes from Class Discussion*	**Lexicalization** "is centered on the belief that reading is a meaning-making activity" (line 17)	Word choice signals that they are particular kinds of teachers—those who have a philosophy about teaching literacy (identities/social languages; significance/situated meanings).	See also lines 9, 11, 12, and 14

"accurately diagnose our students' reading levels" (line 19)	Their word choice signals their membership into a community of literacy specialists. The adverb "accurately" represents a particular kind of teacher (one who is diligent and careful) (identities/social languages).	See also lines 4–6
Voice "if we fail to record linguistic variations at all, then we are missing an important piece of what defines our students as readers" (line 20)	Use of the active voice positions them as agents of instruction.	See also line 21
	Through their word choice they signal that their students have identities as readers (identities/social languages).	See also line 17
Stanza five (lines 21–23) *Guiding Assumptions about Literacy Education* **Pronouns/Verbs** "We believe ..." (line 21) "We are concerned ..." (line 22) "We are struggling" (line 23)	Use of pronoun/verb combination to communicate collective mental processes (belief, concern, and struggle) functions to position them as learners who actively care about their teaching (identities/social languages).	See also lines 6 and 24
Verb Tense "we are struggling"	Present progressive tense signals they are diligent learners and serious about the work of becoming teachers (identities/social languages).	See also lines 5–6, 19, and 24
Voice "We believe that how we record our students' linguistic variations affects our view of the place of culture and language in the classroom" (line 21)	Use of the active voice positions them as agents of instruction (significance/situated meanings).	See also lines 20, 22–23

(Continued)

TABLE 4.3. (Continued)

Stanza	Description of Linguistic Features	Interpretations using the Building Tasks / Associated Theoretical Frame	Connections/Patterns across the Letter
Stanza six (lines 24–27) *The Question*	**Relexicalization** "We are concerned that by not including linguistic variation in running records at all we are discounting our students' cultural and linguistic identities" (line 22).	The students repeat the idea that they expressed in line 18, indicating the importance of the thought (significance/situated meanings).	See also lines 12, 14, 18, and 20
	Intertextuality "Our exposure to your work is limited . . . we have not read all of your writings" (line 24).	They defer to Clay's authority through referencing her body of scholarship (significance/situated meanings; identities/social languages; relationships/intertextuality).	See also line 23
	Mood, Lexicalization "How do you record, interpret, and analyze linguistic variations?" (line 27)	This is the only direct question in the letter. They know enough to ask good questions about how language is represented. They carry stances of teacher researchers. Here, their word choice positions them within the community of practice of literacy educators (significance/situated meanings; identities/social languages).	See also line 12
Stanza seven (line 28) *Closing and Signature*	**Politeness Conventions** "We thank you for your time and consideration . . ."	This functions to reiterate their deference to Clay's expertise and authority (relationships/intertextuality).	See also lines 23 and 24

the reader to get a sense of the data as a whole, without presenting the entire interview, document, and so on. The next column includes a selective represen-tation of the linguistic features that seemed to have some traction in our analy-sis. By this we mean that after we had identified the linguistic resources in each line, we looked for patterns across the letter. We are not interested in isolated instances and we want to be careful not to "feature spot." Featuring spotting is when an analyst analyzes his or her data, only looking for one or two linguistic features, say pronouns or repetition, and attempts to make claims based on this analysis. Notice that in stanza one we focused on the use of pronouns, inter-textuality, the tenses of verbs, and the adverbs used. The third column includes a short, narrative description of our interpretations of these linguistic features connected to the building tasks and associated theoretical frameworks. It is worth repeating that we chose only three of the many building tasks (identities, relationships, and significance) and three of the theoretical frameworks (situated meanings, social languages, and intertextuality). Taking stanza one again as an example, we noted the consistent use of collective pronouns ("we" and "our") that functions to situate the pre-service teachers as part of a community of prac-tice of literacy educators. We argue that this social language is helping them to build a certain kind of identity as a literacy teacher. Finally, the fourth column in Table 4.3 illustrates connections across the letter. Again, we are interested in how these discursive features work together across the letter, building differ-ent storylines about the teachers and the field of literacy education. We noted that the pre-service teachers generated three different kinds of identities— teachers in preparation, practicing teachers, and future teachers. Each identity was brought to life through distinct verb tenses. Thus, in the fourth column we noted the different stanzas where the verb tenses shift. We invite you to follow our analysis stanza by stanza through this chart. Finally, we used this chart to write the findings section.

Part III: Steps in Conducting a Building Tasks Analysis

Appendix 4E: A Guide to Conducting a Building Tasks Analysis

Gee's (2011b, p. 29) approach to discourse analysis, referred to as the "building tasks analysis," brings together his theory of language with devices, or building tasks, for inquiry. Situated meanings, social languages, figured worlds, and Dis-courses are frameworks that analysts use to understand how people use language to accomplish social goals. The building tasks are the things that are being built as people interpret meanings and include questions that guide the analyst. Pro-cedurally, there are a number of steps we went through as we conducted our building tasks analysis. We build on the analytic procedures introduced in Chap-ter 3: creating a transcript, segmenting the text, and locating narrative structure.

From there, we proceed through the following steps, which we described in this Appendix.

(1) Segment the text into stanzas.
(2) Develop research questions.
(3) Identify theoretical frames: figured worlds, cultural models, intertexutality, and situated meanings.
(4) Use the building tasks (and associated questions) to examine the relation-ships between language and the social world: building identities, building relationships, building significance, or other tasks.
(5) Take stock of the linguistic resources used to build the social practices under investigation.
(6) Reconnect discourses practices with social processes, connecting with the-ory and other scholarship in the field.

Appendix 4F: Letter from Dr. Marie Clay to Our Class

Letter to Dr. Rebecca Rogers and her students in Teaching Reading in the Elementary School, from Marie M. Clay, on tour in the USA.

I apologize for the delay in replying to your inquiry because I have been for more than two months on a lecture tour in the USA. The issue you raise is an important one but I do not agree that you have uncovered a problem and I will explain why.

All the instruments that I have devised for teachers to use with children involve standard ways of observing children's behaviors in order to better understand their learning needs and change teaching in response to those learning needs.

A Running Record is a record of the child's behaviour as it occurs at the time the child is observed. It is not a test; it will show you how close a child can come to the author's words. The child may not match the text for any number of reasons—because the child is just a beginning reader and has much to learn about the written code, or because he is learning English at the same time he is learning to read and write, or because, draw-ing upon his oral language control, his home dialect tells him to expect different words and meanings in the text from what is written. It is usually not possible to tell why the child gave a particular response. Whenever he is drawing directly on his oral language skills, learned in his preschool years, there will be a mismatch in what he predicts a book will say, and what it actually says.

So if a Running Record is a result of careful observations it will tell us how close a child's language predictions are to those of an author. Over time there is likely to be a slow change towards the standard dialect of the books as the child develops more and more control over when to use the school's dialect when reading or writing English, and when to use the home dialect he continues to speak in his community and in the playground.

I think a problem arises when you think of a Running Record as an assessment, with a score (% correct), or yielding a "pass" on a book level. Even that is not a problem. It is standard practice for a psychologist administering tests to children to make two assessments and then make a personal judgement. The first assessment is made in the standard way; the second assessment is made in some way that modifies the testing or scoring procedures to suit the special competencies of the child being tested. Then the interpreter of the records makes a comparison and comes to a conclusion of how to teach the child taking both sets of observations (or scoring) into account.

I have deliberately used my personal dialect in this letter. What you have to do is decide what to do with my spelling errors on "behavior" and "judgment."!

Thank you for your inquiry.

Yours sincerely,

Marie M. Clay

Appendix 4G: Additional Reading and Resources to Support a Building Tasks Analysis

Examples of Carrying out Discourse Analysis with the Building Tasks

Alvermann, D. (2006). Ned and Kevin: An online discussion that challenges the "not-yet adult" cultural model. In K. Pahl & J. Rowsell (Eds.), *Travel notes from the new literacy studies: Instances of practices* (pp. 39–56). Clevedon, England: Multilingual Matters Ltd.

Gee, J.P. (2010). *How to do discourse analysis: A toolkit*. New York, NY: Routledge.

Lakshmanan, S. (2011). A critical discourse analysis of neocolonialism in Patricia McCormick's Sold. In Rogers, R. (Ed.), *An introduction to critical discourse analysis in education* (2nd ed.), (pp. 68–92). New York, NY: Routledge.

López-Bonilla, G. (2011). Narratives of exclusion and the construction of self. In Rogers, R. (Ed.), *An introduction to critical discourse analysis in education* (2nd ed.), (pp. 48–67). New York, NY: Routledge.

Marsh, J. & Lammers, J. (2011). Figured worlds and discourses of masculinity: Being a boy in a literacy classroom. In Rogers, R. (Ed.), *An introduction to critical discourse analysis in education* (2nd ed.), (pp. 93–116). New York, NY: Routledge.

Medina, C. (2010). "Reading across communities" in biliteracy practices: Examining translocal discourses and cultural flows in literature discussions. *Reading Research Quarterly, 45(1)*, 40–60.

Wade, S. & Fauske, J. (2004). Dialogue online: Prospective teachers' discourse strategies in computer-mediated classrooms. *Reading Research Quarterly, 39(2)*, 134–160.

Resources for Conducting Descriptive Linguistic Analyses

Fairclough, N. (1992). *Discourse and social change*. Cambridge, UK: Polity Press.

Gee, J. (2006). *An introduction to discourse analysis: Theory and method*. New York, NY: Routledge.

Janks, H. (2005). Language and the design of texts. *English Teaching: Practice and Critique, 4(3)*, 97–110.

Johnston, B. (2008). *Discourse analysis* (2nd ed.). Oxford, UK: Blackwell Publishing.

Stanzas

Gee, J. (2010). *How to do discourse analysis: A tool kit*. New York, NY: Routledge.

Hymes, Dell H. (2003). *Now I know only so far: Essays in ethnopoetics*. Lincoln: University of Nebraska Press.

Johnstone, B. (2010). *Discourse analysis* (2nd ed.). Malden, MA: Blackwell Publishing.

Appendices to Chapter 5

Guide for Conducting Critical Discourse Analysis

Part I: Preparing for the Critical Discourse Analysis

Appendix 5A: Developing Research Questions and Segmenting the Text

As with the other approaches to critically oriented discourse analysis, there are a number of procedural steps that we take in our analysis. We should emphasize that our approach to critical discourse analysis is cumulative. That is, the levels of analysis we have conducted thus far carry with us as we begin our critical discourse analysis. The first stages in preparing to conduct critical discourse analysis repeat the analytic processes we have already described in Chapters 3 and 4. First, the analyst develops research questions. Next, we generated a transcript (see Chapter 3). From there, we segmented the data into meaningful units at the level of stanzas and clauses (see Chapter 4). We often find it useful to analyze the transcript with a narrative framework in mind to see if we can locate a narrative structure (Chapter 3). This gives us additional insights about the form and function of the text. Then, with our research questions and unit of analysis in mind, we survey the linguistic features of the text, line by line. For our analysis of the book club discussion, we asked: What does racial literacy look and sound like in this book club? How are meanings around race, racism, and anti-racism constructed? Fairclough (1993, p. 230) reminds us that "cruces" or conflicts in the data are often productive places to begin analysis because they signal instability in discourse practices. Conversely, locating moments of hope, liberation, and equity are equally as productive and they provide us with a different orientation, a positive one from which to theorize about power and discourse. Table 5.1 is a demonstration of the CDA framework that we use.

TABLE 5.1. Faircloughian CDA Framework

	Genre	*Discourse*	*Style*
Description	*Ways of interacting*	*Ways of representing*	*Ways of being*
Example	Structures such as turn-taking or interruptions.	Themes such as White privilege, oppression.	Positions or identities such as "anti-racist."
Purpose	Organizes talk into recognizable patterns to allow for social work to be done (i.e. I–R–E pattern used for assessing student understanding).	Constructs ideas about the world within the interactional space.	Provides an opportunity for someone to take a position in relation to Discourses.
Analysis	Analyze each line in terms of how the linguistic features of the text signal that it is a particular genre or way of interacting.	Describe the ideas about the world present in each line of talk.	Describe the position that one takes in relation to a discourse. This is often signaled through verbs, modality, and syntactical construction.

Part II: Conducting Critical Discourse Analysis

Appendix 5B: Using the Triparte Schema of Genre, Discourse, and Style

With this framework in mind, we surveyed the linguistic features of the text to get a sense of the organization of the text (e.g., Fairclough, 1993; Gee, 2006; Janks, 2005). Informed by systemic functional linguistics, our analysis operated on the basis that each utterance has both a form and function. Halliday (1994) discusses three functions of language—textual (mode), interpersonal (tenor), and ideational (field). Fairclough (2011) translated these functions into "orders of discourse" and while the language is different, the concepts are the same: genre or "ways of interacting" refers to the mode of language. "Ways of representing" refers to the ideational component of language, or the discourse. And "ways of being," or style, refers to the interpersonal, the tenor. We marked each utterance with its meanings at the level of genre, discourse and style. We color-coded each utterance in terms of genre (blue), discourse (red), and style (green) (see Table 5.1). This helped us look for patterns among genre, discourse, and style, which is our ultimate goal in this analysis.

In the book club discussion we analyzed in Chapter 5, one level of our analysis was a close examination of the "*ways of interacting*" or the *genre* of the book club. At this level, we wondered: What is the participant structure of the book club?

Who controls the topic of conversation? Who speaks the most? What topics ate introduced, appropriated, taken up and dropped by participants? What modes are particularly dense or used often? What aspects of the discussion create coherence, flow, and rhythm or, conversely, conflict and disharmony? In what ways is this discussion intertextual, drawing on the echoes of other texts? When critically analyzing discourse, this kind of descriptive analysis can offer insight into power dynamics that can be studied more closely.

At the level of *discourse* or "*ways of representing*," we asked questions such as: What ideas are represented? What information is foregrounded and back-grounded? How are ideas represented through specific lexical choices, verbs, and pronouns? What information is excluded or silenced? We conducted a few simple lexical counts from words or phrases that we have identified as repeti-tive or potentially relevant to our research question. We developed a codebook to represent the different discourses, styles, and genres that were represented. Throughout our analysis of the discussion, we added and refined this codebook. Ultimately, we examined how each discourse was constructed through associated genres and styles. Here is a sample of our codebook for this book club discus-sion for the discourse of "racism" to illustrate the semiotic resources drawn on by participants.

Genres "Ways of Interacting"
- Embedded speech/Re-voicing
- Piggybacking or chaining
- Humor/Laughter
- Narratives
- Hypothetical situations
- Reference and predication
- Politeness conventions
- False starts and stops
- Cause–effect construction
- Co-constructing
- Overlapping speech
- Changing the topic

Discourse "Ways of Representing"
- Racism is manifested through individuals.
- Racism is manifested through institutional structures and personal beliefs and actions.
- Racism is learned/disrupted through talk.
- Racism is learned/disrupted through actions.
- Racism is conscious/unconscious.
- Racism exists in the present/past.

- Racism includes brutality and violence.
- Racism includes micro-aggressions.

Style "Ways of Being"
- Active construction/Passive construction
- Modality (low or high commitment to the idea)
- Affinity statements (identifying/not identifying with Whiteness; identifying/ not identifying with Blackness)
- Mood (e.g., indicative, imperative, subjunctive, interrogative, or rhetorical)
- Nominalization (e.g., "slaves" versus African-American people who were enslaved)
- Appraisal (communicating appreciation, affect, or judgment of the characters in the book)
- Naming self as reader/teacher as racialized (e.g., "As a White person, I . . .")

Next, we turned to the level of *style* or "*ways of being*" and asked: How do participants represent themselves—as agents or recipients of action? Here, we noticed grammatical aspects such as nominalization, voice, and tense. How are obligation and commitment expressed in this text? Here, we examined the modality of the text. How do the participants evaluate or appraise the themes communicated through judgment, appreciation, and mood? We also closely examined the verbs used to understand how each participant represented ideas, which is central to this level of analysis. Verbs are important because they signal the action in discourse. Our analytic objective was to understand how each participant drew on verbs and what this may mean to the overall meanings being made in the lesson. Procedurally, we underlined verbal phrases, noting the kinds of verbs drawn on in each line for each participant. Tables 5.2 and 5.3 illustrate the verbal processes drawn on by Leslie and Tonya in one portion of the book club.

Our goal was to find connections among genre, discourse, and style, keeping in mind that each level may include multiple modes of semiosis. Table 5.4 is a snapshot that looks across genre, discourse, and style in one excerpt included in Chapter 5.

After analyzing genre, discourse, and style throughout the book club transcript, we looked inductively at the patterns for each participant and then across the participants. This helped us notice how different participants represented their ideas about the place of talk in anti-racist efforts. We created a descriptive portrait of the lesson and wrote a brief summary of the lesson, which reported on these descriptions. We brought theoretical frames to the foreground and were reminded of how people discursively construct the racial worlds they inhabit, bringing them to life (Bell, 1992; Davies and Harré, 1990; Giddens, 1984; Morrison, 1993). Table 5.5 is broken into the three orders of discourse and the associated discursive features that we associate with each. We have also included questions to ask of the text for each level of analysis.

TABLE 5.2. Leslie's Verbal Processes

Possible Positions about Anti-racism/"Social Justice Type Things"	Verbs Used by Leslie	Type of Verb
Anti-racism is carried out through verbal discourse	Talks (lines 11, 13, and 19)	Verbal
Anti-racism is carried out at individual level/that is, learning about racism	Ideas (line 15) Understand (line 23) Remember (line 24)	Mental/Cognitive
Anti-racism is part of relationships or identifications with others	Supporting (line 14) Feel (line 27)	Relational/Affective
Anti-racism involves a redistribution of wealth or power		Material

TABLE 5.3. Tonya's Verbal Processes

Possible Positions about Anti-racism/"Social Justice Type Things"	Verbs Used by Tonya	Type of Verb
Anti-racism is carried out through verbal discourse		Verbal
Anti-racism is carried out at individual level/that is, learning about racism		Mental/Cognitive
Anti-racism is part of relationships or identifications with others	Upset (line 75) Going through emotions (line 83)	Relational/Affective
Anti-racism involves a redistribution of wealth or power	Do anything (line 82)	Material

TABLE 5.4. Looking Across Genre, Discourse, and Style

Clauses	Discourse	Genre	Style
30 Tonya: It kind of reminded me of like,	Inter-racial relationships represented in the book *Iggie's House*.	Book-to-comedy shows intertextual connection.	The marker "like" is used to report a similar situation and allows Tonya to express critique.
31 a lot of times, you know,	Garnering support for her point that knowing Black people doesn't make someone not racist by pointing to a common storyline.	Connection building with her book club partners.	Appraisal of the number of times this happens.
32 if you watch comedy shows or something	Comedy is a vehicle for communicating values around race.	Hypothetical scenario, direct appeal.	Softening stance "or something."
33 and if you watch	Comedy is a vehicle for communicating values around race.	Hypothetical scenario, repetition of the phrase "if you watch" serves as a cohesive device.	Active construction, action verb.
34 Black comics talking about White people	Race is marked; comedy is a vehicle for communicating values around race.	Comics addressing stereotypes.	Active construction, habitual/mental verb.
35 and they will say,	There is a common storyline in comedy about race.	Revoicing comics.	Critique of this position.
36 "Oh, I'm not racist,	Explicitly naming and personalizing racism as "racist."	Revoicing the speech of a comic; intertextuality.	Negative construction of existential verb "to be."

(*Continued*)

TABLE 5.4. (Continued)

Clauses	Discourse	Genre	Style
37 I have a Black friend.	Denial of racism in the hypothetical White person; ordering of words emphasizes race over friendship.	Repetition of the term "Black" creates cohesiveness.	Habitual verb; declarative statement.
38 They come over to my house.	Denial of racism based on personal interaction.	Summarizing the joke.	Habitual verb; declarative statement.
39 I have three Black friends."	Denial of racism based on personal interaction; use of a specific number emphasizes the improbable nature of the friendship.	Repetition of the phrase "Black friend" creates cohesiveness.	Habitual verb; declarative statement.
40 Leslie: uh-huh	Agreement	Cohesion	Affiliation
41 Tonya: That's like the comic jokes	Naming the action as "joking;"	Repetition; summarizing the joke.	Verbal verb "jokes"; making a comparison with the marker "like."
42 because White people will say	White talk includes White people talking about inter-racial friendships that they do not really have.	Parallel construction "they will."	Verbal verb
43 that they have Black friends to prove	Ordering of words privileges race over friends.	Expanding on the comic's joke/ message.	Verbal and belief verbs.
44 that they are not racist or / exclusive	Explicitly naming racism through re-lexicalization.	Denial of racism in the hypothetical White person.	Existential verb signals being racist (or not racist) as an enduring trait.
45 Jenna: uh-huh	Agreement	Cohesion	Affiliation

46 Tonya: But they'll always know	White talk	Conjunctive "but" functions to set up her critique.	Habitual verb; mental verb.
47 how many they have	White talk	Adding on; repetition of "they" creates cohesiveness.	Habitual verb "they have"; third person pronoun; mental/verbal verb.
48 or how many times they have seen them	White talk	Adding on and repetition of "they" creates parallel structure.	Habitual verb; action verb.
49 or exactly what they have talked to them about.	White talk	Adding on and repetition of "they" creates parallel structure.	Habitual verb; verbal verb.
50 So it is just like	"It" refers to White talk and serves as the object of critique.	The repetition of a speech marker of peer group "like" functions to build cohesiveness.	Use of the quotative "like" sets up her reported speech and conveys a mood of critique. Playful tone softens the critique.
51 "come on, now,	Adopts the deictic orientation of someone who is confronting a White person.	Mimicry that conveys expressive content versus precise words.	Mimicry and playful tone serves to soften her critique.
52 that's not your friend."	Knowing a person of color does not make a person not a racist; extending the ideas of the comic.	Mimicry that conveys expressive content versus precise words.	Mimicry and playful tone serves to soften her critique.
53 *Laughter from others in the group*	They understand or can relate to the critique.	Humor	Affinity

TABLE 5.5. Survey of Linguistic Features and Functions Connected to Orders of Discourse

GENRE
"WAYS OF INTERACTING"

Discursive Feature	Description	Questions to Ask of the Text
Turn Taking	Description of the structure and sequence of an interaction.	• What is the sequence of turns? • How many turns are taken? • How long are the turns?
Cohesion	Lexical or grammatical features that help a text to hang together across sentence boundaries and form larger units.	• What relations exist between the clause and the sentence?
Parallel Structure	Similar textual features within the text; at the level of semantics or syntax; across semiotic modes.	• What features of this text function to create flow and rhythm?
Intertextuality	*Manifest intertextuality:* Intertextual features such as: quoted speech, irony, parody, negation; presupposition, and scare quotes. *Constitutive intertextuality:* Interdiscursive features between texts such as: structure, form, and genre.	How does this text draw on other voices, texts, and genres?

DISCOURSE
"WAYS OF REPRESENTING"

Discursive Feature	Description	Questions to Ask of the Text
Information Focus	Themes are represented in the first part of the clause and are generally the known information. Rhemes include the new information and are generally included in the last part of the clause.	• What ideas are represented? • What information is foregrounded by being in the theme position?
Lexical Relations	The relation and classification of experiences through an unfolding series of activities.	• What social categories underlie the lexical strings in the text? • What taxonomies are represented?

TABLE 5.5.

Discursive Feature	Description	Questions to Ask of the Text
Lexicalization	The selection of wordings.	• How are ideas represented through word choice?
Re-lexicalization	Renaming/re-voicing.	• What is the level of formality? • What words or phrases show up again and again in the transcript?
Pronouns	First/second/third person. Inclusive/exclusive pronouns. Sexist/Non-sexist pronouns.	• Which pronouns are used and where?
Exclusion	Suppression of information: topical silence; lexical silence; presuppositional silence.	• What information is being excluded?

STYLE
"WAYS OF BEING"

Discursive Feature	Description	Questions to Ask of the Text
Transitivity	Processes in verbs Verbs of doing (material, behavioral) Verbs of sensing/saying (mental) Verbs of being (relational) Existential verbs ("There is . . .")	• To what degree does an action affect its object?
Tense	Tense sets up when an event occurs in time.	• When is this process occurring?
Voice	Active and passive voice.	• Is the agent represented? Are participants agents or recipients of actions?
Modality	Aspects of grammar that express obligation, permission, and probability (e.g. may, might, can, could, will, should, must, and need).	• How is obligation expressed in this text?
Mood	Grammatical aspects that allow the speaker to express their attitude toward what is being said/written. Indicative (I am here) Imperative (Be here) Subjunctive (If I were here) Interrogative (Is he here?) Rhetorical (Am I here?)	• Through what forms does the speaker express their stance toward what is being said?

(Continued)

TABLE 5.5. (*Continued*)

Discursive Feature	Description	Questions to Ask of the Text
Nominalization	Turning the verb or adjective into a noun.	• Are verb processes turned into nouns in this text? • (For example: Administrators closed ten schools. There were ten school closings.)
Appraisal	Systems of evaluation that are used to negotiate social relationships by communicating attitudes (affect, judgment, and appreciation)	• What kinds of attitudes are negotiated in the text? What is the strength of the feelings involved? How are values sourced and positions aligned?

Part III: Representing the Findings

Appendix 5C: Representational Issues to Consider

At this point, we recontextualize the analysis in the ethnographic context of our classroom and develop a plan for representing our findings. In Chapter 5, we structured the findings through the tension that emerged during one portion of the book club discussion: Should talk be considered action in anti-racist efforts? In each section, we wove our analysis of ways of interacting (genre), ways of representing (discourse), and ways of being (style) and associated multimodality. Representing critical discourse analysis can be tricky, especially given space limitations in journals. When done properly, the reader does not feel lost in the minutiae of the analysis but has a sense of the whole. The challenge for the analyst is finding a way to portray the complexity of linguistic moves while simultaneously being respectful to the ongoing storyline. We find the following craft moves particularly helpful when representing our critical discourse analysis: writing a summary of the overall findings; finding a balance between the micro and macro; and making connections to existing research. We address each in turn.

First, because discourse analysis attends to both linguistic and social structure, it can be difficult for the analyst to present the "big picture" while also attending to the small details of analysis. Providing a summary at the beginning of the findings (or interpretations) section that outlines the key interpretations and how the findings will flow is crucial to guide the reviewer through the article.

Second, balancing the micro- and macro-contexts in the representations/ findings section can be a challenge. Context can be provided in the research de- sign section as well as in the representation of the findings. Often, authors do not provide information about how the excerpts of talk or text are connected to the data set as a whole. Sometimes, the author summarizes the excerpts without real analysis or providing additional context from the study. Presenting fragments of texts leaves readers with unanswered questions about the contextualization of the texts. Indeed, a defining feature of critical discourse analysis is movement beyond describing and interpreting discourse patterns to explaining why and how dis- course practices exist, circulate, are reproduced or challenged. The reader needs to get a sense of the context—through rich descriptions of the local, institutional, and societal domains of practice—to get a sense of the text trajectory of the social practices under investigation.

The third issue to consider in the representation of discourse analysis is the question of: *So what?* How does this analysis connect and contribute to the exist- ing field? Authors can connect to existing scholarship in their findings as well as in the discussion. We also want to emphasize that one of the goals of critical discourse analysis is to open up possible interpretations, recognizing that there are others. To do this, we may provide counter-interpretations or extend an invita- tion to our readers to generate such alternative readings.

Part IV: Steps in Conducting Critical Discourse Analysis

Appendix 5D: A Guide to Conducting Critical Discourse Analysis

(1) Develop research questions.
(2) Create a transcript.
(3) Segment the data:

> Stanzas
> Clauses.

(4) Locate narrative structure.
(5) Survey linguistic features, line by line.
(6) Consult, develop theory.
(7) Organize coding of linguistic features using "orders of discourse." Take each "order of discourse" separately and move through the data set, asking:

> How are "ways of interacting" (genre) expressed?
> What "ways of representing" (discourse) are represented?
> How are "ways of being" (style) communicated?

(8) Locate patterns within and across "orders of discourse," especially places of overlap between all three domains. Create summary charts to illustrate the analysis.

(9) Look across local, institutional, and societal levels of analysis to contextualize the discourse practices under examination.
(10) Represent the findings in a way that balances between the micro and macro and makes connections to existing research.

Appendix 5E: Additional Reading and Resources to Support Critical Discourse Analysis

The second edition of *An Introduction to Critical Discourse Analysis in Education* (Routledge, 2011) includes a companion website with many resources to support those interested in the theories and methods of critical discourse analysis. It can be located at the following url: http://cw.routledge.com/textbooks/9780415874298/

- The website is intended to extend inquiry, exploration, and dialogue beyond the chapters in the book. Some of the resources include:
- Transcripts of original interviews with James Gee, Norman Fairclough, and Gunther Kress, some of the leading scholars in each of the approaches we highlight in this book.
- Four, 15-minute videos that feature many of the leading scholars in critical discourse studies discussing key themes in CDA such as: approaches, procedures, context, and future directions. Guiding questions for each of the videos are provided.
- Resources also include an extensive bibliography, a list of teaching and learning resources, discourse analysis journals and examples of syllabi from leading scholars in the field.

Further Readings in Critical Discourse Analysis

Bartlett, T. (2012). *Hybrid voices and collaborative change: Contextualising Positive Discourse Analysis.* London, UK: Routledge.
Chouliaraki, L. & Fairclough, N. (1999). *Discourse in late modernity—rethinking critical discourse analysis.* Edinburgh, UK: Edinburgh University Press.
Fairclough, N. (1992). *Discourse and social change.* Cambridge, UK: Polity Press.
Fairclough, N. (1995). *Critical discourse analysis.* Boston, MA: Addison Wesley.
Fairclough, N. (2001). *Language and power* (2nd ed.). London, UK: Longman.
Fairclough, N. (2003). *Analysing discourse: Textual analysis for social research.* London, UK: Routledge.
Fairclough, N., & Wodak, R. (1997) Critical discourse analysis. In T.A. van Dijk (ed.), *Discourse studies: A multidisciplinary introduction: Vol. 2. Discourse as social interaction.* London, UK: Sage Publications.
Martin, J. & Rose, D. (2007). *Working with discourse: Meaning beyond the clause* (2nd ed.). London, UK: Continuum Press.
Rogers, R. (2013). Critical discourse analysis: Criteria to consider in reviewing scholarship. In A. Trainor & E. Graue (Eds.), *Publishing qualitative research in the social and*

behavioral sciences: A guide for reviewers and researchers (pp. 66–81). New York, NY: Routledge.

Appendices to Chapter 6

Guide to Conducting Multimodal Discourse Analysis

Part 1: Preparing for the Multimodal Discourse Analysis

Appendix 6A: Creating a Multimodal Transcript

Because our focus in this analysis is on multimodality, we ask: How are meanings being made in this event? The first step in answering this question is to create a multimodal transcript of verbal and nonverbal interactions. We usually begin with the verbal mode because our teacher research questions always ask questions about our participants' linguistic choices. The nonverbal action is inserted as closely to the verbal discourse that overlaps it. This method of transcription allows us to see in a glance how meaning is made in an interaction.

Next, we create clauses as in the example below of Jonah and Tamara's interactions. Clauses, as we described in Appendix 3E, are units of speech that include an action and a participant (in the example below, "So 'I'-participant 'think' - action"). For each speaker, new rows designate verbal turns. The *italicized* discourse is nonverbal.

> 1 Jonah: So I think
> we have time for
> *Reaches for book*
> to look at one more book
> 2 Jonah: so I think
> 3 Tamara: Uhah
> *Reaches for book*
> 4 Jonah: You want
> to look at this one?
> *He puts his hand on the top corner of the book, ready to open the cover. He gazes down at the book.*

In some cases, nonverbal turns will function as turns in an interaction, and the analyst creates new rows for those turns. So in line 3, if Tamara had not said "Uhah" but simply reached for the book, her "turn" would still be placed in a new row.

In order to further analyze the multimodality, we may need a series of images to study and understand how the multiple modes work together (Norris, 2004). We insert additional columns to the table for these images. In our example transcript, we added one column for video freeze frames that illustrated the verbal

TABLE 6.1. Still Frame Transcription

Time Stamp	Partic- ipant	Verbal Nonverbal	Video Freeze Frame	Images/Multimodal Descriptions of Jazz Baby
16:08	Tamara	Uhah Reaches for book		The cover of the book depicts eight diverse characters (four girls and four boys) all of different races and ethnicities. The image illustrates a group of kids dancing, singing, and playing various instruments. Set in bright tones, a lively energetic scene is displayed.

and nonverbal action and one where we could place the images and multimodal descriptions of the pages of *Jazz Baby* that were the focus of the interaction. The video freeze frames were chosen because they illustrated the action that we represented in the transcript and were saved from a video as a still frame. In some rows we needed more than one video freeze frame to capture the ways that modes worked in that turn. In Table 6.1 we use special effects to bring attention to the action we are interested in, as well as to protect the identity of the young participants in our study.[1]

Part II: Conducting the Multimodal Discourse Analysis

Appendix 6B: The Descriptive Analysis of Multimodal Transcripts

After creating a multimodal transcript, we must create a descriptive summary of the interactions. The analyst may choose various entry points into the data, keeping his or her eyes open to what may be interesting. In our example transcript we created a number of descriptive analyses to get a sense of the interaction as a whole.

One way to analyze the interaction is by examining the **turn–taking structure**. Analysis by participant allows the analyst to understand features such as the number of turns, the type of turns, the length of turns, the content of turns, and the number of ideas introduced by each participant. Table 6.2 allows us to see a comparison between Jonah and Tamara's contributions to the turn-taking structure.

At this stage in the analysis, the analyst will develop new questions about **interactional patterns**. For example, the analyst may pay attention to each participant's choice of verbs, as we explained in Chapter 5.

Another tool is a simple **lexical count** of key words and phrases. In Jonah and Tamara's case, we noticed these repetitions:

TABLE 6.2. Jonah and Tamara's Use of Verbs

Participant	Verbs of Doing	Verbs of Sensing/ Saying (Mental)	Verbs of Being (relational)	Existential Verbs ("There is . . .")
Jonah	Look want to try is playing say dancing pound try to read	think remember know look like like says hear	is has	
Tamara	Snap hurted dancing	Like	have got	It's like

"What's that phrase/What's the phrase" was repeated two times.
"Jazz" was repeated 32 times.
"You've got the . . . (language from text)" was repeated seven times.
"Dancing" was repeated five times.

Appendix 6C: Examining Modality

Examining modality is important to the analysis of multimodal transcripts. Charles Pierce classified signs according to the characteristic of the relation that they have to that which they represent (Kress, 2010, p. 63). We might talk about modes as:

Iconic: A mode "resembles" what it represents (e.g., a square for a book).
Indexical: A mode "points to" an object or event (e.g., sitting at a table represents "reading time").
Symbolic: A mode "stands for" a conventionally agreed relation between a form and an object or event (e.g., four walls as house; smile as happiness).

For example, consider an interaction in which a pre-service teacher is explaining what occurred in a previous lesson. As she is telling a story, she lifts her arms, outstretched, with her hands opened toward the sky and says, "I just don't know what I did wrong." The indexical nature of this gesture is that it is emphasizes her words and draws attention to the effect of the statement. To more closely analyze the gesture, we describe **the function** of the sign she is making with her arms.

Modes are arranged in multimodal ensembles of any of the modes of meaning described above (Kress & van Leeuwen, 2001). It is important to attend to the ways that modes work together to construct meanings. We might ask the following questions, as analysts:

1. What modes are drawn upon in this turn?
2. Why does the speaker use multiple modes in this turn?

3. Are the modes dependent on one another, as in a gesture that illuminates an important word, or are they independent, expressing different ideas?
4. How does the "ensemble" of modes of meaning relate to ensembles during other moments in this interaction? Are there patterns of multimodality in the transcript?

As you consider the ways that modes work together, you will find that more questions arise about the ways that meanings are made in the event.

Part III: Steps in Conducting a Multimodal Discourse Analysis

Appendix 6D: Guide to Conducting Multimodal Discourse Analysis

We return to genre, discourse, and style (introduced in Chapter 5) to look more closely at the "ways of interacting," "ways of representing," and "ways of being" that are used in each utterance. The procedures are as follows:

1. Code the interactions, by each idealized line, for ways of interacting, representing, and being. You can do this on paper and transfer it to the computer.

    a. In terms of the **ways of interacting**, or **genre**, we ask how the modes that the participants are drawing upon, such as gestures, gaze, language, and laughter are entry strategies into the conversation and what the function of those entry strategies may be (i.e., an interruption, a topic shift).
    b. In terms of **Discourse** or **ways of representing**, we analyze the ways in which multiple modes construct representations of the world, for example how a teacher reducing the distance between a person and a book indicates an idea about how proximity to a text supports reading.
    c. In terms of **style**, or **ways of being**, we ask how people draw on multiple modes to position themselves in relation to an idea or worldview. For example, a student may look up at her teacher and use her whole body to "pop" out of her seat when she is excited about an illustration or a special word in a story.

Table 6.3 is an example of a line of transcript in which we applied this coding structure.

2. Share your coding with another analyst. Are there discrepant or alternate interpretations?
3. Create a list of codes for key segments of the transcript. For example, in Table 6.4 we listed our codes for a 30-second segment of the transcript.
4. Look closely at this fine-grained analysis next to the descriptive analysis of the interaction. Check for big themes that are noticeable across layers of analysis. Sometimes you may need to return to the data for a closer analysis of a set of interactions or conduct a new lexical count.

TABLE 6.3. Example of Multimodal Transcription and Analysis

Line	Time Stamp	Participant	Verbal Nonverbal	Analysis of Genre, Discourse, and Style	Images from Video
5	17:03	Jonah	Jazz baby Jazz baby Join the band *Tamara looks off into the space in front of them.* You've got the music in your hand. *Looks directly at Tamara.*	Genre: re-reading the first few lines and then adding the rest of the text on the page; Jonah leans in, handles the book. Discourse: supporting the reader by modeling. Gaze at the book indicates affiliation with the text but also draws her into the interaction. Style: Jonah continues to demonstrate his commitment to building print-based literacy. Tamara's gaze indicates that she is listening.	

TABLE 6.4. Codes for a 30-Second Segment of Transcript

Time: 16:06–16:36	Genre Ways of Interacting	Discourse Ways of Representing	Style Ways of Being
Jonah	• "Look at . . ." to draw attention to text • Question posing • Touching book • Correction • Gaze to indicate topic • Reading Tamara's actions • Laughter	• Reading as looking • Student should control text • Decreasing distance between reader and text supports reader • Smooth Jazz • Reading as enjoyment • Drawing on students' background knowledge supports reader	• Guide on the side • Affinity through shared history • Waiting, patient teacher • Affinity for Tamara using smile, laughter, and gaze to indicate enjoyment
Tamara	• Reaching for object and using posture to indicate preference • Sound • Repetition • Smile • Remembering	• Reading as using sounds • Preference for the multimodality of reading	• Control of resources • Affinity for Jonah using smile, gaze, and gesture to show closeness • Connecting with the beat of the music

Appendix 6E: Jonah and Tamara Segments

Table 6.5 is in reference to a page of *Jazz Baby*. There is one female character who has her arms displayed above her head while snapping her fingers. Her eyes are closed and in this background there are musical notes and lines to illustrate her swaying/dancing to the beat. She has a serene look on her face that seems to indicate a deep connection to the music. There is one male character whose hands are placed in a clapping position who looks to the side at others in the band (not shown). Although he is seated, his bent knee suggests that his whole body is also bouncing or moving to the music. The text reads:

> Jazz baby, jazz baby,
> join the band.
> You've got music
> in your hands.

TABLE 6.5. Jonah and Tamara Segment 1

Line	Time Stamp	Partic- ipant	Verbal Nonverbal	Images from Video
1	16:56	Tamara	Jazz. *Slight pause.* *Leans back into her chair with gaze on the text as she reads.* The slight pause. Baby. *Slight pause.* Jazz the baby.	
2	16:57	Jonah	*One hand clutches the side of the book while the other hand points at the text.*	
3	16:59	Jonah	Join the band. *One hand clutches the side of the book while the other hand points at the text.* This actually has a little rhyme to it.	

TABLE 6.5.

Line	Time Stamp	Partic-ipant	Verbal Nonverbal	Images from Video
4	16:59	Tamara	*Leans in and moves closer to book. Her hands are at her side and her gaze is directed at the area where Jonah has pointed.*	
5	17:03	Jonah	Jazz baby Jazz baby Join the band *Tamara looks off into the space in front of them.* You've got the music in your hand. *Looks directly at Tamara.*	
6	17:05	Jonah	Do you hear the rhyme? *Looks directly at Tamara. One hand clutches the side of the book while the other hand points at the page.*	
7	17:07	Tamara	Yeah. *Looks at Jonah.*	

(*Continued*)

TABLE 6.5. *(continued)*

Line	Time Stamp	Partic-ipant	Verbal / Nonverbal	Images from Video
8	17:08	Jonah	Want to try that together? *Gaze still on Tamara.*	
9	17:09	Tamara	Jazz baby. *Swaying.*	
10	17:11	Tamara/ Jonah	Jazz baby / Jazz baby / Join the band *(in unison while both look down at the book).*	
11	17:15	Tamara	You've got the music. *Swaying.* In your haaa–and. *Gazes up at Jonah.*	
12	17:17	Jonah	Where's the music? *Laughs and raises upright clenched fist toward Tamara.*	

TABLE 6.5.

Line	Time Stamp	Partic- ipant	Verbal Nonverbal	Images from Video
13	17:18	Tamara	Haa–and *with sing-song intonation and a big smile on her face.*	
14	17:21	Jonah	*Jonah turns the page while holding the book upright.*	
15	17:22	Tamara	I can snap like that. *Points to the book.*	
16	17:23	Tamara	*Tamara raises both hands up to shoulder level and snaps her fingers.*	

Jonah and Tamara Segment 2

Table 6.6 is an interaction between Jonah and Tamara as they explore a page in *Jazz Baby* that foregrounds one character playing a horn. There are musical notes in the background of the page, the character's cheeks are puffed, and his eyes are squinted to show action. Sound is represented in the picture by lines and movement as well as musical notes. The text reads:

> Jazz baby, jazz baby,
> blow your horn.
> You've got rhythm
> Sure as you're born.

TABLE 6.6. Jonah and Tamara Segment 2

Line	Time Stamp	Participant	Verbal *Nonverbal*	*Images from Video*
1	17:27	Jonah	What's he playing? *Turns the page and looks down at book.*	
2	17:32	Tamara	A . . . *Pauses.* A French horn? *Looks down at book and then up at Jonah.*	
3	17:34	Jonah	Did you say a French horn?	
4	17:36	Tamara	Yeah. *Looking up.*	
5	17:36	Jonah	It's very close to a French horn. *Points with pinky finger at image on the page.*	

Appendix 6F: Tonya and CeCe Segments

Table 6.7 represents Tonya and CeCe's interaction in reference to the first page of *Jazz Baby*, and Table 6.8 represents the interaction in reference to the page that reads "Jazz baby, jazz baby, blow your horn . . ."

TABLE 6.7. Tonya and CeCe Segment 1

Line	Time Stamp	Participant	Verbal Nonverbal	Images from Video
1	25:07	Tonya	OK. Tell me what you're doing in the picture? *CeCe leans in closer to the book.*	
2	25:11	CeCe	Dancing. *Peers into the book.*	
3	25:12	Tonya	It says Jazz Baby Jazz Baby in the band, you've got music in your hands *(reads).*	
4	25:15	CeCe	*Smiling as she looks at the page.*	

(Continued)

TABLE 6.7. *(continued)*

5	25:20	Tonya/ CeCe	So CeCe is dancing to the music. Kind of feelin' it. *CeCe nods, smiling.*	
6	25:21	CeCe	*CeCe nods and her gaze is on the second page.*	
7	25:23	Tonya	*Tonya turns the page.*	

TABLE 6.8. Tonya and CeCe Segment 2

Line	Time Stamp	Partic- ipant	Verbal Nonverbal	*Images from Video*
1	25:24	Tonya	What about here? Where are you? *Hand outstretched in a questioning gesture.*	

TABLE 6.8.

Line	Time Stamp	Partic-ipant	Verbal Nonverbal	Images from Video
2	25:26	CeCe	Nowhere it's just him.	
3	25:27	Tonya	It's just him, he's blowing his horn. What could you be doing right now? *Gazes at CeCe*	
4	25:31	CeCe	Dancing. *Gazes up at Tonya with a big smile.*	
5	25:34	Tonya	You could still be dancing to his horn. *Gazes at book.* To the music he is making with his trumpet.	

Appendix 6G: Additional Reading and Resources to Support Multimodal Discourse Analysis

Examples of CDA with Multimodal Texts

Albers, P. (2007). Visual discourse analysis: An introduction to the analysis of school-generated visual texts. *56th Yearbook of the National Reading Conference*, 81–95.

Crumpler, T.P., Handsfield, L.J., & Dean, T.R. (2011). Constructing difference differently in language and literacy professional development. *Research in the Teaching of English, 46(1),* 55–91.

Marshall, E., & Toohey, K. (2010). Representing family: Community funds of knowledge, bilingualism, and multimodality. *Harvard Educational Review, 80*(2), 221–241.

Mosley, M. & Johnson, A.S. (2007). Examining literacy teaching stories for racial positioning: Pursuing multimodal approaches. *The 56th Yearbook of the National Reading Conference,* 332–344.

Pini, M. (2011). The discourses of educational management organizations: A political design. In Rogers, R. (Ed.), *An Introduction to Critical Discourse Analysis in Education* (2nd ed.), (pp. 267–291). New York, NY: Routledge.

Rogers, R. & Mosley, M. (2008). "A critical discourse analysis of racial literacy in teacher education." *Linguistics and Education, 19,* 107–131.

Schaenen, I. (2010). "Genre means. . . ." A critical discourse analysis of fourth grade talk about genre. *Critical Inquiry into Language Studies, 7(1),* 28–53.

Siegel, M., Kontovourki, S., Schmier, S., & Enriquez, G. (2008). Literacy in motion: A case study of a shape-shifting kindergartner. *Language Arts, 86(2),* 89–98.

Wohlwend, K. (2009). Damsels in discourse: Girls consuming and producing identity texts through Disney princess play. *Reading Research Quarterly, 44(1),* 57–83.

Wohlwend, K. (2011). Mapping modes of children's play and design: An action-oriented approach to critical multimodal analysis. In Rogers, R. (Ed.), *An Introduction to Critical Discourse Analysis in Education* (2nd ed.), (pp. 242–266). New York, NY: Routledge.

Further Reading on Key Concepts in MDA

Hull, G.A., & Nelson, M.E. (2005). Locating the semiotic power of multimodality. *Written Communication, 22,* 224–261.

Norris, S. (2011). *Identity in (Inter)action: Introducing multimodal (inter)action analysis.* Berlin, Germany: DeGruyter Mouton.

O'Halloran, K.L. (2004). *Multimodal discourse analysis: Systemic functional perspectives.* London, UK: Continuum.

Wohlwend, K.E. (2011). *Playing their way into literacies: Reading, writing, and belonging in the early childhood classroom.* New York, NY: Teachers College Press.

Digital Texts and Discourse Analysis

Androutsopoulos, J. (2008). Potentials and limitations of discourse-centered online ethnography. *Language@Internet, 5,* article 8. www.languageatinternet.de/articles/2008/1610/index_html, accessed on May 31, 2012.

Baym, N.K., Zhang, Y.B., & Lin, M-C. (2004). Social interactions across media: Interpersonal communication on the Internet, telephone and face-to-face. *New Media & Society, 6*(3), 299–318.

Herring, S.C. (2007). A faceted classification scheme for computer-mediated discourse. *Language@Internet, 4,* article 1. www.languageatinternet.de/articles/2007/761, accessed on December 26, 2010.

Herring, S.C. (2010). Computer-mediated conversation Part I: Introduction and overview. *Language@Internet, 7,* article 2. urn:nbn:de:0009–7-28011, accessed on May 31, 2012.

Herring, S.C. (2011). Computer-mediated conversation Part II: Introduction and overview. *Language@Internet, 8,* article 2. urn:nbn:de:0009–7-32134, accessed on May 31, 2012.

O'Halloran, K.L. (2009). Multimodal analysis and digital technology. In A. Baldry and E. Montagna (Eds.), *Interdisciplinary perspectives on multimodality: Theory and practice*. Proceedings of the Third International Conference on Multimodality. Campobasso, Italy: Palladino.

Software/Applications to Support (Critical) Discourse Analysis

UAM CorpusTool, PRAAT www.wagsoft.com/software.html

VisualDTA, Dynamic Topic Analysis (DTA) http://info.slis.indiana.edu/~herring/VisualDTA

VisualDTA is an application that can be used to assist DTA by providing a way to visualize the structure of the topic flow within a conversation. After analyzing genre, discourse, and style throughout the book club transcript, we looked inductively at the patterns for each participant and then across the participants. This helped us notice how different participants represented their ideas about the place of talk in anti-racist efforts. We created a descriptive portrait of the lesson and wrote a brief summary of the lesson, which reported on these descriptions. We brought theoretical *frames* to the foreground and were reminded of how people discursively construct the racial worlds they inhabit, bringing them to life (Bell, 1992; Davies, 1990; Giddens, 1984; Morrison, 1993).

Table 5.5 is broken into the three orders of discourse and the associated discursive features that we associate with each. We have also included questions to ask of the text for each level of analysis.

Part IV: Revisiting Critiques of Critical Approaches to Discourse Analysis

As we represent our findings, we find it useful to revisit common critiques of critical approaches to discourse analysis. These can serve as a point of departure for evaluating the merit of our scholarship. We invite you to consider how our work responds to each of these critiques. Some of the common critiques are listed below with the references included as part of the recommended reading list.

- Political and social ideologies are read onto data rather than revealed through the data (Widdowson, 1998).
- There is an unequal balance between social theory and method (van Dijk, 2000).
- Analyses often lack close textual or linguistic analysis (Antaki, Billig, Edwards, & Potter, 2003).
- Analysis tends to be decontextualized (Blommaert & Bulcaen, 2000).
- There is an overemphasis on domination and oppression versus liberation and freedom (Bartlett, 2012; Luke, 2004; Martin, 2004; Mosley & Rogers, 2011).
- There has been little attention to learning and the non-linguistic aspects of interaction such as emotions and activity (Rogers, 2011).

In addition to using the common critiques as a checklist to evaluate our own (and your) scholarship, we may also turn to touchstones for evaluating critical discourse analysis. We introduce eleven touchstones for evaluating critically oriented discourse analysis but refer readers to Rogers (2013) for a full discussion of each. Again, we invite you to consider the analyses we have set forth in this book against each of these touchstones for evaluating the quality of critically oriented discourse analysis. In turn, this list can be used as you conduct your own inquiry.

- The unit of analysis is explicitly addressed and is congruent with the research question and the analytic procedures.
- The theory of language is congruent with the paradigmatic line of inquiry and the analysis.
- Transcription procedures are transparent.
- Treatment of context should be explicit.
- There is no one method of discourse analysis.
- Issues of sampling and over-generalization are addressed.
- Reflexivity should be addressed.
- Analysis should be transparent.
- Issues of representation are considered.
- The findings should extend existing knowledge.
- Commitment to advocacy and social change should be considered.

NOTES

Notes to Chapter 1

1 The book *Iggie's House* (Blume, 1970) is described by Blume as follows on her website www.judyblume.com/books/middle/iggy.php (retrieved July 1, 2008): "When Grove Street gets its first black family, Winnie is a welcoming party of one. . . . The late sixties was a turbulent time in America. Racial tensions were high, especially following the assassination of Martin Luther King. The ongoing fight for racial equality affected all of us, one way or another. At the time, I was almost as naive as Winnie is in this book, wanting to make the world a better place, but not knowing how."

2 For a closer analysis of this event, see Rogers and Mosley (2008).

Notes to Chapter 4

1 Dr. Clay passed away in 2007.

2 It should be noted that Gee (2011a) introduces many more building tasks in his book *How to Do Discourse Analysis: A Toolkit*. We have used only some of the building tasks in our analysis.

3 It is possible, and often preferred, to describe these features not as "deletions" but as standard forms of a language. For example, we could say that in AAVE, plural forms of singular verbs are pronounced as the singular form, or that possessives like "father's" are pronounced as "father." The choice to describe them as deletions takes Standard English as the standard and describes AAVE as a variation, rather than positioning AAVE as a language, as scholars of Ebonics and African-American English have argued (Duncan, 2004; Perry & Delpit, 1998). However, when we were teaching, we used this language of deletions, so we also represent it here.

Notes to Appendices

1 We did obtain permission to use students' images from photos, audio, and video as well as their work in our study, but we still attempt to keep them anonymous when we publish the findings of our study.

REFERENCES

Abendroth, M. (2009). *Cuba's national literacy campaign and critical global citizenship*. Duluth, MN: Litwin Books.

Adorno, T.W., & Horkheimer, M. (2002). *Dialectic of enlightenment*. (E. Jephcott, Trans.). Stanford, CA: Stanford University Press.

Allen, J., Fabregas, V., Hankins, K., Hull, G., Labbo, L., & Lawson, H. (2002). PhOLKS lore: Learning from photographs, families and children. *Language Arts Journal, 79(4)*, 312–322.

Allington, R. (2002). You can't learn much from books you can't read. *Educational Leadership, 60(30)*, 16–19.

Antaki, C., Billig, M., Edwards, D., and Potter, J. (2002) *Discourse analysis means doing analysis: Discourse analysis on-line*, vol. 1, http://extra.shu.ac.uk/daol/articles/v1/n1/a1/antaki2002002-paper.html, accessed October, 2008.

Apple, M.W. (2004). *Ideology and curriculum*. New York, NY: RoutledgeFalmer.

Artiles, A.J., Rueda, R., Salazar, J., & Higareda, I. (2005). Within-group diversity in minority disproportionate representation. *Exceptional Children, 71*, 283–300.

Assaf, L.C. (2005). Exploring identities in a reading specialization program. *Journal of Literacy Research, 37(2)*, 201–236.

Assaf, L.C., & Dooley, C.M. (2006). "Everything they were giving us created tension": Creating and managing tension in a graduate-level multicultural course focused on literacy methods. *Multicultural Education, 14(4)*, 42–49.

Auerbach, E. (2001). "Yes, but . . .": Problematizing participatory ESL pedagogy. In P. Campbell & B. Burnaby (Eds.), *Participatory practices in adult education* (pp. 267–305). Mahwah, NJ: Lawrence Erlbaum Associates.

Bakhtin, M.M. (1986). The problem of the text in linguistics, philology, and the human sciences. (V. McGee, Trans.). In C. Emerson & M. Holquist (Eds.), *Speech genres and other late essays* (pp. 103–131). Austin: University of Texas Press.

Bakhtin, M.M., & Holquist, M. (1981). *The dialogic imagination: Four essays*. Austin: University of Texas Press.

Banks, J.A. (1997). *Educating citizens in a multicultural society*. New York, NY: Teachers College Press.

Barone, D. (1999). *Resilient children*. Newark, DE: International Reading Association.

Bartlett, T. (2012). *Hybrid voices and collaborative change: Contextualizing positive discourse analysis*. London, UK: Routledge.

Baugh, J. (1999). *Out of the mouths of slaves*. Austin, TX: University of Texas Press.

Bear, D.R., Invernizzi, M., Templeton, S., & Johnston, F. (2004). *Words their way: Word study for phonics, vocabulary, and spelling instruction*. Upper Saddle River, NJ: Pearson Merrill Prentice Hall.

Bell, D. (1992). *Faces at the bottom of the well: The permanence of racism*. New York, NY: Basic Books.

Blanchett, W. (2006). Disproportionate representation of African American students in special education: Acknowledging the role of white privilege and racism. *Educational Research, 35(6)*, 24–28.

Bliss, M. (1947, November 18). District rich in history now "Blighted": Cabanne—scene of adventure, romance. *St. Louis Star Times*, p. 13.

Blommaert, J. (2005). *Discourse*. Cambridge, UK: Cambridge University Press.

Blommaert, J. & Bulcaen, C. (2000). Critical discourse analysis. *Annual Review of Anthropology, 29*, 447–466.

Bloome, D., Carter, D., Christian, B., Madrid, S., Otto, S., Stuart-Faris, N., et al. (2008). *On discourse analysis in classrooms: Approaches to language and literacy*. New York, NY: Teachers College Press.

Blume, J. (1970). *Iggie's house*. New York, NY: Bantam Doubleday Dell Books for Young Readers.

Bowles, S., & Gintis, H. (1976). *Schooling in capitalist America*. New York, NY: Basic Books.

Brookfield, S. (2005). *The power of critical theory: Liberating adult learning and teaching*. San Francisco, CA: Jossey-Bass.

Bruner, J. (1991). The narrative construction of reality. *Critical Inquiry, 18(1)*, pp. 1–21

Bruner, J., & Weisser, S. (1991). The invention of self: Autobiography and its forms. In D.R. Olson & N. Torrance (Eds.), *Literacy and orality* (pp. 129–148). Cambridge: Cambridge University Press.

Bunting, E. (1991). Fly away home. New York, NT: Clanon Books.

Burleigh, R. (2001). *Lookin' for bird in the big city*. New York, NY: Harcourt Children's Books.

Burns, L., & Morrell, E. (2005). Critical discourse analysis in literacy research. In B. Maloch, J. Hoffman, D. Schallert, C. Fairbanks, & J. Worthy (Eds.), *54th yearbook of the national reading conference* (Vol. 56, pp. 132–143). Malwah, NJ: Lawrence Erlbaum.

Callinicos, A. (1995). *Race and class*. London: Bookmark publications.

Cambourne, B. (1995). Towards an educationally relevant theory of literacy learning: Twenty years of inquiry. *The Reading Teacher, 53(2)*, 126–127.

Carger, C. (1996). *Of borders and dreams*. NY: Teachers College Press.

Carspecken, P.F. (1996). *Critical ethnography in educational research: A theoretical and practical guide*. New York, NY: Routledge.

Chouliaraki, L., & Fairclough, N. (1999). *Discourse in late modernity: Rethinking critical discourse analysis*. Edinburgh: Edinburgh University Press.

Christie, F. (2002). *Classroom discourse analysis: A functional perspective*. New York, NY: Continuum.

Christie, F., Devlin, B., Freebody, P., Luke, A., Martin, J., Threadgold, T., et al. (1991). *Teaching English literacy: A project of national significance on the pre-service training of teachers*.

Canberra & Darwin: Department of Employment, Education and Training & Northern Territory University Faculty of Education.

Clarence-Fishman, J. (2001). Responding to academic discourse: Developing critical literacy at a South African university. In B. Comber & A. Simpson (Eds.), *Negotiating critical literacies in classrooms* (pp. 273–286). Mahwah, NJ: Lawrence Erlbaum Associates.

Clark, C., & Medina, C. (2000). How reading and writing literacy narratives affect perservice teachers' understandings of literacy, pedagogy and multiculturalism. *Journal of Teacher Education, 51*, 63–76.

Clay, M.M. (1987). Learning to be learning disabled. *New Zealand Journal of Educational Studies, 22(2)*, 155–173.

Clay, M.M. (1991a). *Becoming literate: The construction of inner control.* Portsmouth, NH: Heinemann.

Clay, M.M. (1991b). Introducing a storybook to young readers. *The Reading Teacher, 45(4)*, 264–273.

Clay, M.M. (1994). *Reading recovery: A guide book for teachers in training.* Portsmouth, NH: Heinemann.

Clay, M.M. (2006). *An observation survey of early literacy achievement* (2nd ed.). Portsmouth, NH: Heinemann.

Clements, A. (2003). *The jacket.* New York, NY: Aladdin.

Cochran-Smith, M. (2004). *Walking the road: Race, diversity, and social justice in teacher education.* New York, NY: Teachers College Press.

Cochran-Smith, M., & Lytle, S. (2001). Beyond certainty: Taking an inquiry stance on practice. In A. Lieberman & L. Miller (Eds.), *Teachers caught in the action: Professional development that matters* (pp. 45–60). New York, NY: Teachers College Press.

Comber, B., Thomson, P., & Wells, M. (2001). Critical literacy finds a "place": Writing and social action in a low-income Australian grade 2/3 classroom. *Elementary School Journal, 101(4)*, 451–464.

Commeyras, M. (1994). Were Janell and Neesie in the same classroom? Children's questions as the first order of reality in storybook discussions. *Language Arts, 71*, 517–523.

Compton-Lilly, C. (2005). Nuances of error: Considerations relevant to African American Vernacular English and learning to read. *Literacy Teaching and Learning, 10(1)*, 43–58.

Cooley, R. (2004/2005). New kids on the block: Fifth graders use *Iggie's House* to think about racism, anti-racism, and the importance of acting for justice. *Rethinking Schools, 19(2)*, 48–51.

Cope, B. (1993). *The powers of literacy: A genre approach to teaching writing.* Pittsburg, PA: University of Pittsburg Press.

Cope, B., & Kalantzis, M. (2000). *Multiliteracies: Literacy learning and the design of social futures.* London: Routledge.

Crawford, F., & Bartolomé, L. (2010). Labeling and treating linguistic minority students with disabilities as deficient and outside the normal curve: A pedagogy of exclusion. In C. Dudley-Marling & A. Gurn (Eds.), *Deconstructing the normal curve (and Reconstructing the education for students with disabilities)* (pp. 151–170). New York, NY: Peter Lang.

Davies, B. and Harré, R. (1990) 'Positioning: The discursive production of selves', *Journal for the Theory of Social Behaviour, 20(1),* 44–63.

De Souza Briggs, X.N. (2005). *The geography of opportunity: Race and housing choice in metropolitan America.* Washington D.C.: Brookings Institution Press.

DeBose, C.E., & Faraclas, N. (1993). An Africanist approach to the linguistic study of Black English: Getting to the roots of the tense-aspect-modality and copula systems in Afro-American. In S.S. Mufwene (Ed.), *Africanisms in Afro-American language varieties* (pp. 47–73). Athens, GA: University of Georgia Press.

Degener, S. (2001). Making sense of critical pedagogy in adult literacy learning and teaching. In J. Comings, B. Garner, & C. Smith (Eds.), *Annual review of adult learning and literacy* (pp. 26–62). San Francisco, CA: Jossey-Bass.

Dei, G.J.S. (1996). *Anti-racism education: Theory and practice*. Halifax, UK: Fernwood Publishing.

Delpit, L. (1995). *Other people's children: Cultural conflict in the classroom*. New York, NY: The New Press.

Delpit, L., & Kilgour Dowdy, J. (2002). *The skin that we speak: Thoughts on language and culture in the classroom*. New York, NY: New Press.

Demetrion, G. (2005). *Conflicting paradigms in adult literacy education: In quest of a U.S. democratic politics of literacy*. Malwah, NJ: Lawrence Erlbaum Associates.

Dillard, J.L. (1972). *Black English*. New York, NY: Random House.

Dozier, C., Johnston, P.H., & Rogers, R. (2006). *Critical literacy/critical teaching: Tools for preparing responsive teachers*. New York, NY: Teachers College Press.

Dozier, C., & Rutten, I. (2005–2006). Responsive teaching toward responsive teachers: Mediating transfer through intentionality, enactment, and articulation. *Journal of Literacy Research, 37(4)*, 459–492.

Duckworth, E. (Ed.). (2001). *"Tell me more": Listening to learners explain*. New York, NY: Teachers College Press.

Duncan, G.A. (2004). Ebonics and education: A critical appraisal of the post-1996 research literature. *African American Research Perspectives, 10*. www.rcgd.isr.umich.edu/prba/per spectives/springsummer2004/duncan.pdf, accessed February 8, 2013.

Edwards, P.A. (1999). *A path to follow: Learning to listen to parents*. New York, NY: Heinemann.

Edwards, P.A., McMillon, G.T., & Turner, J.D. (2010). *Change is gonna come: Transforming literacy education for African American students*. New York, NY: Teachers College Press.

Emerson, R., Fretz, R., & Shaw, L. (1995). *Writing ethnographic fieldnotes*. Chicago, ILL: University of Chicago Press.

Fairclough, N. (1992a). *Critical language awareness*. Harlow, Essex, UK: Longman.

Fairclough, N. (1992b). Intertextuality in critical discourse analysis. *Linguistics and Education, 4(3–4)*, 269–293.

Fairclough, N. (1993). *Discourse and social change*. Malden, MA: Polity Press.

Fairclough, N. (1995). *Critical discourse analysis: The critical study of language*. London: Longman.

Fairclough, N. (2003). *Analyzing discourse: Textual analysis for social research*. New York, NY: Routledge.

Fairclough, N. (2011). Semiotic aspects of social tranformation and learning. In Rogers, R. (Ed.), *An introduction to critical discourse analysis in education* (2nd ed.), (pp. 119–126). New York, NY: Routledge.

Ferri, B., & Connor, D. (2006). *Reading resistance: Discourses of exclusion in desegregation and inclusion debates*. New York, NY: Peter Lang.

Finders, M.J. (1997). *Just girls: Hidden literacies and life in junior high*. New York, NY: Teachers College Press.

Fletcher, R., & Portalupi, J. (1999). *Craft lessons: Teaching writing*. New York, NY: Stenhouse.

Flood, J., Lapp, D., Alvarez, D., Romero, A., Ranck-Buhr, W., Moore, J., et al. (1994). *Teacher book clubs: A study of teachers' and student teachers' participation in contemporary multicultural fiction literature discussion groups*. Athens, GA: Universities of Georgia and Maryland.

Florio-Ruane, S. (2000). Culture in literacy education: Thirteen ways of looking at a blackbird. *National Reading Conference Yearbook, 49*, 12–30.

Florio-Ruane, S. (2001). *Teacher education and the cultural imagination: Autobiography, conversation, and narrative*. Malwah, NJ: Lawrence Erlbaum Associates.

Fondrie, S. (2001). "Gentle doses of racism": Whiteness in children's literature. *Journal of Children's Literature, 27(3)*, 9–13.

Fountas, I.C., & Pinnell, G.S. (1996). *Guided reading: Good first teaching for all children*. Portsmouth, NH: Heinemann.

Fountas, I.C., Pinnell, G.S., & Bird, L.B. (1999). *Matching books to readers: Using leveled books in guided reading, K-3*. Portsmouth, NH: Heinemann.

Freire, P. (1970). *Pedagogy of the oppressed*. New York, NY: Bloomsbury Press.

Freire, P. (1973). *Education for critical consciousness*. New York, NY: Seabury Press.

Freire, P. (1983). The importance of the act of reading. *Journal of Education, 165(1)*, 5–11.

Fresche, M.J. (2001). Journal entries as a window on spelling knowledge, *The Reading Teacher, 54(5)*, 500–513.

Fuqua, J.S. (2006). *Darby*. New York, NY: Candlewick Press.

Gay, G. (2002). Preparing for culturally responsive teaching. *Journal of Teacher Education, 53(2)*, 106–116.

Gee, J.P. (1985). The narrativization of experience in the oral style. *Journal of Education, 167(1)*, 9–35.

Gee, J.P. (1991). A linguistic approach to narrative. *Journal of Narrative and Life History, 1(1)*, 15–39.

Gee, J.P. (1996). *Social linguistics and literacies: Ideology in discourses*. London: The Falmer Press.

Gee, J.P. (2000). The new literacy studies: From "socially situated" to the work of the social. In M.H.D. Barton & R. Ivanic (Eds.), *Situated literacies: Reading and writing in context* (pp. 180–196). London: Routledge.

Gee, J.P. (2002). Discourse and socio-cultural studies in reading from the methodology chapters. In M. Kamil, P. Mosenthal, P.D. Pearson, & R. Barr (Eds.), *The handbook of reading research* (pp. 119–132). Malwah, NJ: Lawrence Erlbaum Associates.

Gee, J.P. (2006) *An introduction to discourse analysis: Theory and method* (2nd ed.). New York, NY: Routledge.

Gee, J.P. (2010). *An introduction to discourse analysis: Theory and method* (3rd ed.). London; New York, NY: Routledge.

Gee, J.P. (2011a). *How to do discourse analysis: A toolkit*. New York, NY: Routledge.

Gee, J.P. (2011b). Discourse analysis: What makes it critical? In Rogers, R. (Ed.), *An introduction to critical discourse analysis in education* (2nd ed.), (pp. 23–45). New York, NY: Routledge.

Giddens, A. (1984). *The constitution of society: Outline of the theory of structuration*. Los Angeles, CA: University of California Press.

Giovanni, N. (1994). *Racism 101* (1st ed.). New York, NY: William Morrow.

Giroux, H. (1988). Literacy and the pedagogy of voice and political empowerment. *Educational Theory, 38(1)*, 61–75.

Giroux, H. (1997). Rewriting the discourse of racial identity: Towards a pedagogy and politics of whiteness. *Harvard Educational Review, 67(2)*, 285–320.

Glazier, J.A. (2003). Moving closer to speaking the unspeakable: White teachers talking about race. *Teacher Education Quarterly 30(1)*, 73–94.

González, N., Moll, L.C., & Amanti, C. (Eds.). (2005). *Funds of knowledge: Theorizing practices in households and classrooms*. Malwah, NJ: Lawrence Erlbaum.

Grace, C. (2004). Exploring the African American oral tradition: Instructional implications for literacy learning. *Language Arts, 81(6)*, 481–490.

Green, L.J. (2002). *African American English: A linguistic introduction*. Cambridge, MA: Cambridge University Press.

Greene, S., & Abt-Perkins, D. (2003). *Making race visible: Literacy research for cultural understanding*. New York, NY: Teachers College Press.

Greenfield, E. (1984). Me & Neesie. New York, NY: Harper Collins Publishers.

Guinier, L. (2004). From racial liberation to racial literacy: Brown v. Board of Education and the interest-divergence dilemma. *The Journal of American History, 91(1)*, 92–118.

Gutiérrez, K. (2006). Developing sociocritical literacy in the third space. *Reading Research Quarterly, 43(2)*, 148–164.

Halliday, M.A.K. (1978). *Language as a social semiotic: The social interpretation of language and meaning*. Baltimore, MD: University Park Press.

Halliday, M.A.K. (1994). *An introduction to functional grammar* (2nd ed.). London: Edward Arnold.

Harre, R., & Moghaddam, F.M. (2003). *The self and others: Positioning individuals and groups in personal, political, and cultural contexts.* Westport, CT: Praeger.

Harris, C.I. (1993). Whiteness as property. *Harvard Law Review, 106(8)*, 1707–1791.

Harvey, S., & Goudvis, A. (2000). *Strategies that work: Teaching comprehension to enhance understanding*. New York, NY: Stenhouse.

Harste, J., & Vasquez, V. (1998). The work we do: Journal as audit trail. *Language Arts, 75(4)*, 266–276.

Heaney, G.W., & Uchitelle, S. (2004). *Unending struggle: The long road to an equal education in St. Louis*. St. Louis, MO: Reedy Press.

Heaney, T. (1992). When adult education stood for democracy. *Adult Education Quarterly, 43(1)*, 51–59.

Heath, S.B. (1983). *Ways with words: Language, life, and work in communities and classrooms*. Cambridge: Cambridge University Press.

Heller, M. (2008). Bourdieu "literacy education". In J. Albright & A. Luke (Eds.), *Pierre Bourdieu and literacy education* (pp. 50–67). New York, NY: Routledge.

Hicks, D. (2002). *Reading lives: Working-class children and literacy learning*. New York, NY; London: Teachers College Press.

Holland, D., Lachiocotte, W., Skinner, D. and Cain, C. (1998). *Identity and agency in cultural worlds*. Cambridge, MA: Harvard University Press.

hooks, b. (1994). *Teaching to transgress: Education as the practice of freedom*. New York, NY: Routledge.

hooks, b. (2002). *Be boy buzz*. New York, NY: Hyperion Books.

Hopson, R. (2003). The problem of the language line. *Race Ethnicity and Education, 6(3)*, 227–245.

Horton, M. (1998). *The long haul: An autobiography*. New York, NY: Teachers Collage Press.

Hull, G.A., & Schultz, K. (2002). *School's out!: Bridging out-of-school literacies with classroom practice*. New York, NY: Teachers College Press.

Hymes, D. (1996). *Ethnography, linguistics, narrative inequality: Toward an understanding of voice*. New York, NY: Taylor & Francis.

Janks, H. (2000). Domination, access, diversity and design: A synthesis model for critical literacy education. *Educational Review, 52(2)*, 175–186.

Janks, H. (2002). Critical literacy: Beyond reason. *Australian Educational Researcher, 29*, 7–27.

Janks, H. (2005). Deconstruction and reconstruction: Diversity as a productive resource. *Discourse, 26(1)*, 31–44.

Jargowsky, P.A. (1997). *Poverty and place: Ghettos, barrios, and the American city*. New York, NY: Russell Sage Foundation.

Jewitt, C., & Kress, G. (Eds.). (2003). *Multimodal literacy*. New York, NY: Peter Lang.

Johnson, A. S. (2006). Composing layers of experiences: An autoethnographic inquiry into telling teaching stories. In S. Gruber, N. Barron, & N. Grimm (Eds.), *Social change in diverse teaching contexts: Touchy subjects and routine practices* (pp. 87–102). New York, NY: Peter Lang.

Johnston, P. H. (1997). *Knowing literacy: Constructive literacy assessment*. Portland, ME: Stenhouse Publishers.

Johnston, P. H. (2004). *Choice words: How our language affects children's learning*. Portland, ME: Stenhouse Publishers.

Johnston, P. H. (2012). *Opening minds: Using language to change lives*. Portland, ME: Stenhouse Publishers.

Jones, S. (2006). *Girls, social class, and literacy: What teachers can do to make a difference*. Portsmouth, NH: Heinemann.

Jurow, A. S., & Creighton, L. (2005). Improvisational science discourse: Teaching science in 2 K-1 classrooms. *Linguistics and Education, 16(3)*, 253–362.

Juzwik, M. M. (2006). Performing curriculum: Building ethos through narratives in pedagogical discourse. *Teachers College Record, 108(4)*, 489–528.

Kozol, J. (1978). *Children of the revolution: A Yankee teacher in Cuban schools*. New York, NY: Delta.

Krämer-Dahl, A. (2000). Collective literacy autobiographies: Exploring issues of authority, positioning, and discourse. *Teaching Education, 11(1)*, 99–117.

Kress, G. (2003, May). Reading images: Multimodality, representation and new media. Paper presented at the IIID: Expert forum for knowledge presentation, Chicago, IL.

Kress, G. (2010). *Multimodality: A social semiotic approach to contemporary communication*. London: Routledge Falmer.

Kress, G. (2011). Discourse analysis and education: A multimodal social semiotic approach. In Rogers, R. (ed.), *An introduction to critical discourse analysis in education* (2nd ed.) pp. 205–226. New York, NY: Routledge.

Kress, G., & van Leeuwen, T. (2001). *Multimodal discourse: The modes and media of contemporary communication*. New York, NY: Oxford University Press.

Labadie, M., Mosley Wetzel, M., & Rogers, R. (2013). Opening spaces for critical literacy: Teachers Introducing books to young readers. *The Reading Teacher*, 66(2), 117–127.

Labov, W., & Waletzky, J. (1997). Narrative analysis: Oral versions of personal experience. *Journal of Narrative and Life History, 7(1)*, 3–38.

Ladson-Billings, G. (1994). *The dreamkeepers: Successful teachers of African American children* (1st ed.). San Francisco, CA: Jossey-Bass Publishers.

Ladson-Billings, G. (1999). Preparing teachers for diverse student populations: A critical race theory perspective. *Review of Research in Education, 24*, 211–247.

Ladson-Billings, G. (2001). Crossing over to Canaan: The journey of new teachers in diverse classrooms. San Francisco, CA: Jossey-Bass.

Lee, E. (2010). Taking multicultural, anti-racist education seriously. In Wayne Au, Bill Bigelow, & Stan Karp (Eds.), *Rethinking our classrooms: Teaching for equity and justice* (New Edition ed., Vol. 1), (pp. 9–16), Milwaukee, WI: Rethinking Schools Ltd.

Leland, C., Harste, J., Jackson, C., & Youssef, O. (2001). Making teacher education critical. *National Reading Conference Yearbook, 50*, 382–393.

Lewis, C. (2006). "What's discourse got to do with it?" A meditation on critical discourse analysis in literacy research. *Research in the Teaching of English, 40(3)*, 355–361.

Lewis, C., Enciso, P., & Moje, E.B. (Eds.). (2007). *Identity, agency, and power: Reframing sociocultural research on literacy*. Malwah, NJ: Lawrence Erlbaum.

Lewis, C., & Ketter, J. (2011). Learning as social interaction: Interdiscursivity in a teacher and researcher study group. In Rogers, R. (Ed.), *An introduction to critical discourse analysis in education* (2nd ed.), (pp. 128–153). New York, NY: Routledge.

Lewison, M., Flint, A.S., & Van Sluys, K. (2002). Taking on critical literacy: The journey of newcomers and novices. *Language Arts, 79(5)*, 382–392.

Lewison, M., Leland, C., & Harste, J. (2007). *Creating critical classrooms: K-8 reading and writing with an edge*. New York, NY: Taylor & Francis Group.

Linnell, P. (2005). *The written language bias in linguistics: Its nature, origins and transformations*. London, UK: Routledge.

López-Bonilla, G. (2010). Narratives of exclusion and the construction of the self. In Rogers, R. (Ed.), *An introduction to critical discourse analysis in education* (pp. 46–67). New York, NY: Routledge.

Lowry, L. (1993). *The giver*. New York, NY: Bantam Books.

Luke, A. (2000). Critical literacy in Australia: A matter of context and standpoint. *Journal of Adolescent & Adult and Literacy, 43(5)*, 448–461.

Luke, A. (2003). Literacy and the other: A sociological approach to literacy research and policy in multilingual societies. *Reading Research Quarterly, 38(1)*, 132–141.

Luke, A. (2004). Notes on the future of critical discourse studies. *Critical Discourse Studies, 38(1)*, 132–141.

Luke, A., O'Brien, J., & Comber, B. (1994). Making community texts objects of study. *Australian Journal of Language and Literacy, 17(2)*, 139–142.

Luke, A. (2012). Critical literacy: Foundational notes. *Theory into Practice, 51(1)*, 4–11.

Luke, A., O'Brien, J., & Comber, B. (2001). Making community texts objects of study. In H. Fehring and P. Green (Eds.), *Critical literacy: A collection of articles from the Australian Literacy Educators' Association*, (pp. 112–123), Newark, Delaware: International Reading Association.

Lytle, S.L., & Cochran-Smith, M. (1992). Teacher research as a way of knowing. *Harvard Educational Review, 62(4)*, 447–474.

Macedo, D. (2003). Literacy matters. *Language Arts, 81(1)*, 12–13.

Macgilchrist, F. (2007). Positive discourse analysis: Contesting dominant discourses by reframing the issue. *Critical Approaches to Discourse Across the Disciplines, 1(1)*, 74–94.

Martin, J. (2004). Positive discourse analysis: Power, solidarity and change. *Revista Canaria de Estudios Ingleses*, 49, 179–200.

Martin, J., & Rose, D. (2007). *Working with discourse: Meaning beyond the clause* (2nd ed.). London: Continuum Press.

Maybin, J. (2007). Literacy under and over the desk: Oppositions and heterogeneity. *Language and education, 21(6)*, 515–530.

McEwan, H., & Egan, K. (1995). *Narrative in teaching, learning, and research*. New York, NY: Teachers College Press.

McIntosh, P. (1989). White Privilege: Unpacking the Invisible Knapsack. Peace and Freedom Magazine, July/August, pp.10–12: Women's International League for Peace and Freedom, Philadelphia.

McKinney, M., & Giorgis, C. (2009). Narrating and performing identity: Literacy specialists' writing identities. *Journal of Literacy Research, 41(1)*, 104–149.

McLaren, P. (1988). Culture or canon? Critical pedagogy and the politics of literacy. *Harvard Educational Review, 58(2)*, 213–235.

McVee, M.B. (2004). Narrative and the exploration of culture in teachers' discussions of literacy, identity, self, and other. *Teaching and Teacher Education, 20(8)*, 881–899.

Meier, K.J., Stewart Jr., J., & England, R.E. (1990). *Race, class, and education: The politics of second-generation discrimination*. Madison: University of Wisconsin Press.

Michie, G. (2003). See you when we get there: Young teachers of color working for change. *Rethinking Schools, 18(2)*, 39–42.

Miles, M.B., & Huberman, A.M. (1994). *Qualitative data analysis: An expanded sourcebook* (2nd ed.). Thousand Oaks, CA: Sage Publications.

Millard, K. (2007). *Coming of age in contemporary American fiction*. Edinburgh, UK: Edinburgh University Press Ltd.

Mohr, M., Rogers, R. C., Sanford, B., Nocerino, M.A., & Clawson, S. (2004). *Teacher research for better schools*. New York, NY: Teachers College Press.

Morris, V.G., & Morris, C.L. (2002). *The price they paid: Desegregation in an African American community*. New York, NY: Teachers College Press.

Morrison, T. (1993). *Playing in the dark: Whiteness and the literary imagination*. New York, NY: Vintage Press.

Morrison, T., & Morrison, S. (2002). The big box. New York, NY: Jump at the Sun Publishers.

Mosley, M. (2010). Becoming a literacy teacher: Approximations in critical literacy teaching. *Teaching Education, 21(4)*, 403–426.

Mosley, M., & Johnson, A.S. (2007). Examining literacy teaching stories for racial positioning: Pursuing multimodal approaches. *The National Reading Conference Yearbook, 56*, 332–344.

Mosley, M., & Rogers, R. (2011). Inhabiting the "tragic gap": pre-service teachers practicing racial literacy. *Teaching Education, 22(3)*, 303–324.

New London Group (1996). A pedagogy of multiliteracies. *Harvard Educational Review, 66*, 60–92.

New London Group (2000). A pedagogy of multiliteracies: Designing social futures. In B. Cope & M. Kalantzis (Eds.) *Multiliteracies: Literacy learning and the design of social futures* (pp. 9–37). London: Routledge.

Norris, S. (2004). *Analyzing multimodal interaction: A methodological framework*. New York, NY: Routledge.

Ochs, E., & Capps, L. (2001). *Living narrative: Creating lives in everyday storytelling*. Cambridge, Mass.: Harvard University Press.

Orellana, M., & Hernández, A. (1999). Talking the walk: Children reading urban environmental print. *The Reading Teacher, 52(6)*, 612–619.

Parker, D.C. (2010). Writing and becoming [a teacher]: Teacher candidates' literacy narratives over four years. *Teaching and Teacher Education: An International Journal of Research and Studies, 26(2)*, 1,249–1,260.

Perry, T. (2003). Freedom for literacy and literacy for freedom: The African-American philosophy of education. In T. Perry, C. Steele, & A.G. Hilliard (Eds.), *Young, gifted, and black: Promoting high achievement among African American students* (pp. 11–51). Boston: Beacon Press.

Perry, T., & Delpit, L.D. (1998). *The real ebonics debate: Power, language, and the education of African-American children*. Boston: Beacon Press.

Peterson, B. (2003). Teaching for social justice: One teacher's journey. *Rethinking schools, 18(3)*, 30–39.

Plummer, K. (1995). *Telling sexual stories: Power, change, and social worlds*. New York, NY: Routledge.

Polacco, P. (2001). *Mr. Lincoln's way*. New York, NY: Philomel Books.

Purcell-Gates, V. (1995). *Other people's words: The cycle of low literacy*. Cambridge, MA: Harvard University Press.

Purcell-Gates, V., & Waterman, R. (2000). *Now we read, we see, we speak: Portrait of literacy development in an adult Freirian-based class*. Mahwah, NJ: Lawrence Erlbaum Associates.

Raphael, T.E., Florio-Ruane, S., & George, M. (2001). Book club plus: A conceptual framework to organize literacy instruction. *Language Arts, 79(2)*, 159–168.

Reisigl, M., & Wodak, R. (2001). *Discourse and discrimination: Rhetorics of racism and antisemitism*. London: Routledge.

Rex, L., & Schiller, L. (2009). *Using discourse analysis to improve classroom interaction*. New York, NY: Routledge.

Rex, L.A., & Juzwik, M. (2011). *Narrative discourse analysis for teacher educators*. New York, NY: Hampton Press.

Richardson, E. (2007). "She was workin like foreal": Critical literacy and discourse practices of African American females in the age of hip hop. *Discourse & Society, 18(6)*, 789–809.

Rickford, J. (1999). *African American vernacular English: Features, evolution, educational implications*. Malden, MA: Blackwell Publishers Inc.

Riessman, C.K. (2005). Narrative analysis. In N. Kelly, C. Horrocks, K. Milnes, B. Roberts, & D. Robinson (Eds.), *Narrative, memory & everyday life* (pp. 1–7). Huddersfield, UK: University of Huddersfield.

Rodriguez, T.L., & Cho, H. (2011). Eliciting critical literacy narratives of bi/multilingual teacher candidates across U.S. teacher education contexts. *Teaching and Teacher Education: An International Journal of Research and Studies, 27(3)*, 496–504.

Rogers, R. (2002). Through the eyes of the institution: A critical discourse analysis of decision making in two special education meetings. *Anthropology & Education Quarterly, 33(2)*, 213–237.

Rogers, R. (2011). *An introduction to critical discourse analysis in education* (2nd ed.). New York, NY: Routledge.

Rogers, R. (2013). Critical discourse analysis: Criteria to consider in reviewing scholarship. In A. Trainor & E. Graue (Eds.), *Publishing qualitative research in the social and behavioral sciences: A guide for reviewers and researchers*, pp. 69–81. New York, NY: Routledge.

Rogers, R. (in press). Coaching teachers as they design critical literacy practices. *Reading and Writing Quarterly*.

Rogers, R. & Christian, J. (2007). "What could I say?": A critical discourse analysis of the construction of race in children's literature. *Race, Ethnicity, and Education, 10(1)*, 21–46.

Rogers, R. & Kramer, M.A. (2007). *Adult education teachers: Designing critical literacy practices*. Malwah, NJ: Lawrence Erlbaum Associates Inc.

Rogers, R. & Mosley, M. (2008). A critical discourse analysis of racial literacy in teacher education. *Linguistics and Education, 19*, 107–131.

Rogers, R. & Mosley, M. (2010). Read-alouds as spaces for the deliberation of public sphere issues. *The 59th Yearbook of the National Reading Conference*, 102–116.

Rogers, R. Mosley, M., & Folkes, A. (2010). Focus on policy: Standing up to neoliberalism through critical literacy education. *Language Arts Journal, 87(2)*, 127–138.

Rogers, R., Mosley, M., & Kramer, M.A. (2009). *Designing socially just communities: critical literacy education across a lifespan*. New York, NY: Routledge.

Rogers, R. & Pole, K. (2010). A state takeover: The language of a school district crisis. In L. MacGillvray (Ed.), *Literacy practices in times of crisis* (pp. 138–158). New York, NY: Routledge.

Sawyer, R.K. (2004). Creative teaching: Collaborative discussion as disciplined improvisation. *Educational Researcher, 33(2)*, 12–20.

Schaenen, I. (2010). "Genre means . . .": A critical discourse analysis of fourth grade talk about genre. *Critical Inquiry into Language Studies, 7(1)*, 28–53.

Schiezka, J. (1996). *The True Story of Three Little Pigs*. New York: Puffin Books.

Schneider, J.J. (2001). No blood, guns, or gays allowed!: The silencing of the elementary writer. *Language Arts, 78(5)*, 415–425.

Schwartzer, D. (2001). *Noa's ark: One child's voyage into multiliteracy*. New York, NY: Heinemann.

Scollon, R. (2010). *Analyzing public discourse: Discourse analysis in the making of public policy*. New York, NY: Routledge.

Scollon, R., & Scollon, S. (1981). *Narrative, literacy and face in interethnic communication*. Norwood, NJ: Ablex.

Scollon, R., & Wong Scollon, S. (2004). *Nexus analysis: Discourse and the emerging internet*. New York, NY: Routledge.

Shange, N. (1998). *Whitewash*. New York, NY: Waeker & Company.

Shor, I., & Freire, P. (1987). *Pedagogy for liberation: Dialogues on transforming education*. Westport, CT: Bergin & Garvey.

Sleeter, C.E. (2000–2001). Epistemological diversity in research on preservice teacher preparation for historically underserved children. *Review of Educational Research, 25*, 209–250.

Solorzano, D.G., & Yossi, T.J. (2001). From racial stereotyping and deficit discourse toward a critical race theory in teacher education. *Multicultural Education, 9(1)*, 2–8.

Souto-Manning, M. (2010). Playing with power and privilege: Theatre games in teacher education. *Teaching and Teacher Education, 27*, 997–1,007.

Spinelli, J. (1990). *Maniac magee*. Boston, MA: Little, Brown.

Spradley, J.P. (1979). *The ethnographic interview*. New York, NY: Holt, Rinehart and Winston.

Spradley, J.P. (1980). *Participant observation*. Fort Worth, TX: Harcourt Brace Publishers.

St. Clair, R., & Sandlin, J. (2004). Promoting critical practice in adult education. *New Directions for Adult and Continuing Education, 102*, 25–34.

Street, B.V. (1984). *Literacy in theory and practice*. Cambridge, UK: Cambridge University Press.

Street, B.V. (1993). *Cross-cultural approaches to literacy*. Cambridge, UK; New York, NY: Cambridge University Press.

Sweeney, M. (1997). "No easy road to freedom": Critical literacy in a fourth-grade classroom. *Reading & Writing Quarterly: Overcoming learning difficulties, 13*, 279–290.

Taylor, E., Gilborn, D., & Ladson-Billings, G. (2009). *Foundations of critical race theory in education*. New York, NY: Routledge.

Turner, J.D. (2006). "I want to meet my students where they are!": Preservice teachers' visions of culturally relevant literacy instruction. In J. Hoffman, D.L. Schallert, C.M. Fairbanks, J. Worthy, & B. Maloch (Eds.), *55th Yearbook of the national reading conference*, pp. 309–323.

Twine, F.W. (2004). A white side of black Britain: the concept of racial literacy. *Ethnic and Racial Studies, 27(6)*, 1–30.

Valenzuela, A. (1999). *Subtractive schooling: U.S. -Mexican youth and the politics of caring*. Albany: State University of New York Press.

van Dijk, T.A. (2000). *Critical discourse analysis*. www.discourse-in-society.org/OldArticles/The%20reality%20of%20racism.pdf, accessed March 6, 2003.

Van Maanen, J. (1988). *Tales of the field: On writing ethnography*. Chicago, IL: University of Chicago Press.

Van Sluys, K., Lewison, M., & Flint, A.S. (2006). Researching critical literacy: A critical study of analysis of classroom discourse. *Journal of Literacy Research, 38(2)*, 197–233.

Villegas, A.M., & Lucas, T. (2002). Preparing culturally responsive teachers: Rethinking the curriculum. *Journal of Teacher Education, 53(1)*, 20–32.

Wallace, C. (2001). Critical literacy in the second language classroom: Power and control. In B. Comber & A. Simpson (Eds.), *Negotiating critical literacies in classrooms* (pp. 233–254). Mahwah, NJ: Lawrence Erlbaum Associates.

Weatherford, C.B. (2002). *Jazz baby*. New York, NY: Lee & Low Books.

Webb, S. (2005, December). Navigating the "third space": Positioning and being positioned in classroom discourse. Paper presented at the National Reading Conference.

Weber, R.M. (2001). Historical perspectives on promoting reading: The early Soviet effort. In L. Verhoeven & C. Snow (Eds.), *Literacy and motivation: Reading engagement in individuals and groups* (pp. 275–289). Mahwah, NJ.: Erlbaum Associates.

Wells, G. (2001). *Action, talk and text: Learning and teaching through inquiry*. New York, NY: Teachers College Press.

Wells, A.S., & Crain, R.L. (1997). *Stepping over the color line: African-American students in white suburban schools*. New Haven, CT: Yale University Press.

Wheeler, R., & Swords, R. (2004). Codeswitching: Tools of language and culture transform the dialectically diverse classroom. *Language Arts, 81(6)*, 326–344.

Widdowson, H. (1998). The theory and practice of critical discourse analysis. *Applied Linguistics, 19 (1)*, 136–151.

Williams, L. *The Best Thing*. New York, NY: Lee & Low Books.

Williams, R.L. (1975). *Ebonics: The true language of Black folks*. St. Louis, MO: Williams & Associates.

Wilson, W.J. (1996). *When work disappears: The world of the new urban poor* (1st ed.). New York, NY: Knopf.

Wodak, R., & Meyer, M. (Eds.). (2001). *Methods of critical discourse analysis*. London: Sage Publications.

Wohlwend, K. (2007). Playing to read: A mediated discourse analysis of early literacy apprenticeship. *The National Reading Conference Yearbook, 56*, 377–393.

Woodson, C.G. (1990 [1933]). *The mis-education of the Negro*. Trenton, NJ: Africa World Press.

Wortham, S. (2001). *Narratives in action: A strategy for research and analysis*. New York, NY: Teachers College Press.

Wright, J.A. (2002). *Discovering African American St. Louis: A guide to historic sites* (2nd ed.). St. Louis, MO: Missouri Historical Society Press.

Xu, S. (2000). Preservice teachers integrate understandings of diversity into literacy instruction: An adaptation of the ABC's model. *Journal of Teacher Education, 51*, 135–142.

INDEX

Note: 'N' after a page number indicates a note; 'f' indicates a figure; 't' indicates a table.